STEVE BROOKES

First published in 2011

EMPIRE PUBLICATIONS
1 Newton Street, Manchester M1 1HW

ISBN 1 901 746 86 0

Printed in Great Britain by Martins the Printers

HELP HARRY HELP OTHERS

'Help Harry Help Others' is a campaign supporting Cancer Research UK's brain tumour research. It was started by a young boy called Harry Moseley from Sheldon, Birmingham who was diagnosed with an inoperable brain tumour in 2007 at the age of 7. When his friend Robert Harley became very ill because of his brain tumour, Harry decided to make and sell beaded bracelets to raise money for brain tumour research. The bracelets were a real hit and soon turned into well known campaign.

Sadly Robert, aged 55, died shortly after the campaign started but Harry was dedicated to committing his life to helping others so that they wouldn't have to go through what he and Robert had. Harry single handedly raised over £170,000 for brain tumour research as well as helping Cancer Research UK raise hundreds of thousands of pounds more by appearing in corporate pitches and speaking at events. Harry's cheeky charm and positive attitude was an inspiration to children and adults alike. His supporters came from all walks of life and even a fair few footballers including John Terry, Gareth Barry and Aston Villa's very own Ian Taylor.

Sadly, Harry lost his own battle with cancer on 8th October 2011. It was Harry's wish that the whole of the UK would wear one of his bracelets with pride so Harry's legacy will live on through his campaign to continue the hard work that Harry began.

CONTENTS

FOREWORD

Hi To All You Readers,

We were all happy to be involved with this book as between us we have played for Aston Villa, Birmingham City, Burton Albion, Derby County, Notts County, Northampton Town, Port Vale and West Bromwich Albion.

This book is superbly researched, you can tell a lot of effort was made to get this book completed, It really does relive those memories especially for us as players as results go back to 1980, we have a lot of happy memories and a couple of unfortunate ones but that's football and you can't win them all.

The next few years promise to be exciting with teams gradually improving. All the Midlands clubs have very passionate loyal fans who appreciate their football. We still follow Midlands Football a lot and always will.

Keep up your continued support for your club, and we hope you enjoy the book as much as we did.

All the Best

Ian Taylor, Darren Moore and Michael Johnson,

ACKNOWLEDGEMENTS

Hi All,

It's been a pleasure speaking to a lot of you regarding your views and thoughts on a lot of issues and memories for your club. Fans of Midlands clubs are very passionate fans, there are of course great rivalries but along the way is a lot of great banter too.

I think we should all be proud of our Midlands clubs, they all have a great history and I think a great future.

I would like to thank a number of people for their support in the publication of this book: Ashley Shaw, Ian Taylor, Michael Johnson, Darren Moore, Fiona Hale, Brad Shaw and a lot of journalists and other people in the press and people who work for the clubs featured.

I really hope you all enjoy this book. It was very interesting for me doing all the research and involving the fans as much as I could.

All the Best for the Future,

Steve

THE CLUBS

ASTON VILLA

European Cup:
Winners (1): 1982

European Super Cup:
Winners (1): 1982–83

Intertoto Cup:
Winners (1): 2001

Football League First Division / Premier League
Winners (7): 1894, 1896, 1897, 1899, 1900, 1910, 1981
Runners up (10): 1889, 1903, 1908, 1911, 1913, 1914, 1931, 1933, 1990, 1993

Football League Second Division:
Winners (2): 1938, 1960
Runners up (2): 1975, 1988

Football League Third Division:
Winners (1): 1972

FA Cup:
Winners (7): 1887, 1895, 1897, 1905, 1913, 1920, 1957
Runners up (3): 1892, 1924, 2000

Football League Cup:
Winners (5): 1961, 1975, 1977, 1994, 1996
Runners up (3): 1963, 1971, 2010

FA Charity Shield
Winners (1): 1981 (shared) Runners up (3): 1910, 1957, 1972

Football League War Cup
Winners (1): 1944 (Shared)

Villa previously played at Aston Park from 1874 to 1876 and Perry Barr from 1876 to 1897. In 1897 they moved into the Aston Lower Grounds, Later Renamed Villa Park.

CUP FINALS

FA Cup

1999-2000	Chelsea 1 Aston Villa 0
1956-1957	Aston Villa 2 Manchester United 1

1923-1924	Newcastle United 2 Aston Villa 0
1919-1920	Aston Villa 1 Huddersfield Town 0, aet
1912-1913	Aston Villa 1 Sunderland 0
1904-1905	Aston Villa 2 Newcastle United 0
1896-1897	Aston Villa 3 Everton 2
1894-1895	Aston Villa 1 West Bromwich Albion 0
1891-1892	West Bromwich Albion 3 Aston Villa 0
1886-1887	Aston Villa 2 West Bromwich Albion 0

English League Cup

2009-2010	Manchester United 2 Aston Villa 1
1995-1996	Aston Villa 3 Leeds United 0
1993-1994	Aston Villa 3 Manchester United 1
1976-1977	Aston Villa 3 Everton 2, after 1-1 draw aet, and 0-0 draw
1974-1975	Aston Villa 1 Norwich City 0
1970-1971	Tottenham Hotspur 2 Aston Villa 0
1962-1963	Birmingham City 3 Aston Villa 1, on aggregate: 3-1 home, 0-0 away
1960-1961	Aston Villa 3 Rotherham United 2, on aggregate: 3-0 aet home, 0-2 away

English Charity Shield

1981-1982	Aston Villa 2 Tottenham Hotspur 2 (shared)
1972-1973	Manchester City 1 Aston Villa 0, (at Aston Villa)
1957-1958	Manchester United 4 Aston Villa 0, (at Manchester Utd)
1910-1911	Brighton and Hove A 1 Aston Villa 0

European Champions Cup

1981-1982	Aston Villa 1 Bayern Munich 0

UEFA Super Cup

1982-1983	Aston Villa 3 Barcelona 1, on aggregate: 0-1 away, 3-0 aet home

MANAGERS SINCE 1980

Ron Saunders 1974 - 1982
Tony Barton 1982 - 1984
Graham Turner 1984 - 1986
Billy McNeill 1986 - 1987
Graham Taylor 1987 - 1990
Jozef Vengloš 1990 - 1991
Ron Atkinson 1991 - 1994
Brian Little 1994 - 1998
John Gregory 1998 - 2002
Graham Taylor 2002 - 2003
David O'Leary 2003 - 2006
Martin O'Neill 2006 - 2010
Kevin McDonald – 2010 (Brief)
Gérard Houllier 2010 - 2011
Gary McCallister 2011 (Brief)
Alex Mcleish 2011-

BIRMINGHAM CITY

Football League Second Division: Champions:
1892–93, 1920–21, 1947–48, 1954–55

Runners-up: 1893–94, 1900–01, 1902–03, 1971–72, 1984–85, 2006–07, 2008–09

Play-off winners: 2001–02

Third Division / Division Two (level 3)
Champions: 1994–95; Runners-up: 1991–92

FA Cup: Runners-up: 1931, 1956

League Cup: Winners: 1963, 2011; Runners-up: 2001

Inter-Cities Fairs Cup: Runners-up: 1960, 1961

Associate Members Cup / Football League Trophy: Winners: 1991, 1995

Birmingham Senior Cup: Winners: 1905

Football League South (wartime): Champions: 1945–46

Small Heath Alliance – the original name of Birmingham City Football Club – played their first home games on waste ground off Arthur Street, in the Bordesley Green district. In 1876 they made a temporary move to a fenced-off field in Ladypool Road, Sparkbrook, and a year later they moved again, this time to a rented field in Small Heath, This ground, became known as Muntz Street. St Andrew's was officially opened by Sir John Holder on 26 December 1906

CUP FINALS

FA Cup	1955-1956	Manchester City 3 Birmingham City 1
	1930-1931	West Bromwich Albion 2 Birmingham City 1
League Cup	2010-2011	Birmingham City 2 Arsenal 1
	2000-2001	Liverpool 1 Birmingham City 1, aet, Liverpool won on penalties
	1962-1963	Birmingham City 3 Aston Villa 1, on aggregate: 3-1 home, 0-0 away
Auto Windscreens Shield	1994-1995	Birmingham City 1 Carlisle United 0, aet
English Leyland DAF Cup	1990-1991	Birmingham City 3 Tranmere Rovers 2
Inter-Cities Fairs Cup	1960-1961	Roma 4 Birmingham City 2, on aggregate: 2-2 away, 2-0 home
	1959-1960	Barcelona 4 Birmingham City 1, on aggregate: 0-0 away, 4-1 home

MANAGERS SINCE 1980

1978-82: Jim Smith
1982-86: Ron Saunders
1986-87: John Bond
1987-89 Garry Pendrey
1989-91 Dave Mackay
1991: Lou Macari
1991-93: Terry Cooper
1993-96: Barry Fry
1996-2001: Trevor Francis
2001- 2007: Steve Bruce
2007 - 2011 Alex Mcleish
2011 – Chris Hughton

BURTON ALBION

Football Conference (Level 5)
Winners: 2008-09

Northern Premier League (Level 6)
Winners: 2001-02

Southern Football League Premier Division (Level 6)
Runners-up: 1999-2000, 2000-01

FA Trophy
Runners-up: 1986-87

Southern League Cup
Winners: 1963-64, 1996-97, 1999-2000
Runners-up: 1988-89

Northern Premier League Challenge Cup
Winners: 1982-83
Runners-up: 1986-87

Northern Premier League President's Cup
Runners-up: 1982-83, 1985-86

Staffordshire Senior Cup
Winners: 1955-56
Runners-up: 1976-77

Birmingham Senior Cup
Winners: 1953-54, 1996-97
Runners-up: 1969-70, 1970-71, 1986-87, 2007-08

Bass Charity Vase
Winners: 1954, 1961, 1970-71, 1981, 1986, 1997, 2006, 2007, 2008, 2009, 2011
Runners-up: 1952, 1957, 1973, 1980, 1982, 1983, 1984, 2002, 2003, 2004, 2005, 2010

Albion began life at the Lloyds Foundry ground on Wellington Street but then moved to Eton Park which was built off Derby Road and officially opened on 20 September 1958, from then until its demolition in 2005, the Brewers played all of their home games at Eton Park.

Eton Park was dismantled to make way for housing, as the club had just completed a new stadium, at a cost of £7.2 million. It is situated directly opposite Eton Park and was named the Pirelli Stadium.

MANAGERS SINCE 1980

Ian Storey-Moore 1978 – 1981
Neil Warnock 1981- 1986
Brian Fidler 1986-1988
Vic Halom 1988
Bobby Hope 1988
Chris Wright 1988-1989
Ken Blair 1989-1990
Frank Upton 1990
Steve Powell 1990-1991
Brian Fidler 1991-1992
Brian Kenning 1992-1994
John Barton 1994- 1998
Nigel Clough 1998-2009
Roy Mcfarland 2009
Paul Peschesolido 2009 -

CHELTENHAM

CHELTENHAM TOWN FC

FA Trophy Winners (1997-98)

Football Conference Champions (1998-99); Runners Up (1997-98)

Division Three Play-off Winners (2001-02, 2005-06)

Southern League Champions (1984-85);
Runners Up (1955-56, 1992-93, 1993-94, 1994-95, 1996-97)

Southern League Midland Division Champions (1982-83)

Southern League Division 1 North Runners-Up (1976-77)

Gloucestershire County Cup - Winners 32 times

Leamington Hospital Cup - Winners (1934-35)

Midland Floodlit Cup - Winners (1985-86, 1986-87, 1987-88)

Agg-Gardner's Recreation Ground, Carter's Field and now the Abbey Business Stadium, although it is more commonly known as Whaddon Road.

MANAGERS SINCE 1980

Alan Grundy (1979–82)
Alan Wood (1982–83)
John Murphy (1983–88)
Jim Barron (1988–89)
John Murphy (1990)
Dave Lewis (1990)
Ally Robertson (1991–92)
Lindsay Parsons (1992–95)
Chris Robinson (1995–97)
Steve Cotterill (1997–2002)
Graham Allner (2002–03)
Bobby Gould (2003)
John Ward (2003–07)
Keith Downing (2007–08)
Martin Allen (2008–09)
John Schofield (2009)
Mark Yates (2009–)

COVENTRY

Division 3 (South): 1935-36 Champions
Division 4: 1958-59 Runners up
Division 3: 1963-64 Champions
Division 2: 1966-67 Champions
FA Cup: 1986-87 Winners
FA Youth Cup: 1986-87 Winners
Runners up: 1967-68, 1969-70, 1988-89, 1999-2000
Division 3 (South) Cup: 1935-36
Southern Professional Floodlight Cup: 1959-60

Coventry had a couple of grounds at the start of the formation which started with Dowells Field, they were based there between 1883 and 1887, before moving onto Stoke Road – 1887–1899 then moving onto the home where they were based for 106 years, Highfield Road. They moved into a completely new stadium, The Ricoh Arena, in 2005

CUP FINALS

English FA Cup

1986-1987 Coventry City 3 Tottenham Hotspur 2, aet

English Charity Shield

1987-1988 Everton 1 Coventry City 0

English Division Three South Cup

1935-1936 Coventry City 5 Swindon Town 2, on aggregate: 2-0 away, 3-2 home

MANAGERS SINCE 1980

Gordon Milne 1972 - 1981
Dave Sexton 1981 - 1983
Bobby Gould 1983 - 1984
Donald Mackay 1984 - 1986
George Curtis 1986 -1987
John Sillett 1987 - 1990
Terry Butcher 1990 - 1992
Don Howe 1992
Bobby Gould 1992 - 1993
Phil Neal 1993 -1995
Ron Atkinson 1995 - 1996
Gordon Strachan 1996 - 2001
Roland Nilsson 2001 - 2002
Gary McAllister 2002 - 2003
Eric Black 2003 - 2004
Peter Reid 2004 - 2005
Micky Adams 2005 - 2007
Iain Dowie 2007 - 2008
Chris Coleman 2008 -2010
Aidy Boothroyd2010 - 2011
Andy Thorn 2011 -

DERBY COUNTY

League Division One: Champions: 1972, 1975; Runners-up: 1896, 1930, 1936

Football League Championship and predecessors)
Champions: 1912, 1915, 1969, 1987; Runners-up: 1926, 1996; Play-offs Winners: 2007

Football League One and predecessors: Champions : 1957; Runners-up : 195

FA Cup: Winners: 1946; Runners-up: 1898, 1899, 1903

FA Charity Shield: Winners: 1975

European and International honours: Anglo-Italian Cup; Runners-up: 1992–93

Texaco Cup: Winners: 1972

Watney Cup: Winners: 1971

Derbyshire Senior Cup: Winners: 2011

Midland Cup: Winners: 1946

Derby County's first home stadium was County Cricket Ground, also known as the Racecourse Ground, for matches between 1884 and 1895. When the opportunity to move to Sir Francis Ley's Baseball Ground arose, the club accepted. Commonly referred to amongst supporters as "The BBG", the club moved to The Baseball Ground in 1885 and remained there for the next 102 years, despite opportunities to move in the 1920s and 1940's. Derby's new ground, named Pride Park Stadium, was officially opened by The Queen in 1997.

CUP FINALS

English FA Cup	1945-1946	Derby County 4 Charlton Athletic 1, aet
	1902-1903	Bury 6 Derby County 0
	1898-1899	Sheffield United 4 Derby County 1
	1897-1898	Nottingham Forest 3 Derby County 1
English Charity Shield	1975-1976	Derby County 2 West Ham United 0
Anglo-Italian Cup	1992-1993	Cremonese 3 Derby County 1
English Texaco Cup	1971-1972	Derby County 2 Airdrieonians 1, on aggregate: 0-0 away, 2-1 home
English Watney Cup	1970-1971	Derby County 4 Manchester United 1, (at Derby County)

MANAGERS SINCE 1980

Colin Addison: 1979-1982
John Newman: 1982
Peter Taylor: 1982-1984
Roy McFarland: 1984
Arthur Cox: 1984-1993
Roy McFarland: 1993-95
Jim Smith: 1995-2001
Colin Todd: 2001-2002
John Gregory: 2002-2003
George Burley: 2003-2005
Phil Brown: 2005-2006
Terry Westley: 2006
Billy Davies: 2006-2007
Paul Jewell: 2007-2008
Nigel Clough: 2009-Today

KETTERING TOWN

Football Conference

Conference North champions 2007-08

Conference League Cup 1986-87

Southern League: Champions 1956-57

Premier Division champions 1972-73, 2001-02

Division One North champions 1971-72

Division One champions 1960-61

Eastern Division champions 1927-28, 1928-29

League Cup winners 1974-75

Birmingham League: Champions 1947-48

Northants League: Champions 1904-05

Midland League: Champions 1895-96, 1899-1900

Maunsell Cup: Winners 1912-13, 1919-20, 1923-24,† 1924-25, 1928-29, 1947-48, 1951-52, 1954-55, 1959-60, 1984-85, 1987-88, 1988-89, 1992-93, 1993-94, 1998-99.

Northants Hillier Cup

Winners 1883-84, 1895-86, 1897-98, 1900-01, 1906-07, 1920-21 (reserves), 1931-32, 1932-33, 1935-36, 1938-39, 1946-47, 1952-53 (reserves), 1955-56, 1956-57 (reserves), 1968-69, 1972-73, 1978-79, 1979-80, 1983-84, 1984-85, 1985-86, 1986-87, 1987-88, 1991-92, 1992-93, 1994-95, 1996-97, 2000-01.

† Joint winners with Desborough Town

Kettering currently play at Rockingham Road. They moved to the site in 1897, after spells at North Park and Eldreds Field. Chairman Imraan Ladak has stated the club's intention to move to a new ground in the town. Issues about the lease of the current site have been a concern, as Ladak seeks to secure funding for the new stadium to be built. In June 2011, it was announced that Kettering had reached an agreement with the owners of Nene Park, the home of local rivals Rushden & Diamonds, to secure a lease on the ground that would potentially secure the club's future.

MANAGERS SINCE 1980

Colin Clarke 1979-1982
Jim Conde 1982-1983
Don Masson 1983
David Needham 1983-1986
Alan Buckley 1986-1988
Peter Morris 1988-1992
Dave Cusack 1992
Graham Carr 1992-1995
Gary Johnson 1995-1996
Steve Berry 1996-1998
Peter Morris 1998-2001
Carl Shutt 2001-2003
Nick Platnauer 2003
Domenico Genovese 2003
Kevin Wilson 2003-2006
Paul Gascoigne 2005 (Brief)
Morell Maison 2006-2007
Graham Westley 2007
Mark Cooper 2007-2009
Lee Harper 2009-2010
Morell Maison 2010
Marcus Law 2010-2011
Morell Maison 2011 -

KIDDERMINSTER HARRIERS

Conference Champions: 1994, 2000; Runners-Up: 1997

FA Trophy Winners: 1987, Runners-up: 1991, 1995, 2007

Bob Lord Trophy Winners: 1997, Runners-up 1989

Welsh Cup finalists: 1986, 1989

Southern League Cup Winners: 1980

Worcestershire Senior Cup Winners: 25 times

Birmingham Senior Cup Winners: 7 times

Staffordshire Senior Cup Winners: 4 times

Birmingham & District League/West Midlands (Regional)
League Champions: 6 times; Runners-up: 3 times

Southern League Premier Division Runners-up: 1 time

West Midland League Cup Winners: 7 times

Keys Cup Winners: 7 times

Border Counties Floodlit League Champions: 3 times

Camkin Floodlit Cup Winners: 3 times

Bass County Vase Winners: 1 times

Conference Fair Play Trophy: 4 times

Matches were played at White Wickets on the Franche Road in Kidderminster in the early days, then playing games at Chester Road (the current cricket ground). In 1887–88 the club started playing its matches at Aggborough.

MANAGERS SINCE 1980

John Chambers 1979–1983
Graham Allner 1983–1998
Phil Mullen 1998–1999
Jan Mølby 1999–2002, 2003–2004
Ian Britton 2002–2003
Shaun Cunnington 2004
Stuart Watkiss 2004–2005
Mark Yates 2005–2009
Steve Burr 2010 –

LEICESTER CITY

League Division One Runners-up (1): 1928-29

League Division Two (currently Football League Championship)
Champions (6): 1924-25, 1936-37, 1953-54, 1956-57, 1970-71, 1979-80
Runners-up (2): 1907-08, 2002-03

Play-off Winners (2): 1993-94, 1995-96

League Division Three (currently Football League One): Champions (1): 2008-09

FA Cup: Runners-up (4): 1949, 1961, 1963, 1969

Football League Cup: Winners (3): 1964, 1997, 2000
Runners-up (2): 1965, 1999

FA Charity Shield: Winners (1): 1971

Leicester Fosse began playing on a field near Fosse Road. They moved to Filbert Street in 1891 and played there for 111 years, before relocating to the nearby Walkers Stadium in 2002.

CUP FINALS

English FA Cup	1968-1969	Manchester City 1 Leicester City 0
	1962-1963	Manchester United 3 Leicester City 1
	1960-1961	Tottenham Hotspur 2 Leicester City 0
	1948-1949	Wolverhampton Wndrs 3 Leicester City 1
English League Cup:	1999-2000	Leicester City 2 Tranmere Rovers 1
	1998-1999	Tottenham Hotspur 1 Leicester City 0
	1996-1997	Leicester City 1 Middlesbrough 0, aet, after 1-1 draw aet
	1964-1965	Chelsea 3 Leicester City 2, on aggregate: 3-2 home, 0-0 away
	1963-1964	Leicester City 4 Stoke City 3, on aggregate: 1-1 away, 3-2 home
English Charity Shield	1971-1972	Leicester City 1 Liverpool 0, (at Leicester City)

MANAGERS SINCE 1980

Jock Wallace 1978-1982
Gordon Milne 1982 - 1986
Gordon Milne & Bryan Hamilton 1986 - 1987
Bryan Hamilton 1987
David Pleat 1987 - 1991
Gordon Lee 1991
Brian Little 1991 – 1994
Kevin MacDonald, Tony McAndrew 1994
Mark McGhee 1994 - 1995
David Nish, Chris Turner, Garry Parker, Steve Walsh 1994 – 1995
Martin O'Neill 1995 – 2000
Peter Taylor 2000 - 2001
Garry Parker 2001
Dave Bassett 2001 – 2002
Micky Adams 2002 - 2004
Dave Bassett, Howard Wilkinson 2004
Craig Levein 2004 - 2007
Rob Kelly 2006 - 2007
Nigel Worthington 2007
Martin Allen 2007
Jon Rudkin, Steve Beaglehole, Mike Stowell 2007
Gary Megson 2007
Frank Burrows, Gerry Taggart 2007
Ian Holloway 2007 – 2008
Nigel Pearson 2008 - 2010
Paulo Sousa 2010
Chris Powell, Mike Stowell 2010
Sven-Göran Eriksson 2010 - 2011
Nigel Pearson 2011 -

NORTHAMPTON TOWN

Second Division: Runners-up: 1964–65

Third Division: Champions: 1962–63

Third Division South: Runners-up: 1927–28, 1949–50

Fourth Division: Champions: 1986–87
Runners-up: 1975–76

Promoted: 1960–61, 1999–2000

Play-Off Winners: 1996–97

League Two
Runners-up: 2005–06

Southern Football League: Champions: 1908–09
Runners-up: 1910–11

FA Charity Shield
Runners-up: 1909

Northampton moved to the county ground in 1897, sharing it with Northamptonshire County Cricket Club. The last game to be played at the ground was a 1-0 defeat by Mansfield Town on Tuesday, 12 October 1994. The club then moved to Sixfield's Stadium in 1994. It is a modern all-seater stadium with a capacity of 7,653 and award-winning disabled facilities.

English Charity Shield

1909-1910 Newcastle United 2 Northampton Town 0

MANAGERS SINCE 1980

Clive Walker 1979 - 1980
Bill Dodgin Jnr 1980-1982
Clive Walker 1982 - 1984
Tony Barton 1984 - 1985
Graham Carr 1985 - 1990
Theo Foley 1990 - 1992
Phil Chard 1992 - 1993
John Barnwell 1993 - 1994
Ian Atkins 1995 -1999
Kevin Wilson & Kevan Broadhurst 1999 - 2001
Kevan Broadhurst 2001-2003
Terry Fenwick 2003
Martin Wilkinson 2003
Richard Hill 2003
Colin Calderwood 2003-2006
John Gorman 2006
Ian Sampson & Jim Barron 2006 -2007
Stuart Gray 2007-2009
Ian Sampson 2009 -2011
Gary Johnson 2011

NOTTS COUNTY

FA Cup: Winners: 1894; Finalists: 1891

Second Division (1892–1992), First Division (1992–2004),

The Championship (2004–present): Champions: 1896–97, 1913–14, 1922–23
Runners-Up: 1894–95, 1980–81

Play-off Champions: 1990–91

Third Division (1958–92), Second Division (1992–2004), League One (2004–present)
Runners-Up: 1972–73

Play-off Champions 1989–90

Third Division South (1921–58): Champions: 1930–31, 1949–50

Fourth Division (1958–92), Third Division (1992–2004), League Two (2004–present)
Champions: 1970–71, 1997-98, 2009-10; Runners-Up: 1959–60

Anglo-Italian Cup: Winners: 1994–95; Runners-Up: 1993–94

The club initially played at Park Hollow in the grounds of the old Nottingham Castle. After playing at several grounds, The Magpies settled at Trent Bridge Cricket Ground in 1883. On 3 September 1910, County moved to Meadow Lane

CUP FINALS

English FA Cup

1893-1894 Notts County 4 Bolton Wanderers 1

1890-1891 Blackburn Rovers 3 Notts County 1

Anglo-Italian Cup

1994-1995 Notts County 2 Ascoli 1

1993-1994 Brescia 1 Notts County 0

Anglo-Scottish Cup

1980-1981 Chesterfield 2 Notts County 1, on aggregate: 1-0 home, 1-1 away aet

MANAGERS SINCE 1980

Jimmy Sirrel - 1977 - 1982
Howard Wilkinson - 1982 - 1983
Larry Lloyd - 1983 - 1984
Ritchie Barker - 1984 - 1985
Jimmy Sirrel - 1985 - 1987
John Barnwell - 1987 - 1988
Neil Warnock - 1989 - 1993
Mick Walker - 1993 - 1994
Russell Slade - 1994 - 1995
Howard Kendall - 1995
Colin Murphy - 1995 - 1996
Steve Thompson - 1995 - 1996
Sam Allardyce - 1997 - 1999
Gary Brazil - 1999 - 2000
Jocky Scott - 2000 - 2001
Gary Brazil - 2001 - 2002
Billy Dearden - 2002 - 2004
Gary Mills - 2004
Ian Richardson - 2004 - 2005
Gudjon Thordarson -2005 - 2006
Steve Thompson -2006 - 2007
Ian McParland - 2007 - 2009
Hans Backe - 2009
Steve Cotterill - 2010
Craig Short - 2010
Paul Ince - 2010 - 2011
Martin Allen - 2011 -

NOTTINGHAM FOREST

First Division: Winners: 1977–78; Runners-up: 1966–67, 1978–79

Second Division: Winners: 1906–07, 1921–22, 1997–98
Runners-up: 1956–57, 1993–94

Third Division: Winners: 1950–51; Runners-up: 2007–08

Football Alliance: Winners: 1891–92

FA Cup: Winners: 1898, 1959; Runners-up: 1991

League Cup: Winners: 1978, 1979, 1989, 1990; Runners-up: 1980, 1992

FA Charity Shield: Winners: 1978; Runners-up: 1959

Full Members Cup: Winners: 1989, 1992

European Cup: Winners: 1979, 1980

UEFA Super Cup: Winners: 1979; Runners-up: 1980

Intercontinental Cup: Runners-up: 1980

Anglo-Scottish Cup: Winners: 1977

Bass Charity Vase: Winners: 1899, 2001, 2002

Brian Clough Trophy: Winners: 2009 (29 August), 2010 (29 December), 2011 (22 January)

Dallas Cup: Winners: 2002

Football League Centenary Tournament: Winners: 1988

Nuremberg Tournament: Winners: 1982

Trofeo Colombino Cup: Winners: 1982

Nottingham Forest originally played at the Forest Recreation Ground where they remained until 1879 when they relocated to the Meadows. Following this move, Forest began playing their more important matches at Trent Bridge due to its larger capacity. By 1880, all of Forest's matches were taking place at Trent Bridge but the club secured a site of its own in Lenton in 1882, naming it Parkside.

In 1890, Forest relocated once more, The Town Ground, on the banks of the River Trent, was built in 1890 at a cost of £1,000 before growing success led to a final move across the Trent to the current City Ground site in 1898.

CUP FINALS

English FA Cup

1990-1991	Tottenham Hotspur 2 Nottingham Forest 1, aet
1958-1959	Nottingham Forest 2 Luton Town 1
1897-1898	Nottingham Forest 3 Derby County 1

English League Cup

1991-1992	Manchester United 1 Nottingham Forest 0
1989-1990	Nottingham Forest 1 Oldham Athletic 0

1988-1989	Nottingham Forest 3 Luton Town 1
1979-1980	Wolverhampton Wndrs 1 Nottingham Forest 0
1978-1979	Nottingham Forest 3 Southampton 2
1977-1978	Nottingham Forest 1 Liverpool 0, after 0-0 draw aet

English Zenith Data Systems Cup

1991-1992	Nottingham Forest 3 Southampton 2, aet

English Simod Cup

1988-1989	Nottingham Forest 4 Everton 3, aet

English Charity Shield

1978-1979	Nottingham Forest 5 Ipswich Town 0
1959-1960	Wolverhampton Wndrs 3 Nottingham Forest 1, (at Wolverhampton Wan)

Anglo-Scottish Cup

1976-1977	Nottingham Forest 5 Leyton Orient 1, on aggregate: 1-1 away, 4-0 home

European Champions Cup

1979-1980	Nottingham Forest 1 SV Hamburg 0
1978-1979	Nottingham Forest 1 Malmo 0

UEFA Super Cup

1980-1981	Valencia 2 Nottingham Forest 2, on aggregate: 1-2 away, 1-0 home, Valencia won on away goals
1979-1980	Nottingham Forest 2 Barcelona 1, on aggregate: 1-0 home, 1-1 away

MANAGERS SINCE 1980

Brian Clough 1975 – 93
Frank Clark 1993 – 96
Stuart Pearce 1996 -97
Dave Bassett 1997 -98
Ron Atkinson 1999
David Platt 1999 – 2001
Paul Hart 2001 – 2004
Joe Kinnear 2004
Gary Megson 2005 - 2006
Frank Barlow &
Ian McParland 2006
Colin Calderwood 2006 - 2008
Billy Davies 2009 – 2011
Steve McClaren 2011
Steve Cotterill 2011-

PORT VALE

Football League Third Division / League One (3rd tier)
Runners-up: 1993–94; Play-off winners: 1988–89 (3rd place)

Football League Third Division North: 2 (3rd tier)
Champions: 1929–30, 1953–54; Runners-up: 1952–53

Football League Fourth Division / League Two: 1 (4th tier)
Champions: 1958–59; 3rd place promotion: 1982–83; 4th place promotion: 1969–70, 1985–86

Staffordshire Senior Cup: 2: Winners: 1920, 2001; Runners-up: 1900, 2010

Birmingham Senior Cup: 1: Winners: 1913; Runners-up: 1899, 1900, 1914

Anglo-Italian Cup: Runners-up: 1996

Debenhams Cup: Runners-up: 1977

Football League Trophy: Winners 1993, 2001

Port Vale started its existence at The Meadows in Limekiln Lane, Longport, A basic ground, the club moved on in 1881. They then moved on to Westport Meadows, where they played for three years.

In 1884, the club moved to its third ground, they stayed at Burslem Football and Athletic ground for just two years, the club took the area's name, the club then moved on to the Athletic Ground. It played host to the club for 27 years, It was named due to the fact that it also hosted athletics.

The Rec was Vale's home from 1913 to 1950. The club endured hard financial times during World War II, and sold the ground to the council, who were reluctant to allow the club to rent it back. Vale Park has been Port Vale's home ground since 1950.

CUP FINALS

English LDV Vans Trophy

2000-2001 Port Vale 2 Brentford 1

English Autoglass Trophy

1992-1993 Port Vale 2 Stockport County 1

Anglo-Italian Cup

1995-1996 Genoa 5 Port Vale 2

MANAGERS SINCE 1980

John McGrath 1979-1983
John Rudge 1983-1999
Brian Horton 1999-2004
Martin Foyle 2004-2007
Lee Sinnott 2007-2008
Dean Glover 2008-2009
Micky Adams 2009-2010
Jim Gannon 2011
Mark Grew 2011
Micky Adams 2011 –

SHREWSBURY TOWN

Welsh Cup

Winners 1891, 1938, 1977, 1979, 1984, 1985; runners up 1931, 1948, 1980

Football League Cup Semi Finalists 1961

Football League Trophy runners up 1996, area finalists 2003

Football League Third Division (third tier) champions 1979

Football League Third Division (fourth tier) champions 1994

Football League Fourth Division (fourth tier) runners up 1975

Football League Two (fourth tier) Playoff runners up 2007, 2009 Semi Finalists 2011

Football Conference (fifth tier) Playoff Winners 2004

Midland League (fourth tier midlands) champions 1938, 1946, 1948

Birmingham & District League(fifth tier midlands) champions 1923; runners up 1914, 1924, 1937

Shrewsbury used alot of different grounds when the club was first formed including Racecourse Ground, Monkmoor 1886-1889, then they moved on to Ambler's Field, Copthorne 1889-1893 then after a short stay again moved to Sutton Lane, Sutton Farm 1893-1895, then they spent a good 15 years at Barrack's Ground, Copthorne 1895-1910, then were based at Gay Meadow, Abbey Foregate 1910-2007 before moving to The Greenhous Meadow, Oteley Road, Meole Brace in 2007.

English Auto Windscreens Shield

1995-1996 Rotherham United 2 Shrewsbury Town 1

MANAGERS SINCE 1980

Graham Turner 1978-1984
Chic Bates 1984-1987
Ken Brown 1987
Ian McNeill 1987-1990
Asa Hartford 1990-1991
John Bond 1991-1993
Fred Davies 1993-1997
Jake King 1997-1999
Chic Bates 1999
Kevin Ratcliffe 1999-2003
Mark Atkins 2003
Jimmy Quinn 2003-2004
Chic Bates 2004
Gary Peters 2004-2008
Paul Simpson 2008-2010
Graham Turner 2010 –

STOKE CITY

Football League Championship
Runners-up: 2007–08

Football League Second Division: 3
Champions: 1932–33, 1962–63, 1992–93
Runners-up: 1921–22

Third Place: (Promoted) 1978–79
Play-off Winners: 2001–02

Football League Third Division North: 1
Champions: 1926–27

Football Alliance: 1
Champions: 1890–91

Birmingham & District League: 1
Champions: 1910–11

Southern League Division Two: 2
Champions:1909–10, 1914–15
Runners-up: 1910–11

The Central League (Reserves): 3
Champions: 1927–28, 2003–04

Division Two Champions: 1991–92
United Soccer Association (as Cleveland Stokers)
Runners-up: 1967 (Eastern Division)

FA Cup
Runners-up: 2010–11
Semi-finalists: 1898–99, 1970–71 (3rd place), 1971–72 (4th place)

League Cup: 1
Winners: 1971–72
Runners-up: 1963–64

Football League Trophy: 2
Winners: 1991–92, 1999–2000

Watney Cup: 1
Winners: 1973

Staffordshire Senior Cup: 13
Winners: 1878, 1879, 1904 (Shared), 1914, 1965, 1969 (Shared), 1971, 1975, 1976, 1982, 1993, 1995, 1999
Runners-up: 1883, 1886, 1895, 1901, 1903, 2003, 2006, 2011

Birmingham Senior Cup: 2
Winners: 1901, 1914
Runners-up: 1910, 1915, 1920, 1921

Isle of Man Trophy: 3
Winners: 1987, 1991, 1992
Runners-up: 1985

Bass Charity Vase: 5
Winners: 1980, 1991, 1992, 1995, 1998
Runners-up: 1890, 1894, 1990, 1996

FA Youth Cup
Runners-up: 1983–84

It is unclear where Stoke's original playing fields were located. Their first pitch was certainly in the site of a present burial ground in Lonsdale Street, although there is evidence that they also played on land near to the Copeland Arms public house on Campbell Road. In 1875 they moved to Sweetings Field. Stoke were to stay at Sweetings Field until a merger with the Stoke Victoria Cricket Club in March 1878, when Stoke moved to the Victoria Ground.

By 1995 Stoke drew up plans to make the ground an all seater stadium, to comply with the Taylor Report. However, the club decided it would be better to leave the Victoria Ground and re-locate to a new site.

In 1997 Stoke left the Victoria Ground after 119 years, and moved to the modern 28,384 all seater Britannia Stadium at a cost of £14.7 million.

CUP FINALS

English FA Cup

2010-2011 Manchester City 1 Stoke City 0

English League Cup

1971-1972 Stoke City 2 Chelsea 1
1963-1964 Leicester City 4 Stoke City 3, on aggregate: 1-1 away, 3-2 home

English Auto Windscreens Shield

1999-2000 Stoke City 2 Bristol City 1

English Autoglass Trophy

1991-1992 Stoke City 1 Stockport County 0

English Watney Cup

1973-1974 Stoke City 2 Hull City 0, (at Stoke City)

MANAGERS SINCE 1980

Alan Durban 1978 – 1981
Richie Barker 1981-1983
Bill Asprey 1983-1985
Tony Lacey 1985
Mick Mills 1985-1989
Alan Ball 1989-1991
Graham Paddon 1991
Lou Macari 1991-1993
Joe Jordan 1993-1994
Asa Hartford 1994
Lou Macari 1994-1997
Chic Bates 1997-1998
Chris Kamara 1998
Alan Durban 1998
Brian Little 1998-1999
Gary Megson 1999
Gudjon Thordarson 1999-2002
Steve Cotterill 2002
Dave Kevan 2002
Tony Pulis 2002-2005
Johan Boskamp 2005-2006
Tony Pulis 2006 -

TAMWORTH

Conference North
Champions: 2009

Southern Football League Premier Division
Champions: 2003
Runners-Up: 2002

FA Trophy
Runners-Up: 2003

FA Vase
Champions: 1989

Southern Football League Division One Midlands
Champions: 1997

West Midlands (Regional) League
Champions: 1964, 1966, 1972, 1988

West Midlands League Cup
Champions: 1965, 1966, 1972, 1986, 1988

Birmingham Senior Cup
Champions: 1961, 1966, 1969

Staffordshire Senior Cup
Champions: 1959, 1964, 1966, 2002

Harry Godfrey Trophy
Champions: 1994, 1997

Tamworth have played at The Lamb Ground since 1934. Prior to this, they spent their first season at a ground adjacent to the Jolly Sailor pub. The Lamb Ground takes its name from a pub, the Lamb Inn, which formerly stood nearby.

MANAGERS SINCE 1980

Alan Fogarty 1979-1980
Alan Hampton 1980-1982
Barry Meads 1982
Harry Shepherd 1982-1983
Barry Meads 1983-1984
Dave Seedhouse 1984-1986
Roger Smith 1986-1987
Graham Smith 1987-1991
Frank Dwane & Paul Wood 1992
Sammy Chung 1992-1993
Alan Hampton 1993
Dave Seedhouse 1993
Paul Wood 1993-1994
Les Green 1994-1995
Degsy Bond 1995
Paul Hendrie 1995-2000
Tim Steele 2001
Gary Mills 2001-2002
Darron Gee 2002-2004
Mark Cooper 2004-2007
Adie Smith & Dale Belford 2007
Gary Mills 2007-2010
Des Lyttle 2010-2011
Dale Belford 2011
Marcus Law 2011 -

AFC TELFORD UNITED

Northern Premier League Division 1 Play off winners 2004/2005
Northern Premier League Premier Division Play off winners 2006/2007
Conference North Play off Winners 2010/2011
Setanta Shield Winners 2008/2009

AFC Telford United play their home games at the New Bucks Head. Construction of the stadium commenced in 2000, replacing the Bucks Head ground which had been home to Wellington Town and later Telford United for over a century, The stadium, which could originally hold up to 6,300 supporters, was completed in 2003 and was the 111th largest football ground in England.

MANAGERS SINCE 1980

Bernard McInally 2004-2006
Rob Smith 2006-2010
Andy Sinton 2010 -

WALSALL

Old Division Four Champions : 1959–60

Old Division Three Runners-Up : 1960–61

Old Division Four Runners-Up : 1979–80

Old Division Three Play-Off Winners : 1987–88

Division Three Runners-Up : 1994–95

Division Two Runner-Up : 1998–99

Division Two Play-Off Winners : 2000–01

League Two Champions: 2006–07

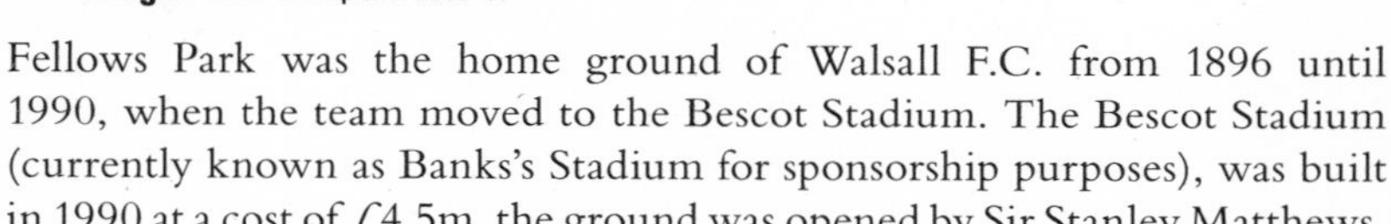
Fellows Park was the home ground of Walsall F.C. from 1896 until 1990, when the team moved to the Bescot Stadium. The Bescot Stadium (currently known as Banks's Stadium for sponsorship purposes), was built in 1990 at a cost of £4.5m, the ground was opened by Sir Stanley Matthews.

MANAGERS SINCE 1980

Alan Buckley 1979-1981
Alan Buckley & Neil Martin 1981-1982
Neil Martin 1982
Alan Buckley 1982-1986
Tommy Coakley 1986-1988
John Barnwell 1989-1990
Kenny Hibbitt 1990-1994
Chris Nicholl 1994-1997
Jan Sorenson 1997-1998
Ray Graydon 1998-2002
Colin Lee 2002-2004
Paul Merson 2004-2006
Mick Halsall 2006
Kevan Broadhurst 2006
Mark Kinsella 2006
Richard Money 2006-2008
Jimmy Mullen 2008-2009
Chris Hutchings 2009-2011
Dean Smith 2011 –

WEST BROMWICH ALBION

Football League First Division (old) Premier League (modern)
Champions: 1919–1920
Runners up: 1924–1925 , 1953–1954
Third Place: 1978-1979

Football League Second Division (old), Division One,
Football League Championship (modern)
Champions: 1901–1902, 1910–1911, 2007–2008
Runners up: 1930–1931 , 1948–1949 , 2001–2002 , 2003–2004 , 2009–2010

Football League Third Division (old), Division Two, Football League One (modern)
Play-off Winners: 1992–1993

FA Cup
Winners: 1888, 1892, 1931, 1954, 1968
Runners up: 1886, 1887, 1895, 1912, 1935

League Cup
Winners: 1966
Runners up: 1967, 1970

FA Charity Shield
Winners: 1920, 1954 (shared with Wolves)
Runners up: 1931, 1968

Bass Charity Vase: 1999, 2000, 2003

FA Youth Cup
Winners: 1976
Runners up: 1955, 1960

Tennent Caledonian Cup: 1977

Birmingham Senior Cup
Winners: 1886, 1895, 1988, 1990, 1991
Runners up: 1887, 1888, 1890, 1892, 1894, 1903, 1905, 2002

Staffordshire Senior Cup: 1883, 1886, 1887, 1889, 1900, 1902, 1903, 1924, 1926, 1932, 1933, 1951, 1969 (shared with Stoke City)

Watney Cup
Runners up: 1971

The Baggies' first ground was Cooper's Hill, where they played from 1878 to 1879. From 1879 to 1881 they alternated between Cooper's Hill and Dartmouth Park.During the 1881–82 season they played at Bunn's Field, also known as The Birches. From 1882 to 1885, Albion rented the Four Acres ground from West Bromwich Dartmouth Cricket Club. From 1885 to 1900 Albion played at Stoney Lane.

By 1900, they moved to a new ground called The Hawthorns, The Hawthorns became an all-seater stadium in the 1990s, in order to comply with the recommendations of the Taylor Report.

CUP FINALS

English FA Cup

1967-1968	West Bromwich Albion 1 Everton 0, aet
1953-1954	West Bromwich Albion 3 Preston North End 2
1934-1935	Sheffield Wednesday 4 West Bromwich Albion 2
1930-1931	West Bromwich Albion 2 Birmingham City 1
1911-1912	Barnsley 1 West Bromwich Albion 0, aet, after 0-0 draw
1894-1895	Aston Villa 1 West Bromwich Albion 0
1891-1892	West Bromwich Albion 3 Aston Villa 0
1887-1888	West Bromwich Albion 2 Preston North End 1
1886-1887	Aston Villa 2 West Bromwich Albion 0
1885-1886	Blackburn Rovers 2 West Bromwich Albion 0, after 0-0 draw

English League Cup

1969-1970	Manchester City 2 West Bromwich Albion 1, aet
1966-1967	Queens Park Rangers 3 West Bromwich Albion 2
1965-1966	West Bromwich Albion 5 West Ham United 3, on aggregate: 1-2 away, 4-1 home

English Charity Shield

1968-1969	Manchester City 6 West Bromwich Albion 1, (at Manchester City)
1954-1955	Wolverhampton Wndrs 4 West Bromwich Albion 4 (shared), (at Wolverhampton Wan)
1931-1932	Arsenal 1 West Bromwich Albion 0
1920-1921	West Bromwich Albion 2 Tottenham Hotspur 0, (at Tottenham H)

English Watney Cup

1971-1972	Colchester United 4 West Bromwich Albion 4, aet, Colchester Utd won on penalties (at West Brom Alb)

MANAGERS SINCE 1980

Ron Atkinson 1978-1981
Ronnie Allen 1981-1982
Ron Wylie 1982-1984
Johnny Giles 1984-1985
Nobby Stiles 1985-1986
Ron Saunders 1986-1987
Ron Atkinson 1987-1988
Brian Talbot 1988-1991
Stuart Pearson 1991
Bobby Gould 1991-1992
Osvaldo Ardiles 1992-1993
Keith Burkinshaw 1993-1994
Alan Buckley 1994-1997
Arthur Mann 1997
Ray Harford 1997
Richie Barker 1997
John Trewick 1997
Denis Smith 1997-1999
Cyrille Regis & John Gorman 1999
Brian Little 1999-2000
Cyrille Regis & Allan Evans 2000
Gary Megson 2000-2004
Frank Burrows 2004
Bryan Robson 2004-2006
Nigel Pearson 2006
Craig Shakespeare 2006
Tony Mowbray 2006-2009
Roberto Di Matteo 2009-2011
Roy Hodgson 2011 –

WOLVES

First Division
Champions: 1953–54, 1957–58, 1958–59

Championship / Second Division
Champions: 1931–32, 1976–77, 2008–09
Play-off winners: 2003

Third Division (North) / Third Division
Champions: 1923–24, 1988–89

Fourth Division
Champions: 1987–88

UEFA Cup
Runners-up: 1972

FA Cup
Winners: 1893, 1908, 1949, 1960
Runners-up: 1889, 1896, 1921, 1939
Third-place: 1973
Semi-finalists: 1890, 1951, 1979, 1981, 1998

Football League Cup
Winners: 1974, 1980
Semi-finalists: 1973

FA Charity Shield
Winners: 1949*, 1954*, 1959, 1960* (* joint holders)
Runners-up: 1958

Football League Trophy
Winners: 1988
Texaco Cup
Winners: 1971

Football League War Cup
Winners: 1942

FA Youth Cup
Winners: 1958
Runners-up: 1953, 1954, 1962, 1976

United Soccer Association
Champions 1967 – playing as Los Angeles Wolves

North American Soccer League International Cup
Winners 1969 – playing as Kansas City Spurs

The Central League
Winners 1931–32, 1950–51, 1951–52, 1952–53, 1957–58, 1958–59

Birmingham Senior Cup
Winners 1891-92, 1892-93, 1893-94, 1899-1900, 1901-02, 1923-24, 1986-87
Runners-up 1888-89, 1896-97, 1897-98, 1903-04, 1906-07, 1908-09, 1912-13, 1998-99, 2003-04

Birmingham Football Combination
Winners 1934-35

Birmingham and District League
Winners 1892-93, 1897-98, 1898-99, 1900-01, 1953-54, 1957-58, 1958-59

Worcestershire Football Combination
Winners 1957-58

Staffordshire Senior Cup
Winners 1887-88, 1893-94, 1966-67
Runners Up 1884-85

Walsall Senior Cup
Runners Up 1885-86

Wrekin Cup
Winners 1884 (First ever Trophy)

Gothia World Youth Cup
Winners 2009

Wolverhampton Wanderers have played at Molineux, Whitmore Reans, since 1889. Their previous home was in the Blakenhall area, and although no signs of the ground remain, a nearby road is called Wanderers Avenue. The Molineux name originates from Benjamin Molineux, a local merchant who built his home on the grounds.

In 1953, the stadium became one of the first to install floodlights, at an estimated cost of £10,000. The first ever floodlit game was held on 30 September 1953, as Wolves won 3–1 against South Africa.

CUP FINALS

English FA Cup

1959-1960	Wolverhampton Wndrs 3 Blackburn Rovers 0
1948-1949	Wolverhampton Wndrs 3 Leicester City 1
1938-1939	Portsmouth 4 Wolverhampton Wndrs 1
1920-1921	Tottenham Hotspur 1 Wolverhampton Wndrs 0
1907-1908	Wolverhampton Wndrs 3 Newcastle United 1
1895-1896	Sheffield Wednesday 2 Wolverhampton Wndrs 1
1892-1893	Wolverhampton Wndrs 1 Everton 0
1888-1889	Preston North End 3 Wolverhampton Wndrs 0

English League Cup

1979-1980	Wolverhampton Wndrs 1 Nottingham Forest 0
1973-1974	Wolverhampton Wndrs 2 Manchester City 1

English Sherpa Vans Trophy

1987-1988	Wolverhampton Wndrs 2 Burnley 0

English Charity Shield

1960-1961	Burnley 2 Wolverhampton Wndrs 2 (shared), (at Burnley)
1959-1960	Wolverhampton Wndrs 3 Nottingham Forest 1, (at Wolverhampton Wan)
1958-1959	Bolton Wanderers 4 Wolverhampton Wndrs 1, (at Bolton)
1954-1955	Wolverhampton Wndrs 4 West Bromwich Albion 4 (shared), (at Wolverhampton Wan)

1949-1950 Portsmouth 1 Wolverhampton Wndrs 1 (shared), (at Portsmouth)

English Texaco Cup

1970-1971 Wolverhampton Wndrs 3 Heart of Midlothian 2, on aggregate: 3-1 away, 0-1 home

UEFA Cup

1971-1972 Tottenham Hotspur 3 Wolverhampton Wndrs 2, on aggregate: 2-1 away, 1-1 home

MANAGERS SINCE 1980

John Barnwell 1978-1982
Ian Greaves 1982
Graham Hawkins 1982-1984
Tommy Docherty 1984-1985
Bill McGarry 1985
Sammy Chapman 1985-1986
Graham Turner 1986-1994
Graham Taylor 1994-1995
Mark McGhee 1995-1998
Colin Lee 1998-2000
Dave Jones 2001-2004
Glenn Hoddle 2004-2006
Mick McCarthy 2006 -

CLUB LEGENDS

(In no particular order, chosen by the fans)

ASTON VILLA

PAUL MCGRATH

1989-1996 - 252 apps, 9 goals

'Macca' played some of the best football of his career at Villa Park, despite recurrent knee problems which meant he hardly trained. Villa came close to winning the title in his first season. He won the PFA Player of the Year award in his time there and also helped the club defeat Manchester United in the 1993–94 Football League Cup final.

McGrath left in 1996 after Villa won another League Cup and he is widely regarded one of the greatest players in the club's history. His nickname was 'God' by Villa fans, who still remember him by singing a terrace chant every matchday to the tune of "Kumbaya". Paul has since started a musical career.

IAN TAYLOR

1994-2003 - 234 apps, 28 goals

Ian played in the Aston Villa side that won the 1996 League Cup final 3–0 against Leeds United and 'Tails' got on the scoresheet. He scored important goals in Villa's 1997–1998 UEFA Cup run, when they would eventually be knocked out to Atlético Madrid on away goals at the quarter-final stage. He also helped Villa reach the 2000 FA Cup Final.

A lifelong supporter of the club he used to stand on the famous Holte End as a kid. It is perhaps for this reason, combined with his utterly committed displays and knack of scoring crucial goals, that he quickly became a fans' favourite. He is often seen at away games and sits with the fans, he is now an Ambassador for the club.

Ian was released by manager Graham Taylor in the summer of 2003

TONY MORLEY

1979-1983 - 137 apps, 25 gls

Tony joined Villa for £200,000 in June 1979. A skilful winger, he enjoyed the best days of his career here. He was seen as a wayward genius but was moulded by Ron Saunders into one of the most dangerous players around. He was famed for scoring spectacular goals.

A vital part of the Villa side that won the League Championship in 1980–81, and later the European Cup in 1982, Tony crossed the ball in for Peter Withe to score the famous winning goal.

Morley won six caps also for England before he was transferred to local rivals West Bromwich Albion. Tony is still involved with the club and does radio work in his spare time too.

MARTIN LAURSEN

2004-2009 - 84 apps, 8 gls

Martin arrived for a fee of £3 million, on a four-year contract. He made an impression in early games but he was plagued with knee injuries which meant he missed a lot of games early in his Villa career.

Laursen became an effective goalscorer for Villa during the 2007–08 season, scoring six times, not bad for a centre half. That season he was also voted Supporters' Player of the Year.

Laursen became club captain when Gareth Barry left. In May 2009 Martin announced his decision to retire from football rather than undergo major surgery. He was included in the "Villa Legends" section on Aston Villa's official website. He will always be remembered fondly by the Villa Faithful.

PETER WITHE

1980-1985 - 182 apps, 74 goals

Ron Saunders brought Peter to Villa Park on the eve of the 1980–81 season when they forked out £500,000, the club's record signing at the time. Peter scored 20 times in 36 games to finish joint-top scorer in the league with Tottenham Hotspur's Steve Archibald helping Villa secure the title. Withe was also the scorer of Villa's famous winner against Bayern Munich in the European Cup final of 1982.

After 5 years, he moved on to Sheffield United, in what he later described as "the biggest wrench of my career." Capped by England 11 times, Withe scored once, and was also the first-ever English player representing Aston Villa to feature in a World Cup Finals squad in 1982. He has done a lot of coaching since finishing playing.

Also High on the list by fans were ...
Olof Mellberg, Dean Saunders, Ashley Young, Gordon Cowans

★

BIRMINGHAM CITY

MARTIN GRAINGER

1996-2005 - 225 apps, 25 goals

The popular defender left in December 2004. He was an attacking left back who could also play further up the field or even as a winger and was a dead ball specialist. Martini joined Birmingham City on 25th March 1996 and quickly became an inspirational player due to his continued consistency and ability from set-pieces.

He picked up the fans' Player of the Season award for 1999–2000 and played for Birmingham in the 2001 Football League Cup Final defeat to Liverpool, where he unfortunately missed one of the spot kicks in the shootout

Grainger retired from football on 1 January 2005, having spent 13 years as a player. His goal-scoring appearance against Manchester United on 10 April 2004, proved to be his final professional fixture.

MIKAEL FORSSELL

2003-2008 - 101 apps, 30 goals

Mikael joined in 2005 on a three-year deal for a fee of £3 million, he unfortunately had a few injuries in his time at St Andrews.

His 2007–08 pre-season performances were good and he scored five goals in five games. He scored his first hat-trick on 1st March 2008 in the 4–1 win over Tottenham Hotspur. In his final season at the Blues, he finished the season as their top scorer with nine goals as the club were relegated from the Premier League

GEOFF HORSFIELD

2000-2003 - 108 apps, 23 goals

In July 2000, Geoff signed a five-year contract with the Blues, who paid a club record fee of £2.25 million, He was their top scorer in his first season, finding the net on twelve occasions.

In the 2001–02 season, Horsfield was chosen as Player of the Year by both fans and players. Horsfield's first Premier League goal came in the September 2002 local derby defeat of Aston Villa. He also scored in the return fixture at Villa Park, an eventful game in which he ended up keeping goal when Nico Vaesen was injured after Birmingham had used all their substitutes.

PAUL TAIT

1988-1999 - 170 apps, 14 goals

Paul was born and bred in Sutton Coldfield. As a young lad he played as a striker but spent most of his playing career as a midfielder. He turned professional with the Blues in 1988 and played for the club for eleven years. He got into trouble during the 1995 Auto Windscreens Shield final when, after scoring the winner, he revealed a t-shirt reading "Shit on the Villa". He was fined two weeks' wages for the incident that was a mad moment that caused a stir.

NIGEL GLEGHORN

1989-1992 - 142 apps, 33 goals

After being at Manchester City, Nigel signed for Blues, recently relegated to the Third Division, for a relatively big fee of £175,000. He stayed for three seasons, helping them to victory in the Leyland DAF Cup final in 1991 and promotion to Division One in 1991–92. In that season he was Blues' top scorer with 22 goals and scored the winner against Shrewsbury Town in the last home game of the season when the club needed a win to be sure of automatic promotion.

Also High on the list by fans were...
Christophe Dugarry, Darren Purse, Stan Lazaridis

BURTON ALBION

DARREN STRIDE

1993-2010 - 654 apps, 124 goals

Darren captained the side for 12 years, He had been part of the first team since progressing from the youth team and had become the club's record holder for most appearances. He had also played in every single position during his time at the club, even pulling on the goalkeeping jersey in an emergency. Definitely a team player!

Stride was released at the end of the 2009–10 after 17 years with the club. He joined Alfreton Town on a one-year deal in August 2010.

SIMON REDFERN

1986-1998 - 457 apps, 86 goals

Simon was a great character and really popular with his team mates and the club's fans. He had so many great performances and played in a lot of really big games always performing well. He will always be a fans' favourite and loved forever.

JOHN BRAYFORD

2005-2008 - 100 apps, 8 goals

John progressed through the youth ranks at 'The Brewers' after spending time as a boy with both Manchester City and Stoke City. He was a part of the England Schools FA team that faced Australia in February 2006. Having signed professional forms, John made his first team debut for Burton just two months later against Ebbsfleet United.

A right back, John also played in the centre of defence and in midfield, he was known for scoring goals having scored five for Burton in the 2007/2008 season

AARON WEBSTER

1998 - present 436 apps, 77 goals

Aaron made his first team debut in September 1998. He was in the first team when as a 17 year old and, under the guidance of former manager Nigel Clough, he became one of the most accomplished left sided players in the non-league game starting as a winger and turning into a cultured left back with a knack of scoring important goals. He is now third in Albion's all time appearances.

PHIL ANNABLE

1970-1980 & 1981-1983 - 567 apps, 70 goals

Phil was a big tough Defender and a popular player who had two spells with the club. He had a great relationship with the Brewers fans.

★

CHELTENHAM TOWN

JAMIE VICTORY

1996-2007 - 258 apps, 22 goals

Jamie signed on at Cheltenham Town on a free from Bournemouth in 1995. At the start of the 2006–07 season, Jamie had a testimonial game featuring the current team against a team of Cheltenham legends including Julian Alsop, Mike Duff, Martin Devaney, and Steve Book among others.

In May 2007, he was released by Cheltenham after eleven years with the club.

JULIAN ALSOP

2000-2003 & 2009-2010 - 222 apps, 39 goals

Julian signed for Cheltenham Town from Swansea and wasn't really prolific in his first season, but his second year proved to be a revelation. Alsop scored 26 goals, including the second goal as Cheltenham beat Rushden and Diamonds 3–1 in the Division Three play-off final. He left Cheltenham for Oxford United at the end of 2002–03.

On 20 July 2009, Alsop signed a month-by month agreement and returned with Cheltenham Town, after playing in the first three pre-season friendlies for the club.

NEIL GRAYSON

1998-2002 - 162 apps, 48 goals

Cheltenham Town made a £15,000 bid for Neil in March 1998. He was instrumental in Cheltenham's promotion to the Football League in 1998-99. He was subsequently named Conference Player of the Year. His last appearances for the club were in the successful 2001-02 playoff campaign, He was soon released by the club and then joined non-league side Forest Green Rovers.

CHRIS BANKS

1994-2004 - 397 apps, 1 goal

In July 1994 Chris made the move to Cheltenham and went on to captain the side as they rose from the Southern League to the Football League. While playing part-time he worked as a tiler he turned to full-time football on Cheltenham's promotion to the Football League. He was forced to retire through injury in November 2004.

LEE HOWELLS

1991-2004 - 367 apps, 66 goals

Lee was a popular midfielder in his time at Cheltenham Town and played a key role in a number of important games. He also spent time in his career in Australia. He was with the club for 13 years.

★

COVENTRY CITY

DION DUBLIN

1994-1998 - 145 apps, 61 goals

In four-and-a-half years with Coventry, Dion established himself as one of the Premier League's top strikers, In the 1997–98 season, he equalled the Coventry City record for most goals in a top division season with 23 goals in all competitions.

The 1997/98 season also saw Dublin share elite status as the Premier League's top scorer with Blackburn's Chris Sutton and Liverpool's Michael Owen – each Englishman scoring 18 league goals.

No City fan would deny the enormous contribution that Dion Dublin made to the club's fortunes. No other Coventry City player has scored more goals for the Sky Blues in England's top division.

STEVE OGRIZOVIC

1984-2000 - 504 apps, 1 goal

Steve achieved fame during 16 years at Coventry City. He holds the record at Coventry for the most appearances as a player at 601 in all competitions (504 in the league) and he played in the winning FA Cup team of 1987. Fans will never forget him. I remember watching him a lot on Match of the Day as a child, he always stood out, Steve was a fantastic keeper.

MICK QUINN

1992-1994 - 64 apps, 25 goals

On 20th November 1992, Micky arrived at Coventry City. Bobby Gould paid £250,000 for his services.

During his first six months at Highfield Road, Quinn scored 17 Premier League goals – 10 of them in his first 6 games. Scoring in his first four games makes him one of only six players to perform this feat, of which he scored a brace against each of Crystal Palace, Liverpool and Aston Villa

Eventually he was pushed further down the pecking order by the arrival of £2 million striker Dion Dublin from Manchester United.

TREVOR PEAKE

1983-1991 - 335 apps, 7 goals

Trevor moved to Coventry City for £100,000 on July 6th 1983. He really made his name in football. It was the FA Cup that brought Trevor the best moment of his career. Coventry reached the FA Cup final in 1987 where they played Tottenham Hotspur at Wembley. A 3-2 victory saw Coventry achieve the best moment in their history and Trevor was a part of it. However, he also experienced the lows of the FA Cup when he was in the Coventry team that were beaten 2-1 by non-league Sutton United.

GARY MCALLISTER

1996-2000 - 119 apps, 20 goals & 2002-2004 - 55 apps, 10 goals

McAllister joined Coventry City on 26th July 1996, for a fee of £3,000,000. He stayed there for four seasons. His final season at the club started poorly – including defeat by Tranmere Rovers in the league cup – followed by a stylish and creditable finish. Some of the home form is regarded by many City fans as among the best of the previous decade with Robbie Keane and Cedric Roussel leading the attack. Having experienced a difficult start at the club, McAllister won over the fans and remains a respected figure at Coventry City.

Also High on the list by fans were …
Darren Huckerby, Richard Shaw, Marcus Hall,
Peter Ndlovu, Moustapha Hadji, Yousef Chippo

DERBY COUNTY

IGOR ŠTIMAC

1995-1999 - 84 apps, 3 goals

Štimac arrived on the 31st October 1995 for a fee of £1.5 million from Hajduk Split. He scored a goal on his debut for the Rams away at Tranmere but the Rams suffered a 5-1 defeat. The rest of the season, Derby gained promotion and was unbeaten in 20 consecutive matches. Igor was sold on 29th August 1999 to West Ham United for £600,000.

In all, Štimac made 84 league appearances for the Rams, In 2009 he was voted into a fans' greatest ever Derby County team, by readers of the *Derby Evening Telegraph.*

PAULO WANCHOPE

1996-1999 - 72 apps, 23 goals

Paulo went to England and Derby County on 27th March 1997. He cost Derby £600,000.

Wanchope marked his debut for Derby in impressive fashion, scoring a memorable goal which I remember very well, it was against Manchester United at Old Trafford, beating four United players before slotting past Peter Schmeichel during a 3–2 win – the goal was later voted the greatest in the club's history by the Derby fans as part of the club's 125th Anniversary Celebrations.

Wanchope was eventually sold to West Ham United for £3.5 million on 28th July 1999.

ALIJOSA ASANOVIC

1997 - 38 apps, 7 goals

An undeniably talented attacking midfielder who played a big part in the Rams' first Premiership season, Alijosa was a very popular player with Rams Fans.

ROY MCFARLAND

1967-1981 - 434 apps, 44 goals & 1983-1984 - 8 apps, 0 goals

Roy signed for Derby on 25th August 1967, as they were preparing for a challenge to win promotion to the First Division.

He was famous during the late 1960s and 1970s as a central defender in the Derby side which won promotion to the First Division in 1969 and followed this success with two league titles; the first under Cloughie in 1972 and the second under Dave Mackay in 1975. He also won 28 caps for England.

COLIN TODD

1971-1978 - 293 apps, 6 goals

After 191 appearances and three goals in all competitions for Sunderland, Todd rejoined Cloughie at Derby County in February 1971.

On joining Derby, he had cost them a record transfer fee for a defender of £175,000. When linked with Derby, Cloughie famously remarked "We're not signing Colin Todd, we can't afford him". He then signed him that same day. Cloughie sent the chairman Sam Longson a telegram informing him of the signing and the size of the fee: £175,000.

Colin helped Derby win the First Division title in his first full season at the Baseball Ground and collected a second title winner's medal under Dave Mackay in 1975. He also won the PFA Players' Player of the Year award in 1975.

★

KETTERING TOWN

RENE HOWE

2006-2007 - 40 apps, 25 goals

Howe was signed by Kettering Town in 2006. After scoring 25 goals and helping Kettering to finish as runners-up in the Conference North, he then moved to Peterborough United on 2nd May 2007 for an undisclosed fee.

KEITH ALEXANDER

1984-1986 - 74 apps, 11 goals

Keith joined Kettering Town just before the start of the 1983–84 season, where he spent two seasons and played 74 games scoring

11 times. During his time at Kettering, Alexander had a brief, but successful, loan spell at Wisbech Town, and was instrumental in the club's FA Vase run that year. Keith was a real top guy and a good professional.

CARL SHUTT

1999-2003 - 76 apps, 5 goals

Carl joined non-league Kettering Town, initially as a player. In February 2001 he took over as caretaker manager. Though unable to avoid relegation, his position was made permanent and he led them back to the Conference at the first attempt. In the 2002–03 season, he managed the club through a difficult period with the club up for sale and facing the prospect of administration. It was a losing battle and when they were relegated, the club decided to terminate his contract.

CARL ALFORD

1994-1996 - 94 apps, 54 goals & 2001 (Loan) - 2 apps, 0 goals

Carl scored a number of cracking goals and was a real competitive player, After scoring 54 goals for Kettering Town in 18 months, Rushden & Diamonds offer of £85,000, a non-league record, was enough to persuade the Poppies to sell and he arrived at Nene Park at the end of March 1996. After a period on loan back at Kettering Town in January 2001, he joined Yeovil Town in the summer helping them to lift the FA Trophy in 2002.

CRAIG WESTCARR

2006-2009 - 102 apps, 23 goals

Craig spent two successful seasons at Kettering. He made an instant impact, winning Conference North Player of the Month in the first few weeks of the season, Kettering finally finished second and lost in the promotion play-offs.

In Westcarr's second season, he was played mostly as a winger, but as Kettering's striking situation got desperate, he tried the position and ended the season as the club's top goalscorer, in a season that saw them win the league in April to clinch promotion to the Conference National. He ended up leaving for Stevenage.

KIDDERMINSTER HARRIERS

MARK YATES

1994-1999 & 2004 - 249 apps, 42 goals

Mark Yates dropped out of the Football League to sign for Conference side Kidderminster Harriers in 1994, going on to become captain. In his first season at the club Kidderminster reached the final of the FA Trophy, losing 2-1 to Woking. In 1997 Yates seemed set for a return to League football as Kidderminster led the Conference by a significant margin going into the final months of the season, but ended up losing out to Macclesfield Town.

In January 1999 Yates left Kidderminster to join local rivals Cheltenham Town for a fee of £25,000, After falling out of favour, Yates returned to Kidderminster in 2004.

PAUL JONES

1986-1991 - 242 apps, 0 goals

Paul started his career with the Harriers as a real solid young goalkeeper before he moved to Wolverhampton Wanderers for a fee of £60,000. He played less than 50 games for Wolves before moving to Stockport County.

JUSTIN RICHARDS

2007-2009 - 65 apps, 22 goals

At the end of the 2006–07 season, Justin signed on a free transfer. He was considered a big signing for the club at the time and he scored 6 goals in 22 appearances in his opening season. In January 2008, he joined Oxford United on loan until the end of the season. He managed just one goal in fifteen appearances.

Richards returned to Kidderminster and decided to stay on at the club for the 2008–09 season. He enjoyed his second most prolific season in the Conference, hitting seventeen goals in all competitions.

BRIAN SMIKLE

2006-2010 - 137 apps, 21 goals

In May 2006, West Bromwich Albion announced that Smikle's contract would not be renewed. He left the Baggies and late in July

2006, he signed for Kidderminster Harriers where he stayed until May 2010, he was a fine winger at the club, popular with the Harriers fans

ADIE SMITH

1997-2004 - 211 apps, 12 goals

Adie joined on 1st August 1997 for £19,000. Smith became a fans' favourite at Kidderminster and, after just two seasons in the Conference, Harriers won the Conference title in the 1999-00 season, and were promoted to the Third Division.

He stayed with Kidderminster for another three seasons in the Third Division.

★

LEICESTER CITY

MATT ELLIOTT

1997-2005 - 245 apps, 26 goals

Matt signed for Leicester City in early 1997 for a transfer fee of £1.6 million. He was one of the most memorable players in the Premier League, he seemed to score every other game, he was always in the news. He was a great defender chipping in with the odd goal.

Elliott signed the last contract of his career in August 2001, which would last until June 2005.

He had a loan spell at Ipswich Town before his retirement. Elliott retired from football in January 2005.

MUZZY IZZET

1996-2004 - 269 apps, 38 goals

Izzet joined Leicester on loan originally but was then able to make his move permanent for a fee of £800,000. He started off well when they came 9th in the Premier League and won the League Cup. Izzet formed a great partnership in midfield with Neil Lennon, which proved vital for Leicester.

In the 1998–99 season, The Foxes came 10th in the league, and reached the League Cup final again, but lost out to spurs. The following season, Leicester came 8th, and again got to the League Cup

Final, this time coming up against Tranmere Rovers, of Division One. This time they won 2–1, with Matt Elliott getting both goals. His time at Leicester drew interest from West Ham and Middlesbrough, but he did not leave the club.

Muzzy was a very creative player and will always be remembered as one of The Foxes' better players.

NEIL LENNON

1996-2000 - 170 apps, 6 goals

Neil was a great battling midlfielder, he had a great partnership with Muzzy Izzet and also played alongside Robbie Savage, Matt Elliott, and Steve Walsh. He was part of a great team and enjoyed a lot of success, he was a fans' favourite before moving to Celtic in December 2000. Lennon became Celtic captain in 2005 and later became their manager, which was a very brave move considering his background.

ROBBIE SAVAGE

1997-2002 - 172 apps, 8 goals

Robbie joined Leicester City for a fee of £400,000, managed by Martin O'Neill in July 1997. Savage spent five years at Leicester, where he made his name as a reliable, competitive and fiery midfielder.

One of the most memorable moments involving Robbie was when he was head butted by Dion Dublin in one of the Villa v Birmingham City Derby games.

Robbie is now working in the media and involved in live football coverage with ESPN and recently involved in Strictly Come Dancing.

GARY LINEKER

1978 -1985 - 194 apps, 95 goals

Gary began his football career at Leicester City and became known as a prolific goalscorer. He finished as the First Division's joint top goalscorer in 1984–85, earning his first England cap. He moved to Everton where he remained a clinical finisher, scoring 38 goals in 52 games before moving to Barcelona. Famous for his international career, Gary has since worked for the BBC covering World Cups, European Championships and Match of the Day programmes and also hosting Sport Relief and Sports Personality of the Year and the odd Walkers Crisps adverts. Very Tasteful!

Also High on the list by fans were... Steve Claridge, Steve Walsh.

NORTHAMPTON TOWN

IAN SAMPSON

1994-2004 - 392 apps, 26 goals

Ian joined Northampton in 1994 after a loan spell. He played for the Cobblers for 10 years. Sampson retired from the game at the end of the 2003–04 season.

ANDY WOODMAN

1995 – 1999 - 160 apps, 0 goals

Andy Woodman signed from Exeter City. Woodman is regarded as something of a cult figure and he was granted a testimonial by the club in summer 2007.

JOHN FRAIN

1997-2003 - 219 apps, 5 goals

In January 1997 John joined Northampton Town on loan, he instantly became a big hero in the club's history by scoring a stoppage-time winner from a free kick in that season's Football League Two play-off final. His free-transfer move to the club was made permanent at the end of that season. He later played his part in the club winning automatic promotion back to League Two in 1999–2000

Frain retired as a player at the end of the 2004–05 season due to a persistent knee injury.

JAMIE FORRESTER

2000-2003 - 121 apps, 45 goals

In terms of success, Forrester's spell at Northampton was very similar to that at his previous club Scunthorpe. Scoring a goal every other game and winning promotion with The Cobblers he rivalled his success at The Iron. His impressive displays led Hull City, to hand him a contract.

EDDIE MCGOLDRICK

1986-1988 - 107 apps, 9 goals

Eddie started out at non league side Kettering Town, before moving into the Football League with another one of our Midlands Teams Northampton Town, where he collected a Fourth Division title medal in 1987.

NOTTS COUNTY

LEE HUGHES

2009- present - 74 apps, 44 goals

Lee signed for League Two team Notts County on a two-year contract on 22 July 2009, on the same day that Sven-Göran Eriksson arrived at the club as director of football. On his debut he scored a hat-trick in a 5–0 win over Bradford City. He then got his second hat-trick against Northampton Town. In December, during a 4–1 win over Burton Albion, Hughes scored another hat-trick, adding to his impressive goal tally. On 1st May, Hughes added another two goals in County's final home game of the season making him the first Notts player to score 30 league goals since Tommy Lawton in the 1949–50 season.

In an interview on the club's official website, Hughes said that he loved the city, the club, and the fans. Hughes also declared that he would "love" to end his career there.

In September 2011, Lee scored the only goal for County in the 1-1 game v Juventus at the famous Italian club's new stadium. . He signed a new 18 month contract to stay at the club on 4th October 2011.

GARY McSWEGAN

1993-1995 - 62 apps, 21 goals

Gary was a striker who began his career with Rangers. His first team opportunities at Ibrox were limited and in 1993 he joined Notts County for £400,000. Two seasons later he returned to Scotland with Dundee United for £375,000.

TOMMY JOHNSON

1989-1992 - 118 apps, 47 goals

Tommy started his career with Notts County in the summer of 1987, joining them as an apprentice on leaving school. He was a first-team regular and a professional by the end of the decade, when still only 18 years old, and his prolific goalscoring saw County reach the First Division in 1991 after two successive promotion playoff triumphs. Tommy was involved with the club after he retired, he is still very popular with the fans.

IAN MCPARLAND

1980-1989 - 221 apps, 69 goals

Ian was with Notts County from 1980 to 1988, and had caught the eye of then Forest manager Brian Clough who wanted to bring him to Forest as a player, but he didn't end up there, Ian is well known more for his time at County, with a lot of very good goals, a great battling striker.

MARK DRAPER

1988-1994 - 222 apps, 40 goals

Mark began his career at Notts County, making his debut in December 1988. He came through the youth system and was a talented midfielder, he became recognized by County supporters as one of the greatest young players ever developed at the club. Draper was finally sold during the 1994 close season to Leicester City for £1.25 million - a record fee for the club at the time.

★

NOTTINGHAM FOREST

STAN COLLYMORE

1993-1995 - 65 apps, 41 goals

In June 1993, Stan signed for Forest in an initial £2 million deal rising to £2.75 million based on certain clauses. He was signed by newly-appointed boss Frank Clark, who had just taken over as manager at the end of Brian Clough's 18-year reign. Frank has recently taken over as the new chairman in October 2011. Forest had just been relegated from the Premier League, but Stan's good form in the 1993–94 season helped them back to the top flight as Division One runners-up. He scored 22 Premier League goals in 1994–95 as Forest finished third in the league and achieved UEFA Cup Qualification.

He held the British transfer record when he moved from Nottingham Forest to Liverpool for £8.5 million in 1995.

STUART PEARCE

1985-1997 - 401 apps, 63 goals

'Psycho' was brought to Nottingham Forest by Cloughie in a £300,000 deal. Pearce spent 12 years at Forest, most of it as club captain.

Appointed caretaker player-manager of Forest in December 1996, Stuart's first game in charge was at home to Arsenal. He admitted in an interview with Match of the Day, that in his first attempt at picking a starting eleven, he did not realise until it was pointed out to him by his wife that he had omitted the goalkeeper. Forest won the game 2–1, Despite Stuart winning Manager of the Month in January 1997, the club were relegated from the Premier League.

He opted to leave the club at the end of the 1996–97 season after twelve years at the City Ground. Stuart was involved with Manchester City before the big takeover and is now currently coach of the England Under 21s.

DES WALKER

1984-1992 - 264 apps, 1 goal & 2002-2004 - 57 apps, 0 goals

Walker, a hard-tackling central defender, was signed by Forest in 1980 as an apprentice. Cloughie gave Walker his debut in March 1984 at the age of 18, just two months before the end of the 1983-84 First Division campaign in which Forest finished third and qualified for the UEFA Cup.

Walker was a certain name on the list of 22 players whom Robson took to the 1990 FIFA World Cup in Italy, he made some great performances, and emerged as one of the players of that tournament.

Walker then travelled with the England squad to Euro 92 in Sweden but England failed to get beyond the group stages, very disappointing..

He briefly trained with his ex-Forest team-mate Nigel Clough later in his career at Burton Albion and a short stint in the U.S. playing for the New York Metro Stars in their 9/11 benefit matches against DC United. Forest manager Paul Hart then asked if Walker could train with Forest, who were now struggling in the second tier of English football. In July 2002, Walker signed for Forest on a permanent basis which was a welcome return.

Walker made almost 60 more appearances in his second spell for

Forest. His final competitive appearance for Forest came against Wigan Athletic on 7th August 2004

A testimonial match was held in his honour - this drew thousands of spectators. He became first team coach at Forest afterwards but left in January 2005 when Gary Megson was put in charge.

STEVE STONE

1989-1999 - 229 apps, 23 goals

Stone began his career at Nottingham Forest, he had some bad injuries but ended up being a very vital player, he was also in the England squad for Euro 96.

He ended up signing for Aston Villa after leaving Forest for £5.5 million in 1999, having made 229 appearances for Forest.

MARK CROSSLEY

1989-2000 - 303 apps, 0 goals

"Norm", as he was known by Nottingham Forest fans during his stay at the City Ground, started his football career in 1987 as a trainee with Forest. He had a loan spell at Manchester United during the 1989-90 season but was never used in the first team.

He was a huge favourite with the fans, despite making the occasional mistake; he became first-choice 'keeper at the start of the 1990-91 season

Mark had a knack of saving penalties and he is the only 'keeper ever to have denied Matthew Le Tissier from the penalty spot. He also has the dubious distinction of scoring the first Premier League own goal, in Forest's 4–1 loss against Blackburn Rovers on 5th September 1992.

He was granted a testimonial match during the 1999–2000 season by Nottingham Forest. During that season, Mark found himself on the bench numerous times, playing second choice to Dave Beasant. He was finally released from Forest, against his will, in 2000 as the club's financial troubles required them to reduce the wage bill.

Also High on the list by fans were...
Ian Woan, Pierre Van Hoiijdonk. Bryan Roy.

PORT VALE

MARTIN FOYLE

1991-2000 - 296 apps, 83 goals

Martin signed for Port Vale in June 1991 for a club record fee of £375,000. His first game was against former club Oxford, and he scored both goals in a 2–1 win

Martin was the Valiant's Top Scorer for a number of seasons. Some of Martin's important goals include a late equaliser in a League Cup tie at Anfield in 1991, two at Brighton which sealed promotion in 1994 and another in a game at Huddersfield Town in 1998 which saved the club from relegation, what a day that was!

ROBBIE EARLE

1982-1991 - 294 apps, 77 goals

During his early career, Robbie suffered from a broken leg and was released by Stoke, at which point he was snapped up by local rivals Port Vale, where he turned professional in 1982.

He made his Vale debut in a 1–0 defeat at Swindon Town on 28th August 1982, He was an ever-present in the 1985–86 Fourth Division promotion squad making 142 consecutive appearances between September 1984 and January 1987, the run coming to an end due to a groin strain.

In all, 'The Black Pearl', as he was known by the Valiant's supporters was considered one of the best midfielders ever to play for the club. In July 1991 he was transferred to Wimbledon for a fee of £775,000 (and 30% of any future transfer fee)

It was later reported that Wimbledon chairman Sam Hammam had locked Earle in a room during transfer negotiations and only let him out when he agreed to sign for Wimbledon.

RAY WALKER

1984 (Loan) - 15 apps, 1 goal & 1986-1997 - 351 apps, 33 goals

Ray played for Port Vale in all competitions between 1984 and 1997, A fine gifted player who was twice voted the club's Player of the Season.

ANDY PORTER

1986-1998 - 357 apps, 22 goals & 2004-2006 - 4 apps, 0 goals

Andy made his Football League debut in December 1986. It marked the beginning of a long association with the Vale Park club, as more than 350 Football League appearances were made before he departed for Wigan Athletic in July 1998. He enjoyed a testimonial match against Derby County in 1996. As of 2009, he has the 6th most league appearances of any Vale player. His appearances in all competitions mean he has the 5th most appearances of any Vale player over all competitions.

DEAN GLOVER

1989-1998 - 363 apps, 15 goals

Port Vale became Glover's main club in his playing days as he remained at the Potteries side for ten seasons, for the majority of his playing career.

He formed an excellent partnership with fellow centre half Neil Aspin. He was part of the Vale side that won the Autoglass Trophy in 1993. He was a big part of the promotion campaign of the 1993–94 season which saw Vale return to the second tier and was an ever-present and selected in the PFA's Second Division team.

Glover left Vale at the end of the 1997–98 season as Vale stayed up with a final day 4–0 win at Huddersfield. Dean became a crowd favourite in the process for his committed displays at centre half and right back. He ended up getting a Testimonial with the club in which Take That's Robbie Williams played. As of 2009, he has the fifth most league appearances of any Vale player.

SHREWSBURY TOWN

MICKY BROWN

1986-1991 - 190 apps, 9 goals & 1992-1994 - 67 apps, 11 goals & 1996-2001 - 161 apps, 16 goals

Mickey was best known for playing for Shrewsbury Town during the late 80's and 90's when he joined the club three times. His most famous moment at the club is most likely scoring the goal which kept Shrewsbury in the Football League in May 2000. He is also the record league appearance holder at Shrewsbury. It was after he left Shrewsbury for the final time that his career took him to many other lower division clubs but he didn't stay very long with any of them.

JOE HART

2003-2006 - 54 apps, 0 goals

Joe Hart, what a great Goalkeeper, easily England's No.1. Whilst Joe was still a Year 11 pupil at school, he travelled with the first team squad of his hometown club, Shrewsbury Town, to Exeter City on 1st February 2003. He was a non-playing substitute on that occasion and fulfilled that role again versus Rochdale at Gay Meadow on 1st March 2003, still some six weeks short of his 16th birthday. Joe made his senior debut on 20th April 2004, a day after his 17th birthday. He played the full 90 minutes in the match against Gravesend & Northfleet. Four days later, he played at Morecambe.

Hart did not play again until April of the following year, as Scott Howie dominated in goal. With Shrewsbury back in the Football League (the newly-renamed League Two) and struggling, Hart played six matches.

From the start of the 2005–06 season, Hart made the step up into the first team, and became the club's first choice goalkeeper, claiming the number 1 shirt.

On 7 February 2006, he was announced as the top League Two player in the PFA Fans' Player of the Month Awards for January 2006. Football fans voted him as the best player in the division via the PFA's website. At the PFA Awards ceremony on 23 March 2006, it was announced that Hart had been voted as League Two's best goalkeeper for 2005–06 by his fellow professionals, earning him a place in the

PFA League Two Team of the Year, His life has certainly changed since then.

GRANT HOLT

2008-2009 - 43 apps, 20 goals

On 24th June 2008, Shrewsbury Town broke their club transfer record by signing Holt for £175,000. He opened his scoring account for the Shrews on his debut, scoring from the penalty spot against Macclesfield Town in a game they won 4–0.

Holt has now scored in his career on his debut for Sheffield Wednesday, Barrow, Nottingham Forest and Shrewsbury Town.

On 7th October 2008, in a Football League Trophy 2nd Round match against Wycombe Wanderers, Holt scored five of the seven goals scoring in the Shrews' 7–0 win.

BEN DAVIES

2006- 2009 - 115 apps, 30 goals

Ben's club debut was in the 2006–07 opener against Mansfield Town, which finished 2–2. He scored a total of 12 times over the course of the season. He was a reliable player who ended up being club captain before he left the club.

BEN SMITH

2004-2006 - 24 apps, 4 goals

An injury to his shoulder meant Ben required an operation in March 2004, shortly before joining Shrewsbury Town. He made 24 league appearances for the Shropshire club before making the move to Weymouth in January 2006 but he was voted as a favourite.

STOKE CITY

ROBERT HUTH

2009- present - 70 apps, 9 goals

On 27th August 2009, Robert signed for Stoke City for £5 million. He made his Stoke debut in a 1–0 win over Sunderland on 29th August 2009 He celebrated his 100th League appearance by scoring his first Stoke goal on 4th October 2009 against Everton. He was given the captain's armband for Stoke's FA Cup Quarter Final tie at his old club Chelsea which he described as a proud moment. After a successful season for Huth for 2010/11 he was named as player of the year.

MICKEY THOMAS

1982-1984 - 57 apps, 14 goals & 1990-1991 - 46 apps, 7 goals

Mickey had a great career, He played for a lot of big clubs, he had two spells at Stoke City, they were not long spells but they were very effective - he was a great talent to watch weekly and very popular.

PETER HOEKSTRA

2001-2004 - 78 apps, 11 goals

Hoekstra signed for English Division Two side Stoke City in August 2001. Hoekstra's skill caused problems for many defences and he was often subject to heavy tackles. He often produced his most eye catching displays for Stoke against Reading. He retired in 2004.

He was voted as the best Stoke player to play in the first ten years at the Britannia Stadium in 2008. He is now a youth coach at FC Groningen with whom he made a visit to Stoke with in April 2011.

MARK STEIN

1991-1993 - 97 apps, 55 goals & 1996-97 (Loan) 11 apps, 4 goals

In 1991–92, Mark was taken to Stoke from Oxford United for £100,000 by Lou Macari following an impressive loan spell

In 1992–93 Stein scored 26 league goals to fire the side to the newly-renamed Division Two championship, racking up 93 points in a season which included a 25-game run without defeat.

He joined Chelsea late in 1993 for £1,600,000, shortly after

Macari had left Stoke to manage Celtic. Mark returned to Stoke on a short-term loan, scoring four goals in 11 games in 1996–97, the club's final season at the Victoria Ground.

RICARDO FULLER

2006 - present - 169 apps, 43 goals

Fuller joined Stoke City for a fee of £500,000 and in his first season he was the top goalscorer with 11 goals but he also had the worst disciplinary record.

In the 2007–08 season, Fuller became a vital part of Stoke promotion wining side becoming a firm fan favourite in the process. He scored 15 goals during the 2007–08 season as Stoke won promotion to the big time, he also won the club's goal of the season award for his sole effort against Wolverhampton Wanderers.

Fuller scored Stoke City's first-ever Premier League goal, a late consolation in a 3–1 defeat to Bolton Wanderers on the opening day of the 2008–09 season. He followed this up with another goal in Stoke's 3–2 win over Aston Villa in their first ever Premier League home match. This goal won Match of the Day's 'Goal of the Month' for August. His goal against Villa would win him the goal of the season award the second time, he has proved to be a very effective player.

★

AFC TELFORD

JIM BENTLEY

1997-2002 - 161 apps, 0 goals

Bentley, who debuted for Telford United in 1997, moved to Morecambe in 2002. He was a real good consistent defender.

ANDY BROWN

2008 - present - 88 apps, 52 goals

Andy joined the club in 2008, He was Telford's top goal-scorer in 2010 and his goal at Harrogate in February 2010 saw him overtake Lee Moore as the Bucks leading all-time scorer. Although injured in a vehicle accident in October of 2010, Andy has recovered and helped secure Telford a spot in the Blue Square Bet North play-offs.

SHANE KILLOCK

2009 - present - 77 apps, 3 goals

At the start of the 2009–10 season, Shane joined Conference North side Telford United on loan. The move was made permanent in November 2009.

Killock was named Telford United captain in August 2010, and that season captained the Bucks to promotion via the play offs to the Blue Square Bet Premier division, he also won a player of the season award.

LEE MOORE

2006-2009 - 91 apps, 35 goals

Lee scored a number of great goals for the side and involved in a lot of big games but eventually left the club in 2009.

SAM RICKETTS

2003-2004 - 41 apps, 4 goals

During Sam's time at Oxford United he had a brief spell on loan at Nuneaton Borough before being released from his professional contract to sign for Conference National side Telford United in the summer of 2003. His form for Telford led him to be selected for the England non-League XI that season.

★

TAMWORTH

BOB TAYLOR

2004-2006 - 60 apps, 19 goals

Bob joined Tamworth in 2004. A highlight of his time there was a 10-minute 2nd-half hat-trick in a 3–2 win at Leigh RMI on 6 November 2004. In 2005 Taylor signed for Tamworth for a further 12 months. Following his release from Tamworth in May 2006, Taylor linked up with Kidderminster Harriers for pre-season training and signed a non-contract deal with the club in September 2006, and has since set up his own promotions company, Super Bob Events.

ADIE SMITH

2004-2008 - 167 apps, 8 goals

On 6th February 2004, Tamworth manager Darron Gee announced the signing of Smith on an 18-month contract. Smith completed the remainder of the season with Tamworth, with the club finishing in 17th position and avoiding relegation.

In Smith's second season with Tamworth, they defied the odds to finish 15th and make history with The Lambs gaining their highest league position in their history, although by the end of this season, Smith's contract had run out.

On 14th April 2005, Smith showed his loyalty to the club by signing a new contract. By this point, he had become the club's captain and led The Lambs to another historic feat, when they made the FA Cup Third Round. The club drew Stoke City and managed to take them to a replay at the Lamb, before going out on penalties.

Smith and Tamworth started the 2006-07 season and finished it pretty much the same as they did the previous season. He and goalkeeping coach Dale Belford took charge of the first team in January 2007, another disappointing league campaign though saw Tamworth finish 22nd and be relegated from the Conference National.

Despite their relegation from the Conference, Smith signed a new one-year contract with the Staffordshire club on 4th May 2007. Smith explained that his decision was an easy one, due to his love for the club, fans and people at the club.

ALEX RODMAN

2008-2011 - 91 apps, 24 goals

Rodman signed for The Lambs from Nuneaton Borough on 30 May 2008. One of Rodman's last games for Tamworth was against Newport County in which he scored a hat-trick, of which impressed County's outgoing manager at the time Dean Holdsworth

CARL HEGGS

2005-2006 - 25 apps, 4 goals & 2007 6 apps, 0 goals

On June 1, 2005 Carl joined the club. During his season with The

Lambs, Carl became a firm favourite with the fans, and was often referred to as "Heggsie" or "Heggo".

His time at Tamworth saw him involved in two notable goals. A 25-yard screamer against Halifax Town, in a 2-1 defeat and a powerful and determined run through the heart of the Stoke City defence, laying off a perfect pass for Nathan Jackson to slot into the empty net for the opening goal of the replay, however, Tamworth lost the game on penalties after drawing 1-1 in normal time.

JAKE SHERIDAN

2007-2011 - 81 apps, 7 goals

On 2nd July 2007 Sheridan teamed up with his former Notts County manager Gary Mills at Conference North side Tamworth, agreeing a one-year deal. In his first season with the Lambs, the club recorded a disappointing 15th place finish in the Conference North.

Following promotion to the Conference National later on, Sherdian was one of five players who agreed a new deal with The Lambs. Jake proved to be an important member of the squad.

He will always be regarded in Tamworth folklore, after scoring what proved to be the winner on the final day of the 2010–11 in a home fixture against Forest Green Rovers. Jake left the club along with Aaron Farrell, a few weeks prior to his contract expiring, in a bid to start looking for a new club for the 2011–12 season.

★

WALSALL

DEAN KEATES

1995-2002 - 159 apps, 9 goals & 2006-2007 53 apps, 15 goals

Beginning his career with his hometown club Walsall, Dean became a regular in the side at the age of 19. Keates was a key member of the Saddlers' midfield in a successful 1998–99 season, playing in all but three games as Walsall won promotion to Division One as runners-up. He was eventually released in July 2002.

He moved back to Walsall on 31st January 2006, Richard Money was appointed as the Saddlers' new manager in May 2006 and under him, Keates was appointed captain. He played a key role in Walsall's promotion as champions back to League One in the 2006–07 season, scoring 13 goals. Keates was named in the PFA League Two Team of the Year for the 2006–07 season, as well as being named Walsall's Player of the Season.

JIMMY WALKER

1993-2004 - 403 apps, 0 goals & 2010 - apps 30, 0 goals

Jimmy is a cult hero at Bescot Stadium. He was a key player in three promotion seasons and won their Player of the Season award twice. He was awarded a testimonial in the summer of 2003. Walker's successes at Walsall included promotion from Division Three in 1995 and from Division Two in 1999 and again 2001.

On 29th October 2010 Walker re-signed for Walsall, on a short-term contract due to end in January 2011. On 28th January 2011 he extended his contract to the end of the 2010/2011 season. On 12th April 2011 Walker made his 500th appearance for The Saddlers, against Brentford, which ended in a 3-2 win for Walsall. On 8 June 2011, Jimmy Walker signed a one year deal at Walsall.

JORGE LEITÃO

2000-2005 - 230 apps, 57 goals

In July 2000, Jorge moved to England with Walsall, who paid £150,000 for his services after three impressive trial games.

Leitão scored a career-best 18 goals in 44 games in his first season with Walsall, He was also named in the Division Two Player's Team of the Year. The 2002–03 season was Walsall's most successful in the league since the 1950s and Jorge scored a lot of goals in that period.

PAUL MERSON

2003-2006 - 77 apps, 6 goals

Paul was of course a very gifted creative skilful player, he scored a few goals and made a lot of inspiring performances before becoming manager.

DAVID KELLY

1983-1988 - 147 apps, 63 goals

David was a top goal scorer for Walsall when they won promotion to the Second Division via the playoffs in 1988, but was transferred to West Ham United soon afterwards, having scored 63 goals in 147 games for Walsall since making his debut for them in 1983.

★

WEST BROMWICH ALBION

BOB TAYLOR

1992-1998 - 238 apps, 96 goals & 2000-2003 86 apps, 17 goals

It was Albion manager Bobby Gould who brought him to The Hawthorns for a £300,000 fee in January 1992. Taylor was seen as a replacement for Don Goodman, who had been sold to Sunderland earlier in the season. Taylor scored on his debut against Brentford in a 2–0 Hawthorns win, and added another two on his away debut as Albion beat local rivals Birmingham City 3–0 at St. Andrews. Initially nicknamed "Trigger" (due to a perceived resemblance to the character in the television comedy Only Fools and Horses), Taylor soon became known as "Super Bob", a moniker he was first given by fans of Bristol City during his spell there, and scored eight times in 19 games during the second half of 1991–92.

During the 1992–93 season, Taylor capitalised fully on the attacking football Albion played under manager Ossie Ardilles finishing as Division Two's top goalscorer with 30 league goals, and scoring 37 in all competitions. This was despite having a succession of different strike partners throughout the season, including Simon Garner, Luther Blissett, David Speedie and even midfielder Gary Robson. However when Andy Hunt arrived at Albion in March 1993, he and Taylor quickly forged a successful striking partnership that would last several seasons. Hunt and Taylor were part of the Baggies team that beat Port Vale at Wembley in the Division Two playoff final, to secure promotion to Division One. In the second half, with the game still goalless, Taylor was through on goal when he was brought down by former Leeds team-mate Peter Swan. Swan's subsequent dismissal proved to be the turning point in the game, with Hunt scoring the first goal in a 3–0 victory.

Taylor was the club's top league goalscorer once again in 1993–94, scoring 18 goals. Albion however struggled in Division One and only avoided relegation on the last day of the season. Taylor scored several goals in local derbies during his time at Albion, including a diving header against Wolves to seal a 2–0 win in March 1995; he later described it as the best goal of his career. His only hat-trick for Albion, in a 4–4 draw against Watford on 12 March 1996, helped him to finished as Albion's top league goal scorer for the third time, finding the net on 17 occasions in 1995–96. He captained the side for the second half of that season and scored his 100th goal for the club in the final league game of the campaign, against Derby County. Things changed however in 1998, when Denis Smith succeeded Ray Harford as manager. Recovering from an ankle injury and struggling with his fitness, Taylor was sent out on loan to Premiership club Bolton Wanderers.

With West Bromwich Albion struggling near the foot of Division One, manager Gary Megson signed Taylor in a £90,000 deal, making the striker one of four deadline-day signings by the club. Taylor's return to the Hawthorns paid off as he scored five goals in eight games, including one in a last day 2–0 victory over Charlton Athletic, to keep Albion in Division 1. His goal against former club Bolton – an overhead kick in a 4–4 draw – was voted as Albion's goal of the season for 1999–2000. The following season (2000–01) then saw Albion exceed all expectations, reaching the Division 1 playoffs, where they lost in the semi-final to Bolton.

Taylor became the 100th Albion player to be sent off in a first team match when he received a red card against Barnsley on 28 October 2001. After scoring vital goals in the final few games of the 2001–02 season against Nottingham Forest, Coventry and Rotherham, he sealed Albion's promotion to the Premiership with the second goal in a final-day 2–0 win over Crystal Palace. Albion struggled in their first season in the Premiership however, with Taylor starting only one game. In March 2003, he expressed his unhappiness at his lack of first team action, saying that he was forced to train with the Albion youth team, and that he hadn't spoken to manager Gary Megson for four months. Albion were already relegated by the time Bob Taylor made his 377th and final appearance for them, in a 2–2 draw against Newcastle United on 11 May 2003. In what was only his second start of the season, Taylor was substituted due to injury after half an hour, but left the field to a standing ovation.

YOUSSOUF MULUMBU

2009- present - 80 apps, 10 goals

On 2 February 2009, Youssouf joined them on loan with a view to a permanent deal at the end of the season. Mulumbu's first term at The Hawthorns was interrupted by injuries and he had to wait until April to make his Barclays Premier League debut, coming on as a sub in a 2-2 draw at Portsmouth. He signed for West Brom permanently on a one-year contract for a fee of £175,000 on 10 July and extended that deal one month later by another year. Mulumbu scored his first goal in West Brom's 2–0 win over Ipswich Town on 22 August 2009. Mulumbu decided to boycott international football after he claimed his national team, DR Congo, lacked professionalism. Soon after this, he bagged his third goal of the season with a stunning 25 yard strike in West Brom's 3–1 win over Reading on 17 October 2009.

Mulumbu signed a new-and-improved contract in January 2011, committing his furture to the Baggies until June 2014, after penning a two-and-a-half year deal, plus a further year's option in the club's favour. It was his second one-year extension in seven months and was a reward for his impressive form in his first full Premier League season. Mulumbu has formed an effective defensive midfield partnership with Austrian international Paul Scharner, who was recently moved back to his favoured position of central midfield, having covered for the injured Jonas Olsson. This brought out a string of improved performances from Mulumbu, including both he and Scharner scoring in their 3–1 away victory against Birmingham City and again both scoring against Sunderland. Mulumbu scored the winning goal, in the 86th minute, against West Midland rivals Aston Villa on 30 April 2011, the 2–1 win was the first win for West Brom against Aston Villa since 1985. He was named West Brom's Player of the Year by both the club and the fans at the end of the season, and signed his third contract extension in 13 months on 25 July 2011, tying himself to the club until 2015 (with the option of an extra year).

PETER ODEMWINGIE

2010- present - 32 apps, 15 goals

On 20 August 2010 Odemwingie signed for the Baggies for an undisclosed fee on a two-year contract, with the option of a third year in the club's favour. A day later, he scored the 81st-minute winning goal on his Premier League debut, a 1–0 win against Sunderland. Shortly after signing for West Brom, photographs showed Lokomotiv Moscow fans celebrating the sale of Odemwingie through the use of racist banners targeted at the player. One banner included the image of a banana and read "Thanks West Brom". Before West Brom's game against Tottenham Hotspur in September 2010, it was announced that West Brom fans would unfurl a banner to counter the racist one, the banner read 'Thanks Lokomotiv' and is accompanied by a picture of Odemwingie celebrating his winner on his debut against Sunderland. Odemwingie scored again for West Brom as they defeated Arsenal 3–2 at the Emirates Stadium on 25 September 2010 and scored a brace for West Brom on 5 December 2010, as they defeated fellow promoted side Newcastle United 3–1 at the Hawthorns.

On 19 March 2011, Arsenal travelled to The Hawthorns. The reverse fixture saw West Brom win 3–2 away from home, this time they were able to secure a 2–2 draw.Odemwingie scored the second goal for West Brom which brought his season tally in the Premier League to 10 goals, only two behind Robert Earnshaw's Premier League record for the club. 9 April saw West Brom travel to the Stadium of Light to play Sunderland. Odemwingie continued to impress and scored a goal in the 29th minute to level the scores. His side eventually won 3–2, three points significantly helping his side's survival hopes.

After the game, he announced his desire to keep on playing well for West Brom by aiming to score 15 league goals. On 16 April Odemwingie edged closer to this personal target when he became West Brom's joint top goalscorer ever in a single season in the Premier League with a goal against Chelsea, bringing his tally to 12. Because of his continued success in his debut season in England, Odemwingie was reportedly targeted by a number of big clubs but he shunned these moves, saying that he desires to play for West Brom next season and that he is happy there.

Odemwingie continued his fine form, scoring a lovely curling effort with his left foot in the fifth minute against Tottenham Hotspur. This brought him on to 13 league goals for the season, and meant that he had scored four in his last five games. On 30 April, Odemwingie became the first player in West Brom's Premier League history to score in four consecutive games. This goal came against Aston Villa and meant he had scored 15 goals thus far in his debut season. It would also contribute to Odemwingie's second Premier League Player of the Month award of the season. Odemwingie is only the sixth man to have received the accolade twice in a season in the award's history. Odemwingie ended the 2010–11 season as West Bromwich Albion's top goal scorer with a club record of 15 league goals.

On 18 August it was announced that Odemwingie had signed a new three-year agreement with West Bromwich Albion, after a £4 m bid from Wigan Athletic was turned down by the club.

After some injury setbacks, he scored his first goal of the 2011-12 season away to Norwich City, pouncing on a confusion between Richie De Laet and Declan Rudd.

CYRILLE REGIS

1977-1984 - 237 apps, 82 goals

Cyrille scored on his debut for West Bromwich Albion's reserve team in a Central League match against Sheffield Wednesday reserves and made his first team debut in a League Cup match against Rotherham United on 31 August 1977, scoring twice in a 4–0 win. Three days later he made his league debut in a 2–1 victory over Middlesbrough. Again he found the net, taking the ball from the halfway line to the penalty area before scoring with a right-foot drive. Middlesbrough's David Mills, who later became a team-mate of Regis at Albion, described it as "a goal of sheer brilliance".

Regis also scored in his first FA Cup match in January 1978, helping Albion to beat Blackpool 4–1. A few days later, Albion appointed a new manager, Ron Atkinson. Ronnie Allen had departed in late-December to manage the Saudi Arabia national team and John Wylie, the club's captain, had acted as caretaker manager in the interim.

Regis teamed up with two other black players, Laurie Cunningham and Brendon Batson. It was very unusual for an English club to simultaneously field three black players. Although not by any means the first black footballers to play professionally in England, the Three Degrees (a reference to The Three Degrees contemporary vocal trio of the same name) were an integral part of their acceptance in the English leagues.

A strong and fast traditional centre-forward, Regis was voted PFA Young Player of the Year in 1978 and earned the Goal of the Season award in 1981–82, for his powerful long-range shot against Norwich City in the FA Cup. He finished his stint at West Brom with 112 goals (League and Cup) in 301 total appearances, though never secured a major honour at the Hawthorns. The team came close: FA Cup semi finalists in 1978 (Ipswich) & 1982 (QPR) and League Cup Semi Finalists (1982). They finished third in the First Division in 1979 and fourth in 1981. Many people (including then manager Ron Atkinson) regard the 5-3 away win at Old Trafford on 30 December 1978 as the quintessential WBA game from the period, with Regis hitting the final goal with typical gusto in the second half.

RICHARD SNEEKES

1996-2001 - 251 apps, 34 goals

Alan Buckley signed the Dutchman for West Bromwich Albion in March 1996 for £400,000. Despite Buckley claiming it would be a while before he made any difference, Sneekes almost immediately became a cult hero at The Hawthorns. He was quite literally an overnight sensation, and many of the Baggies crowd took to wearing long blond wigs as gestures of worship - even the club shop was selling them. Sneekes finished his first season with ten goals from thirteen games, arguably for some Albion fans saving them from relegation. Sneekes spent seven seasons at West Brom before finally being transferred at the start of the 2001–02 season. After Sneekes' retirement in 2007, he went on to captain West Bromwich Albion in the Midlands 'Masters' and has done so ever since. He scored in the 2008 and 2011 tournaments.

WOLVES

STEVE BULL

1986-1999 - 474 apps, 250 goals

In over 13 years at Wolves, Bull broke no less than four of the club's goal scoring records. He became their all-time leading goal scorer with 306 goals in competitive games (250 of them in the Football League, also a club record) and became their highest goalscorer in a single season when he scored 52 goals in competitive games during the 1987–88 season.

He also scored a club record of 18 hat-tricks - the first of them against Hartlepool United in a 4-1 Fourth Division home win on 9 May 1987, the last on 17 August 1996 in a 3-0 Division One away win over Grimsby Town

His debut for Wolves, then languishing in the Fourth Division, was against Wrexham on 22 November 1986. He went on to make 464 league appearances for the club, 561 appearances in total.

He is regarded as such a legend at the club that one of the main stands at their home ground, Molineux is named after him. This commemoration was made in June 2003, with the stand having previously being known as the John Ireland Stand.

In his first season at the club, 1986-87, he scored 19 goals for Wolves - 15 of them in the Fourth Division, in which they finished fourth - although they lost out on promotion after being beaten by Aldershot in the playoffs. Bull scored 52 goals in all competitions during the 1987-88 season as Wolves won the Fourth Division championship and became the first of only three teams (later matched by Burnley and Preston North End) to have been champions of all four divisions in the English league.

On 11 February 1989, after just over two years at the club, he surprassed the 100-goal margin for Wolves when scoring a hat-trick in a Third Division game against fellow promotion contenders Fulham at the Molineux, which Wolves won 5-2. In 1988-89, he inspired Wolves to a second successive promotion, this time as Third Division champions, with 50 goals — marking a tally of 102 goals in two seasons. While still playing in the Third Division, he was selected for the England team and scored on his debut against Scotland at

Hampden Park.

Late in the 1991-92 season, he scored his 195th competitive goal for Wolves after just over five years at the club, breaking the club's decade-old goalscoring record set by John Richards. Early in the following season he scored his 200th goal for the club.

Bull remained a prolific goalscorer second tier of the English league and stayed loyal to his Midlands roots despite interest from the likes of Coventry City and Newcastle United. In fact, when former England manager Graham Taylor was manager at Molineux in 1995, he had agreed with then Coventry City boss, Ron Atkinson the sale of Bull to the Highfield Road club. The outcry from the gold and black sector of the Black Country was prolific, the local Express and Star newspaper even launching a campaign to keep Bull at Wolves. Whether it was a prick of guilt, or a tug at the old heart-strings, no-one will ever know, but Bull backed out of the deal and his transfer to Coventry never happened.

Bull played only one game in the English top flight — coming on as a substitute, replacing Andy Thompson, for West Bromwich Albion in 1986 — the rest of his career was spent in the lower divisions. He came close to achieving his ambition of reaching the Premier League in 1995 and 1997, but Wolves lost in the play-offs both times.

During his final two seasons at Molineux, his chances of first-team football were reduced by a series of knee injuries. He reached the 300-goal milestone on 18 February 1998, scoring in a 2-0 home win over Bradford City in the league.

Bull's final goal for the club came against Bury on 26 September 1998 and his final competitive appearance for the club came on the last day of the 1998-99 season against Bradford City. In July 1999, the 34-year-old Bull finally gave in and announced his retirement. However, he soon returned to playing as player-coach of Hereford United for a season in the Conference, working with Graham Turner, the manager who had signed him for Wolves.

Known by his fans as 'Bully' for his club loyalty, rapport with supporters and passion for the game and also known as the "Tipton Skin" for his trademark closely cropped haircut, he received an MBE for services to football in December 1999, shortly after retiring as a first class player.

In May 2003, Bull appeared in a testimonial game for West Bromwich Albion's Bob Taylor at The Hawthorns. He amused many of the Albion fans in attendance by dramatically falling to the ground when the chant went up, "Stand up if you hate the Wolves".

On 29 July 2006, Bull made one final appearance for Wolves in his 20th anniversary testimonial game against Aston Villa at Molineux playing the first seven minutes of the match.

JOHN DE WOLF

1994-1996 - 28 apps, 5 goals

John signed for Wolves in December 1995 for £600,000. He was swiftly made captain of the side by manager Graham Taylor, and helped them reach the FA Cup quarter-finals, as well as remarkably scoring a hat-trick from centre-back in one game against Port Vale. However, he soon suffered a knee injury that ruled him out of the promotion run-in, where the team would ultimately lose to Bolton in the play-offs.

The following season, however, he missed most games as Wolves finished a lowly 20th in the final table. The Dutchman fell out with new manager Mark McGhee who attempted to select to him for the reserve side, only for De Wolf to speak out and claim that he should not be fielded in the reserves as he was an experienced player who had not been injured. He left the club soon afterwards and returned to his homeland with VVV Venlo of the second division.

MATT MURRAY,

1998-2010 - 87 apps, 0 goals

Murray progressed through Wolves academy system to sign professional forms in 1998. The five year contract he was given, aged 17, is the longest in the club's history for an academy graduate.

However, his career failed to find its stride immediately as he was largely out of contention through injury. He suffered a cruciate knee injury just twenty minutes into a loan spell at non-league Kingstonian in October 2000 where he made his first professional appearance.

He was promoted into Wolves' first team on 31 August 2002 against Wimbledon, deputising for the injured Michael Oakes, and then keeping his place through that season. The season ended with him producing a man-of-the-match performance in the Play-off final in May 2003, where he produced a number of vital saves to help the club win promotion to the Premier League, the pick being a second-half penalty save from Michael Brown.

He followed this up by debuting for England Under-21s, against Slovakia U21, the first of five under-21 caps. However, a back problem then a foot fracture wrecked his second season. In the three years that followed the success of 2002–03, he only played seven games for Wolves due to a variety of injuries.

The goalkeeper next played in January 2005 but soon suffered another break to his foot, ruling him out for a further year. By March 2006 he was fit enough to be sent on loan to Tranmere Rovers, but was called back to Wolves within a month because of possible injuries to other goalkeepers.

He started his first game for Wolves in almost sixteen months on the final day of the season at Norwich City, and managed to retain his place at the beginning of the 2006–07 season, where he was largely credited with Wolves' impressive start to the season, due to a catalogue of good performances allowing for five of their first seven games to end 1–0.

His performances were given further recognition as he won the PFA Championship Player of the Month award in December 2006, and, as the campaign ended, he was named in the Championship Team of the Year at the 2006–07 PFA Awards dinner and also voted the PFA Fans' Player of the Year for the division. He was also voted Wolves' Player of the Season as they reached the play-offs. The season ended on a sour note though as he broke his shoulder on the eve of his club's vital play-off game against local rivals West Bromwich Albion.

After spending the summer recuperating from his shoulder injury, he suffered another setback from a cruciate (left) knee injury in pre-season training. He underwent two operations for this, and missed the whole of the 2007–08 campaign while undergoing rehabilitation with the aim of returning for the new season. However, inflammation in his knee then delayed his comeback further still. By the time he recovered, fellow academy graduate Wayne Hennessey had established himself as first choice.

In November 2008, he joined League One Hereford United on loan, but only played two full games before injury again struck suffering a ruptured patella tendon in his right knee during a match against MK Dons. In November 2009 Murray started his first game back for Wolves playing in a reserve game, but he felt discomfort in his knee and was substituted after just 23 minutes. This was to prove his last appearance in a Wolves shirt.

He announced his playing retirement on 26 August 2010 aged 29. In total he made 87 appearances for Wolves.

On 26 September 2010, at half-time in a match between Wolves and Aston Villa, he gave a speech to the crowd, announcing his retirement and thanking the fans. He has since continued working for Wolves in an "Ambassador" role while making occasional appearances on Sky Sports as a pundit.

JOLEON LESCOTT

2000-2006 - 169 apps, 8 goals

Joleon's first-team debut came as a 17-year-old in the 2000–01 season against Sheffield Wednesday at Molineux on 13 August 2000. At the end of his first season, Lescott was named the Supporters' Young Player of the Year by the Wolves' fans; an award he also won in the subsequent 2001–02 season.

Lescott started to become a regular fixture in the Wolves' team. During the 2002–03 season he missed only one league match and played in each of the club's FA Cup fixtures. He was also a member of the team that defeated Sheffield United 3–0 at the Millennium Stadium to win promotion to the FA Premier League for the 2003–04 season. Lescott declared this to be the proudest moment of his career.

Despite Wolves gaining promotion, Lescott along with Matt Murray was unable to participate in the 2003–04 season due to knee surgery, preventing him from competing in the Premier League. Wolves were subsequently relegated and, upon completing his rehabilitation, Lescott returned to compete in the Championship.

In October 2005, Lescott agreed a two-and-a-half-year extension to his contract at Wolves. At the conclusion of the 2005–06 season he was named in the Championship team of the season, voted for by his fellow professionals, and also picked up the Wolves' Player of the Year award.

He has since done very well at Everton and now Manchester City, and being in England Squads regularly.

ANDY THOMPSON

1986-1997 - 376 apps, 43 goals

Andy began his career as a midfielder with West Bromwich Albion, where he made his debut in the Full Members Cup in November 1985. He scored in the penalty shoot-out, although Albion lost to Chelsea, who went on to win the competition.

Thompson moved to rivals Wolverhampton Wanderers with Steve Bull in November 1986 for a combined fee of £65,000, and made the transition to full-back. 'Thommo' became a fans' favourite at Molineux, known for his speed and penalty taking. He was an integral part of the team that won back-to-back promotions to the (old) Second Division in the late 1980s (also lifting the Sherpa Van Trophy). He remained a vital player in the team as they twice failed in the play-offs, as they tried to break into the Premier League during the 1990s. He eventually left the club in 1997 to join Tranmere Rovers, after making a total of 451 appearances for the Midlanders.

MIDLANDS DERBIES

ASTON VILLA VS. BIRMINGHAM

	VILLA	DRAWS	BLUES
League	45	29	36
League Cup	4	1	2
FA Cup	2	1	0
Total	51	31	38

2010/2011

FAPL	Su 16Jan 2011	Birmingham 1 - 1 Aston Villa
LC	We 01Dec 2010	Birmingham 2 - 1 Aston Villa
FAPL	Su 31Oct 2010	Aston Villa 0 - 0 Birmingham

2009/2010

FAPL	Su 25Apr 2010	Aston Villa 1 - 0 Birmingham
FAPL	Su 13Sep 2009	Birmingham 0 - 1 Aston Villa

2007/2008

FAPL	Su 20Apr 2008	Aston Villa 5 - 1 Birmingham
FAPL	Su 11Nov 2007	Birmingham 1 - 2 Aston Villa

2005/2006

FAPL	Su 16Apr 2006	Aston Villa 3 - 1 Birmingham
FAPL	Su 16Oct 2005	Birmingham 0 - 1 Aston Villa

2004/2005

FAPL	Su 20Mar 2005	Birmingham 2 - 0 Aston Villa
FAPL	Su 12Dec 2004	Aston Villa 1 - 2 Birmingham

2003/2004

FAPL	Su 22Feb 2004	Aston Villa 2 - 2 Birmingham
FAPL	Su 19Oct 2003	Birmingham 0 - 0 Aston Villa

2002/2003

FAPL	Mo 03Mar 2003	Aston Villa 0 - 2 Birmingham
FAPL	Mo 16Sep 2002	Birmingham 3 - 0 Aston Villa

1993/1994

LC	We 06Oct 1993	Aston Villa 1 - 0 Birmingham
LC	Tu 21Sep 1993	Birmingham 0 - 1 Aston Villa

1988/1989

LC	We 12Oct 1988	Aston Villa 5 - 0 Birmingham
LC	Tu 27Sep 1988	Birmingham 0 - 2 Aston Villa

1987/1988

DIV 2	Sa 12Dec 1987	Birmingham 1 - 2 Aston Villa
DIV 2	Sa 22Aug 1987	Aston Villa 0 - 2 Birmingham

1985/1986

DIV 1	Sa 22Mar 1986	Aston Villa 0 - 3 Birmingham
DIV 1	Sa 07Sep 1985	Birmingham 0 - 0 Aston Villa

1983/1984

DIV 1	Sa 31Mar 1984	Birmingham 2 - 1 Aston Villa
DIV 1	Sa 15Oct 1983	Aston Villa 1 - 0 Birmingham

1982/1983

DIV 1	Mo 04Apr 1983	Aston Villa 1 - 0 Birmingham
DIV 1	Mo 27Dec 1982	Birmingham 3 - 0 Aston Villa

1981/1982

DIV 1	Sa 20Feb 1982	Birmingham 0 - 1 Aston Villa
DIV 1	Sa 26Sep 1981	Aston Villa 0 - 0 Birmingham

1980/1981

DIV 1	Sa 13Dec 1980	Aston Villa 3 - 0 Birmingham
DIV 1	Sa 11Oct 1980	Birmingham 1 - 2 Aston Villa

1978/1979

DIV 1	Sa 03Mar 1979	Aston Villa 1 - 0 Birmingham
DIV 1	Sa 21Oct 1978	Birmingham 0 - 1 Aston Villa

1977/1978

DIV 1	Sa 25Feb 1978	Birmingham 1 - 0 Aston Villa
DIV 1	Sa 01Oct 1977	Aston Villa 0 - 1 Birmingham

1976/1977

DIV 1	Tu 10May 1977	Birmingham 2 - 1 Aston Villa
DIV 1	Sa 18Sep 1976	Aston Villa 1 - 2 Birmingham

1975/1976

DIV 1	Sa 03Apr 1976	Birmingham 3 - 2 Aston Villa
DIV 1	Sa 27Sep 1975	Aston Villa 2 - 1 Birmingham

1969/1970

DIV 2	Mo 30Mar 1970	Birmingham 0 - 2 Aston Villa
DIV 2	Sa 18Oct 1969	Aston Villa 0 - 0 Birmingham

1968/1969

DIV 2	Sa 12Apr 1969	Aston Villa 1 - 0 Birmingham
DIV 2	Sa 21Sep 1968	Birmingham 4 - 0 Aston Villa

1967/1968

DIV 2	Sa 24Feb 1968	Birmingham 2 - 1 Aston Villa
DIV 2	Sa 07Oct 1967	Aston Villa 2 - 4 Birmingham

1964/1965

DIV 1	Mo 12Apr 1965	Aston Villa 3 - 0 Birmingham
DIV 1	Sa 13Feb 1965	Birmingham 0 - 1 Aston Villa

1963/1964
DIV 1 Tu 31Mar 1964 Birmingham 3 - 3 Aston Villa
DIV 1 Mo 30Mar 1964 Aston Villa 0 - 3 Birmingham
1962/1963
LC Mo 27May 1963 Aston Villa 0 - 0 Birmingham
LC Th 23May 1963 Birmingham 3 - 1 Aston Villa
DIV 1 Sa 16Mar 1963 Aston Villa 4 - 0 Birmingham
DIV 1 Sa 27Oct 1962 Birmingham 3 - 2 Aston Villa
1961/1962
DIV 1 Sa 17Mar 1962 Birmingham 0 - 2 Aston Villa
DIV 1 Sa 28Oct 1961 Aston Villa 1 - 3 Birmingham
1960/1961
DIV 1 Sa 11Mar 1961 Birmingham 1 - 1 Aston Villa
DIV 1 Sa 22Oct 1960 Aston Villa 6 - 2 Birmingham
1958/1959
DIV 1 Sa 20Dec 1958 Birmingham 4 - 1 Aston Villa
DIV 1 Sa 23Aug 1958 Aston Villa 1 - 1 Birmingham
1957/1958
DIV 1 Sa 21Dec 1957 Aston Villa 0 - 2 Birmingham
DIV 1 Sa 24Aug 1957 Birmingham 3 - 1 Aston Villa
1956/1957
DIV 1 We 10Apr 1957 Birmingham 1 - 2 Aston Villa
DIV 1 Sa 27Oct 1956 Aston Villa 3 - 1 Birmingham
1955/1956
DIV 1 We 21Sep 1955 Birmingham 2 - 2 Aston Villa
DIV 1 Mo 05Sep 1955 Aston Villa 0 - 0 Birmingham
1949/1950
DIV 1 Sa 29Apr 1950 Birmingham 2 - 2 Aston Villa
DIV 1 Sa 10Dec 1949 Aston Villa 1 - 1 Birmingham
1948/1949
DIV 1 Sa 30Apr 1949 Birmingham 0 - 1 Aston Villa
DIV 1 Sa 04Dec 1948 Aston Villa 0 - 3 Birmingham
1938/1939
DIV 1 Sa 04Mar 1939 Aston Villa 5 - 1 Birmingham
DIV 1 Sa 29Oct 1938 Birmingham 3 - 0 Aston Villa
1935/1936
DIV 1 Sa 28Mar 1936 Aston Villa 2 - 1 Birmingham
DIV 1 Sa 23Nov 1935 Birmingham 2 - 2 Aston Villa
1934/1935
DIV 1 Sa 29Dec 1934 Aston Villa 2 - 2 Birmingham
DIV 1 Sa 25Aug 1934 Birmingham 2 - 1 Aston Villa
1933/1934
DIV 1 Sa 14Apr 1934 Aston Villa 1 - 1 Birmingham
DIV 1 Sa 02Dec 1933 Birmingham 0 - 0 Aston Villa
1932/1933
DIV 1 We 08Mar 1933 Birmingham 3 - 2 Aston Villa
DIV 1 Sa 22Oct 1932 Aston Villa 1 - 0 Birmingham
1931/1932
DIV 1 Sa 02Apr 1932 Birmingham 1 - 1 Aston Villa
DIV 1 Sa 21Nov 1931 Aston Villa 3 - 2 Birmingham
1930/1931
DIV 1 Sa 21Feb 1931 Birmingham 0 - 4 Aston Villa
DIV 1 Sa 18Oct 1930 Aston Villa 1 - 1 Birmingham
1929/1930
DIV 1 Sa 28Dec 1929 Birmingham 1 - 1 Aston Villa
DIV 1 Sa 31Aug 1929 Aston Villa 2 - 1 Birmingham
1928/1929
DIV 1 Sa 09Mar 1929 Aston Villa 1 - 2 Birmingham
DIV 1 Sa 27Oct 1928 Birmingham 2 - 4 Aston Villa
1927/1928
DIV 1 Sa 17Mar 1928 Aston Villa 1 - 1 Birmingham
DIV 1 Sa 05Nov 1927 Birmingham 1 - 1 Aston Villa
1926/1927
DIV 1 Sa 19Mar 1927 Aston Villa 4 - 2 Birmingham
DIV 1 Sa 30Oct 1926 Birmingham 1 - 2 Aston Villa
1925/1926
DIV 1 Sa 27Feb 1926 Birmingham 2 - 1 Aston Villa
DIV 1 Sa 17Oct 1925 Aston Villa 3 - 3 Birmingham
1924/1925
DIV 1 Sa 14Feb 1925 Aston Villa 1 - 0 Birmingham
DIV 1 Sa 11Oct 1924 Birmingham 1 - 0 Aston Villa
1923/1924
DIV 1 Sa 01Sep 1923 Aston Villa 0 - 0 Birmingham
DIV 1 Sa 25Aug 1923 Birmingham 3 - 0 Aston Villa
1922/1923
DIV 1 Sa 24Mar 1923 Aston Villa 3 - 0 Birmingham
DIV 1 Sa 17Mar 1923 Birmingham 1 - 0 Aston Villa
1921/1922
DIV 1 We 15Mar 1922 Birmingham 1 - 0 Aston Villa
DIV 1 Sa 11Mar 1922 Aston Villa 1 - 1 Birmingham
1907/1908
DIV 1 Sa 18Jan 1908 Aston Villa 2 - 3 Birmingham
DIV 1 Sa 21Sep 1907 Birmingham 2 - 3 Aston Villa
1906/1907
DIV 1 Sa 19Jan 1907 Birmingham 3 - 2 Aston Villa
DIV 1 Sa 15Sep 1906 Aston Villa 4 - 1 Birmingham
1905/1906
DIV 1 Sa 20Jan 1906 Aston Villa 1 - 3 Birmingham
DIV 1 Sa 16Sep 1905 Birmingham 2 - 0 Aston Villa
1904/1905
DIV 1 Sa 25Feb 1905 Birmingham 0 - 3 Aston Villa
DIV 1 Sa 29Oct 1904 Aston Villa 2 - 1 Birmingham
1903/1904
DIV 1 Sa 16Jan 1904 Aston Villa 1 - 1 Birmingham
DIV 1 Sa 19Sep 1903 Birmingham 2 - 2 Aston Villa
1901/1902
DIV 1 Th 26Dec 1901 Aston Villa 1 - 0 Birmingham
DIV 1 Sa 12Oct 1901 Birmingham 0 - 2 Aston Villa

1900/1901

FA CUP	We 27Mar 1901	Aston Villa 1 - 0 Birmingham	
FA CUP	Sa 23Mar 1901	Birmingham 0 - 0 Aston Villa	

1895/1896

DIV 1	Sa 26Oct 1895	Birmingham 1 - 4 Aston Villa
DIV 1	Sa 07Sep 1895	Aston Villa 7 - 3 Birmingham

1894/1895

DIV 1	Sa 20Oct 1894	Birmingham 2 - 2 Aston Villa
DIV 1	Sa 01Sep 1894	Aston Villa 2 - 1 Birmingham

1887/1888

FA CUP	Sa 05Nov 1887	Aston Villa 4 - 0 Birmingham

ASTON VILLA V COVENTRY

	VILLA WINS	DRAWS	COV.WINS
League	29	17	8
FA Cup	2	0	2
Total	31	17	10

2000/2001

FAPL	Sa 05May 2001	Villa	3 - 2	Coventry
FAPL	Sa 25Nov 2000	Coventry	1 - 1	Villa

1999/2000

FAPL	Sa 11Mar 2000	Villa	1 - 0	Coventry
FAPL	Mo 22Nov 1999	Coventry	2 - 1	Villa

1998/1999

FAPL	Sa 27Feb 1999	Villa	1 - 4	Coventry
FAPL	Sa 03Oct 1998	Coventry	1 - 2	Villa

1997/1998

FAPL	Sa 11Apr 1998	Coventry	1 - 2	Villa
FA CUP	Sa 14Feb 1998	Villa	0 - 1	Coventry
FAPL	Sa 06Dec 1997	Villa	3 - 0	Coventry

1996/1997

FAPL	We 19Feb 1997	Villa	2 - 1	Coventry
FAPL	Sa 23Nov 1996	Coventry	1 - 2	Villa

1995/1996

FAPL	Sa 16Dec 1995	Villa	4 - 1	Coventry
FAPL	Sa 30Sep 1995	Coventry	0 - 3	Villa

1994/1995

FAPL	Mo 06Mar 1995	Villa	0 - 0	Coventry
FAPL	Mo 29Aug 1994	Coventry	0 - 1	Villa

1993/1994

FAPL	Su 06Mar 1994	Coventry	0 - 1	Villa
FAPL	Sa 11Sep 1993	Villa	0 - 0	Coventry

1992/1993

FAPL	Sa 10Apr 1993	Villa	0 - 0	Coventry
FAPL	Sa 26Dec 1992	Coventry	3 - 0	Villa

1991/1992

DIV 1	Sa 02May 1992	Villa	2 - 0	Coventry
DIV 1	Sa 28Sep 1991	Coventry	1 - 0	Villa

1990/1991

DIV 1	Sa 19Jan 1991	Coventry	2 - 1	Villa
DIV 1	Sa 08Sep 1990	Villa	2 - 1	Coventry

1989/1990

DIV 1	Su 04Mar 1990	Coventry	2 - 0	Villa
DIV 1	Sa 18Nov 1989	Villa	4 - 1	Coventry

1988/1989

DIV 1	Sa 13May 1989	Villa	1 - 1	Coventry
DIV 1	Sa 26Nov 1988	Coventry	2 - 1	Villa

1986/1987

DIV 1	Sa 28Mar 1987	Villa	1 - 0	Coventry
DIV 1	Sa 04Oct 1986	Coventry	0 - 1	Villa

1985/1986

DIV 1	Sa 11Jan 1986	Coventry	3 - 3	Villa
DIV 1	Sa 14Sep 1985	Villa	1 - 1	Coventry

1984/1985

DIV 1	Sa 19Jan 1985	Coventry	0 - 3	Villa
DIV 1	Sa 25Aug 1984	Villa	1 - 0	Coventry

1983/1984

DIV 1	Sa 07Apr 1984	Villa	2 - 0	Coventry
DIV 1	Tu 13Mar 1984	Coventry	3 - 3	Villa

1982/1983

DIV 1	Sa 19Mar 1983	Villa	4 - 0	Coventry
DIV 1	Sa 06Nov 1982	Coventry	0 - 0	Villa

1981/1982

DIV 1	Sa 27Feb 1982	Villa	2 - 1	Coventry
DIV 1	Sa 10Oct 1981	Coventry	1 - 1	Villa

1980/1981

DIV 1	Sa 17Jan 1981	Coventry	1 - 2	Villa
DIV 1	Sa 30Aug 1980	Villa	1 - 0	Coventry

1979/1980

DIV 1	Tu 29Apr 1980	Coventry	1 - 2	Villa
DIV 1	We 19Dec 1979	Villa	3 - 0	Coventry

1978/1979

DIV 1	Sa 07Apr 1979	Coventry	1 - 1	Villa
DIV 1	We 28Mar 1979	Villa	1 - 1	Coventry

1977/1978

DIV 1	Tu 21Mar 1978	Coventry	2 - 3	Villa
DIV 1	Mo 26Dec 1977	Villa	1 - 1	Coventry

1976/1977

DIV 1	Sa 16Apr 1977	Coventry	2 - 3	Villa
DIV 1	Sa 20Nov 1976	Villa	2 - 2	Coventry

1975/1976

DIV 1	Tu 13Apr 1976	Coventry	1 - 1	Villa
DIV 1	Sa 30Aug 1975	Villa	1 - 0	Coventry

1964/1965

FA CUP	Sa 09Jan 1965	Villa	3 - 0	Coventry

1945/1946

FA CUP	Tu 08Jan 1946	Villa	2 - 0	Coventry
FA CUP	Sa 05Jan 1946	Coventry	2 - 1	Villa

1937/1938

DIV 2	Sa 12Mar 1938	Coventry	0 - 1	Villa
DIV 2	Sa 30Oct 1937	Villa	1 - 1	Coventry

1936/1937

DIV 2	Sa 06Feb 1937	Coventry	1 - 0	Villa
DIV 2	Sa 03Oct 1936	Villa	0 - 0	Coventry

ASTON VILLA V DERBY

	VILLA WINS	DRAWS	DERBY WINS
League	60	21	37
FA Cup	6	1	5
League Cup	1	1	0
Total	67	23	42

2007/2008

FAPL	Sa 12Apr 2008	Derby	0 - 6	Villa
FAPL	Sa 03Nov 2007	Villa	2 - 0	Derby

2001/2002

FAPL	Sa 12Jan 2002	Villa	2 - 1	Derby
FAPL	Sa 22Dec 2001	Derby	3 - 1	Villa

2000/2001

FAPL	Sa 24Feb 2001	Derby	1 - 0	Villa
FAPL	Sa 30Sep 2000	Villa	4 - 1	Derby

1999/2000

FAPL	Sa 25Mar 2000	Villa	2 - 0	Derby
FAPL	Su 26Dec 1999	Derby	0 - 2	Villa

1998/1999

FAPL	We 10Mar 1999	Derby	2 - 1	Villa
FAPL	Sa 26Sep 1998	Villa	1 - 0	Derby

1997/1998

FAPL	Sa 07Feb 1998	Derby	0 - 1	Villa
FAPL	Sa 20Sep 1997	Villa	2 - 1	Derby

1996/1997

FAPL	Sa 12Apr 1997	Derby	2 - 1	Villa
FA CUP	Sa 25Jan 1997	Derby	3 - 1	Villa
FAPL	Sa 24Aug 1996	Villa	2 - 0	Derby

1991/1992

FA CUP	We 05Feb 1992	Derby	3 - 4	Villa

1990/1991

DIV 1	Sa 02Feb 1991	Villa	3 - 2	Derby
DIV 1	Sa 15Sep 1990	Derby	0 - 2	Villa

1989/1990

DIV 1	Sa 17Mar 1990	Derby	0 - 1	Villa
DIV 1	Sa 30Sep 1989	Villa	1 - 0	Derby

1988/1989

DIV 1	Sa 06May 1989	Derby	2 - 1	Villa
DIV 1	Sa 19Nov 1988	Villa	1 - 2	Derby

1986/1987

LC	Tu 04Nov 1986	Villa	2 - 1	Derby
LC	We 29Oct 1986	Derby	1 - 1	Villa

1979/1980

DIV 1	Sa 01Mar 1980	Villa	1 - 0	Derby
DIV 1	Sa 20Oct 1979	Derby	1 - 3	Villa

1978/1979

DIV 1	We 11Apr 1979	Villa	3 - 3	Derby
DIV 1	Sa 23Dec 1978	Derby	0 - 0	Villa

1977/1978

DIV 1	Sa 25Mar 1978	Villa	0 - 0	Derby
DIV 1	Tu 27Dec 1977	Derby	0 - 3	Villa

1976/1977

DIV 1	Sa 09Apr 1977	Derby	2 - 1	Villa
DIV 1	We 02Mar 1977	Villa	4 - 0	Derby

1975/1976

DIV 1	Mo 19Apr 1976	Villa	1 - 0	Derby
DIV 1	Sa 27Dec 1975	Derby	2 - 0	Villa

1968/1969

DIV 2	Sa 29Mar 1969	Villa	0 - 1	Derby
DIV 2	Sa 07Sep 1968	Derby	3 - 1	Villa

1967/1968

DIV 2	Sa 06Jan 1968	Villa	2 - 1	Derby
DIV 2	Sa 02Sep 1967	Derby	3 - 1	Villa

1959/1960

DIV 2	Tu 15Mar 1960	Villa	3 - 2	Derby
DIV 2	Sa 24Oct 1959	Derby	2 - 2	Villa

1952/1953

DIV 1	Sa 03Jan 1953	Villa	3 - 0	Derby
DIV 1	Sa 30Aug 1952	Derby	0 - 1	Villa

1951/1952

DIV 1	Sa 22Dec 1951	Derby	1 - 1	Villa
DIV 1	Sa 25Aug 1951	Villa	4 - 1	Derby

1950/1951

DIV 1	Sa 23Dec 1950	Villa	1 - 1	Derby
DIV 1	Sa 26Aug 1950	Derby	4 - 2	Villa

1949/1950

DIV 1	We 31Aug 1949	Derby	3 - 2	Villa
DIV 1	Tu 23Aug 1949	Villa	1 - 1	Derby

1948/1949

DIV 1	We 27Apr 1949	Derby	2 - 2	Villa
DIV 1	Sa 04Sep 1948	Villa	1 - 1	Derby

1947/1948

DIV 1	We 07Apr 1948	Villa	2 - 2	Derby
DIV 1	Sa 20Sep 1947	Derby	1 - 3	Villa

1946/1947

DIV 1	Sa 04Jan 1947	Villa	2 - 0	Derby
DIV 1	Sa 07Sep 1946	Derby	1 - 2	Villa

1945/1946

FA CUP	Sa 09Mar 1946	Derby	1 - 1	Villa
FA CUP	Sa 02Mar 1946	Villa	3 - 4	Derby

1938/1939

DIV 1	Sa 31Dec 1938	Derby	2 - 1	Villa

DIV 1 Sa 03Sep 1938 Villa 0 - 1 Derby
1935/1936
DIV 1 Sa 01Feb 1936 Derby 1 - 3 Villa
DIV 1 Sa 28Sep 1935 Villa 0 - 2 Derby
1934/1935
DIV 1 Sa 05Jan 1935 Derby 1 - 1 Villa
DIV 1 Sa 01Sep 1934 Villa 3 - 2 Derby
1933/1934
DIV 1 Sa 21Apr 1934 Derby 1 - 1 Villa
DIV 1 Sa 09Dec 1933 Villa 0 - 2 Derby
1932/1933
DIV 1 Sa 06May 1933 Villa 2 - 0 Derby
DIV 1 Sa 24Dec 1932 Derby 0 - 0 Villa
1931/1932
DIV 1 Sa 16Apr 1932 Derby 3 - 1 Villa
DIV 1 Sa 05Dec 1931 Villa 2 - 0 Derby
1930/1931
DIV 1 Sa 21Mar 1931 Derby 1 - 1 Villa
DIV 1 Sa 15Nov 1930 Villa 4 - 6 Derby
1929/1930
DIV 1 Mo 09Sep 1929 Villa 2 - 2 Derby
DIV 1 We 04Sep 1929 Derby 4 - 0 Villa
1928/1929
DIV 1 Sa 16Mar 1929 Derby 1 - 0 Villa
DIV 1 Sa 03Nov 1928 Villa 2 - 3 Derby
1927/1928
DIV 1 Tu 27Dec 1927 Villa 0 - 1 Derby
DIV 1 Mo 26Dec 1927 Derby 5 - 0 Villa
1926/1927
DIV 1 Sa 26Feb 1927 Derby 2 - 3 Villa
DIV 1 Sa 09Oct 1926 Villa 3 - 1 Derby
1921/1922
FA CUP Sa 07Jan 1922 Villa 6 - 1 Derby
1920/1921
DIV 1 Sa 30Apr 1921 Villa 1 - 0 Derby
DIV 1 Sa 23Apr 1921 Derby 2 - 3 Villa
1919/1920
DIV 1 Mo 08Sep 1919 Derby 1 - 0 Villa
DIV 1 Mo 01Sep 1919 Villa 2 - 2 Derby
1913/1914
DIV 1 Mo 13Apr 1914 Villa 3 - 2 Derby
DIV 1 Th 25Dec 1913 Derby 0 - 2 Villa
1912/1913
DIV 1 We 12Mar 1913 Derby 0 - 1 Villa
FA CUP We 15Jan 1913 Derby 1 - 3 Villa
DIV 1 Sa 19Oct 1912 Villa 5 - 1 Derby
1909/1910
FA CUP Mo 02May 1910 Villa 6 - 1 Derby
1906/1907
DIV 1 Sa 23Mar 1907 Villa 2 - 0 Derby
DIV 1 Sa 17Nov 1906 Derby 0 - 1 Villa
1905/1906
DIV 1 Mo 16Apr 1906 Villa 6 - 0 Derby
DIV 1 Sa 30Sep 1905 Derby 1 - 0 Villa
1904/1905
DIV 1 Sa 11Feb 1905 Derby 0 - 2 Villa
DIV 1 Sa 15Oct 1904 Villa 0 - 2 Derby
1903/1904
DIV 1 Mo 28Dec 1903 Derby 2 - 2 Villa
DIV 1 Sa 10Oct 1903 Villa 3 - 0 Derby
1902/1903
DIV 1 Sa 03Jan 1903 Derby 2 - 0 Villa
DIV 1 Sa 06Sep 1902 Villa 0 - 0 Derby
1901/1902
DIV 1 Sa 15Feb 1902 Villa 3 - 2 Derby
DIV 1 Sa 19Oct 1901 Derby 1 - 0 Villa
1900/1901
DIV 1 Mo 22Apr 1901 Derby 3 - 0 Villa
DIV 1 Sa 29Sep 1900 Villa 2 - 1 Derby
1899/1900
DIV 1 Sa 03Feb 1900 Villa 3 - 2 Derby
DIV 1 Sa 30Sep 1899 Derby 2 - 0 Villa
1898/1899
DIV 1 Sa 04Mar 1899 Derby 1 - 1 Villa
DIV 1 Sa 05Nov 1898 Villa 7 - 1 Derby
1897/1898
DIV 1 Sa 05Mar 1898 Villa 4 - 1 Derby
FA CUP Sa 29Jan 1898 Derby 1 - 0 Villa
DIV 1 Sa 22Jan 1898 Derby 3 - 1 Villa
1896/1897
DIV 1 Sa 24Oct 1896 Villa 2 - 1 Derby
DIV 1 Sa 17Oct 1896 Derby 1 - 3 Villa
1895/1896
DIV 1 Sa 08Feb 1896 Derby 2 - 2 Villa
FA CUP Sa 01Feb 1896 Derby 4 - 2 Villa
DIV 1 Sa 21Sep 1895 Villa 4 - 1 Derby
1894/1895
FA CUP Sa 02Feb 1895 Villa 2 - 1 Derby
DIV 1 Sa 05Jan 1895 Villa 4 - 0 Derby
DIV 1 Sa 22Sep 1894 Derby 0 - 2 Villa
1893/1894
DIV 1 Sa 02Dec 1893 Derby 0 - 3 Villa
DIV 1 Sa 30Sep 1893 Villa 1 - 1 Derby
1892/1893
DIV 1 Sa 17Dec 1892 Derby 2 - 1 Villa
DIV 1 Sa 29Oct 1892 Villa 6 - 1 Derby
1891/1892
DIV 1 Sa 09Jan 1892 Villa 6 - 0 Derby
DIV 1 Sa 03Oct 1891 Derby 4 - 2 Villa

1890/1891
DIV 1 Sa 25Oct 1890 Villa 4 - 0 Derby
DIV 1 Sa 18Oct 1890 Derby 5 - 4 Villa
1889/1890
DIV 1 Sa 28Dec 1889 Derby 5 - 0 Villa
DIV 1 Sa 12Oct 1889 Villa 7 - 1 Derby
1888/1889
DIV 1 Sa 09Mar 1889 Derby 5 - 2 Villa
FA CUP Sa 16Feb 1889 Villa 5 - 3 Derby
DIV 1 Sa 29Dec 1888 Villa 4 - 2 Derby
1885/1886
FA CUP Sa 14Nov 1885 Derby 2 - 0 Villa

ASTON VILLA V LEICESTER

	VILLA WINS	DRAWS	LEICESTER WINS
League Cup	3	2	2
League	26	21	35
FA Cup	2	0	2
Total	31	23	39

2007/2008
LC We 26Sep 2007 Villa 0 - 1 Leicester
2006/2007
LC Tu 24Oct 2006 Leicester 2 - 3 Villa
2003/2004
FAPL Sa 31Jan 2004 Leicester 0 - 5 Villa
LC We 29Oct 2003 Villa 1 - 0 Leicester
FAPL Sa 30Aug 2003 Villa 3 - 1 Leicester
2001/2002
FAPL Sa 20Apr 2002 Leicester 2 - 2 VillaFAPL
Sa 01Dec 2001 Villa 0 - 2 Leicester
2000/2001
FAPL We 04Apr 2001 Villa 2 - 1 Leicester
FA CUP Sa 27Jan 2001 Villa 1 - 2 Leicester
FAPL Sa 19Aug 2000 Leicester 0 - 0 Villa
1999/2000
FAPL Sa 22Apr 2000 Villa 2 - 2 Leicester
LC We 02Feb 2000 Leicester 1 - 0 Villa
LC Tu 25Jan 2000 Villa 0 - 0 Leicester
FAPL Sa 25Sep 1999 Leicester 3 - 1 Villa
1998/1999
FAPL Tu 06Apr 1999 Leicester 2 - 2 Villa
FAPL Sa 24Oct 1998 Villa 1 - 1 Leicester
1997/1998
FAPL Sa 10Jan 1998 Villa 1 - 1 Leicester
FAPL Sa 09Aug 1997 Leicester 1 - 0 Villa
1996/1997
FAPL We 05Mar 1997 Leicester 1 - 0 Villa
FAPL Sa 16Nov 1996 Villa 1 - 3 Leicester
1994/1995
FAPL We 22Feb 1995 Villa 4 - 4 Leicester
FAPL Sa 03Dec 1994 Leicester 1 - 1 Villa
1987/1988
DIV 2 Sa 06Feb 1988 Villa 2 - 1 Leicester
DIV 2 Sa 05Sep 1987 Leicester 0 - 2 Villa
1986/1987
DIV 1 Sa 11Apr 1987 Leicester 1 - 1 Villa
DIV 1 Sa 01Nov 1986 Villa 2 - 0 Leicester
1985/1986
DIV 1 Mo 31Mar 1986 Villa 1 - 0 Leicester
DIV 1 Th 26Dec 1985 Leicester 3 - 1 Villa
1984/1985
DIV 1 Sa 02Mar 1985 Villa 0 - 1 Leicester
DIV 1 Sa 27Oct 1984 Leicester 5 - 0 Villa
1983/1984
DIV 1 Sa 14Apr 1984 Leicester 2 - 0 Villa
DIV 1 Sa 19Nov 1983 Villa 3 - 1 Leicester
1981/1982
LC Fr 01Jan 1982 Leicester 0 - 0 Villa
LC Fr 01Jan 1982 Villa 2 - 0 Leicester
1980/1981
DIV 1 Sa 04Apr 1981 Leicester 2 - 4 VillaDIV 1
Sa 01Nov 1980 Villa 2 - 0 Leicester
1977/1978
DIV 1 Sa 04Mar 1978 Villa 0 - 0 Leicester
DIV 1 Sa 08Oct 1977 Leicester 0 - 2 Villa
1976/1977
DIV 1 Sa 05Mar 1977 Leicester 1 - 1 Villa
FA CUP Sa 08Jan 1977 Leicester 0 - 1 Villa
DIV 1 Sa 25Sep 1976 Villa 2 - 0 Leicester
1975/1976
DIV 1 Sa 20Mar 1976 Leicester 2 - 2 Villa
DIV 1 Sa 29Nov 1975 Villa 1 - 1 Leicester
1969/1970
DIV 2 Sa 04Apr 1970 Leicester 1 - 0 Villa
DIV 2 We 27Aug 1969 Villa 0 - 1 Leicester
1966/1967
DIV 1 Sa 04Feb 1967 Villa 0 - 1 Leicester
DIV 1 Sa 24Sep 1966 Leicester 5 - 0 Villa
1965/1966
DIV 1 Sa 05Feb 1966 Leicester 2 - 1 Villa
FA CUP Sa 22Jan 1966 Villa 1 - 2 Leicester
DIV 1 Sa 28Aug 1965 Villa 2 - 2 Leicester
1964/1965
DIV 1 Tu 20Apr 1965 Villa 1 - 0 Leicester
DIV 1 Mo 19Apr 1965 Leicester 1 - 1 Villa
1963/1964
DIV 1 Sa 18Apr 1964 Villa 1 - 3 Leicester
DIV 1 Sa 07Dec 1963 Leicester 0 - 0 Villa

1962/1963
DIV 1 We 15May 1963 Villa 3 - 1 Leicester
DIV 1 Sa 08Dec 1962 Leicester 3 - 3 Villa
1961/1962
DIV 1 Sa 21Apr 1962 Villa 8 - 3 Leicester
DIV 1 Sa 02Dec 1961 Leicester 0 - 2 Villa
1960/1961
DIV 1 We 19Apr 1961 Leicester 3 - 1 Villa
DIV 1 Sa 01Oct 1960 Villa 1 - 3 Leicester
1958/1959
DIV 1 Sa 04Apr 1959 Villa 1 - 2 Leicester
DIV 1 Sa 15Nov 1958 Leicester 6 - 3 Villa
1957/1958
DIV 1 Sa 08Feb 1958 Leicester 6 - 1 Villa
DIV 1 Sa 28Sep 1957 Villa 5 - 1 Leicester
1954/1955
DIV 1 Sa 26Mar 1955 Leicester 4 - 2 Villa
DIV 1 Sa 06Nov 1954 Villa 2 - 5
Leicester1938/1939
DIV 1 Sa 25Feb 1939 Leicester 1 - 1 Villa
DIV 1 Sa 22Oct 1938 Villa 1 - 2
Leicester1936/1937
DIV 2 Sa 10Apr 1937 Leicester 1 - 0 Villa
DIV 2 Sa 05Dec 1936 Villa 1 - 3
Leicester1934/1935
DIV 1 Sa 19Jan 1935 Villa 5 - 0 Leicester
DIV 1 Sa 08Sep 1934 Leicester 5 - 0 Villa
1933/1934
DIV 1 Sa 30Dec 1933 Leicester 1 - 1 Villa
DIV 1 Sa 26Aug 1933 Villa 2 - 3 Leicester
1932/1933
DIV 1 Th 09Feb 1933 Leicester 3 - 0 Villa
DIV 1 Sa 17Sep 1932 Villa 4 - 2 Leicester
1931/1932
DIV 1 Sa 02Jan 1932 Leicester 3 - 8 Villa
DIV 1 Sa 29Aug 1931 Villa 3 - 2 Leicester
1930/1931
DIV 1 Sa 28Feb 1931 Villa 4 - 2 Leicester
DIV 1 Sa 25Oct 1930 Leicester 4 - 1 Villa
1929/1930
DIV 1 Sa 22Feb 1930 Leicester 4 - 3 Villa
DIV 1 Sa 19Oct 1929 Villa 3 - 0 Leicester
1928/1929
DIV 1 Tu 02Apr 1929 Villa 4 - 2 Leicester
DIV 1 Mo 01Apr 1929 Leicester 4 - 1 Villa
1927/1928
DIV 1 Sa 31Dec 1927 Leicester 3 - 0 Villa
DIV 1 Sa 27Aug 1927 Villa 0 - 3 Leicester
1926/1927
DIV 1 Sa 16Apr 1927 Villa 2 - 0 Leicester
DIV 1 Sa 27Nov 1926 Leicester 5 - 1 Villa
1925/1926
DIV 1 We 10Mar 1926 Villa 2 - 2 Leicester
DIV 1 Sa 10Oct 1925 Leicester 1 - 2 Villa
1908/1909
DIV 1 Sa 27Mar 1909 Leicester 4 - 2 Villa
DIV 1 Sa 31Oct 1908 Villa 1 - 1 Leicester
1904/1905
FA CUP Sa 04Feb 1905 Villa 5 - 1 Leicester

ASTON VILLA VS. NOTTM FOREST

	VILLA WINS	DRAWS	FOREST WINS
League	50	27	31
FA Cup	5	1	4
League Cup	1	0	1
Total	56	28	36

1998/1999
FAPL Sa 24Apr 1999 Villa 2 - 0 Forest
FAPL Sa 28Nov 1998 Forest 2 - 2 Villa
1996/1997
FAPL Sa 22Feb 1997 Forest 0 - 0 Villa
FAPL Sa 02Nov 1996 Villa 2 - 0 Forest
1995/1996
FA CUP We 13Mar 1996 Forest 0 - 1 Villa
FAPL Su 10Dec 1995 Forest 1 - 1 Villa
FAPL Sa 23Sep 1995 Villa 1 - 1 Forest
1994/1995
FAPL Sa 21Jan 1995 Forest 1 - 2 Villa
FAPL Sa 22Oct 1994 Villa 0 - 2 Forest
1992/1993
FAPL Su 04Apr 1993 Forest 0 - 1 Villa
FAPL Sa 12Dec 1992 Villa 2 - 1 Forest
1991/1992
DIV 1 Sa 18Apr 1992 Forest 2 - 0 Villa
DIV 1 Sa 21Sep 1991 Villa 3 - 1 Forest
1990/1991
DIV 1 Sa 23Feb 1991 Forest 2 - 2 Villa
DIV 1 Sa 10Nov 1990 Villa 1 - 1 Forest
1989/1990
DIV 1 Sa 02Dec 1989 Villa 2 - 1 Forest
DIV 1 Sa 19Aug 1989 Forest 1 - 1 Villa
1988/1989
DIV 1 Sa 21Jan 1989 Forest 4 - 0 Villa
DIV 1 Sa 24Sep 1988 Villa 1 - 1 Forest
1986/1987
DIV 1 Sa 03Jan 1987 Villa 0 - 0 Forest
DIV 1 Sa 13Sep 1986 Forest 6 - 0 Villa

1985/1986
DIV 1 Sa 15Mar 1986 Forest 1 - 1 Villa
DIV 1 Sa 12Oct 1985 Villa 1 - 2 Forest
1984/1985
DIV 1 Sa 29Dec 1984 Forest 3 - 2 Villa
DIV 1 We 05Sep 1984 Villa 0 - 5 Forest
1983/1984
DIV 1 Sa 17Mar 1984 Villa 1 - 0 Forest
DIV 1 We 07Sep 1983 Forest 2 - 2 Villa
1982/1983
DIV 1 Sa 05Feb 1983 Forest 1 - 2 Villa
DIV 1 Sa 11Sep 1982 Villa 4 - 1 Forest
1981/1982
DIV 1 Sa 24Apr 1982 Forest 1 - 1 Villa
DIV 1 Sa 28Nov 1981 Villa 3 - 1 Forest
1980/1981
DIV 1 Sa 18Apr 1981 Villa 2 - 0 Forest
DIV 1 Sa 27Dec 1980 Forest 2 - 2 Villa
1979/1980
DIV 1 Sa 05Apr 1980 Villa 3 - 2 Forest
DIV 1 We 26Dec 1979 Forest 2 - 1 Villa
1978/1979
DIV 1 We 04Apr 1979 Forest 4 - 0 Villa
FA CUP Mo 01Jan 1979 Forest 2 - 0 Villa
DIV 1 Sa 30Sep 1978 Villa 1 - 2 Forest
1977/1978
DIV 1 We 05Apr 1978 Villa 0 - 1 Forest
LC Su 01Jan 1978 Forest 4 - 2 Villa
DIV 1 Sa 17Sep 1977 Forest 2 - 0 Villa
1974/1975
DIV 2 Sa 08Mar 1975 Forest 2 - 3 Villa
DIV 2 We 02Oct 1974 Villa 3 - 0 Forest
1973/1974
DIV 2 We 24Apr 1974 Villa 3 - 1 Forest
DIV 2 Sa 27Oct 1973 Forest 1 - 2 Villa
1972/1973
LC Mo 01Jan 1973 Forest 0 - 1 Villa
DIV 2 Tu 26Dec 1972 Villa 2 - 2 Forest
DIV 2 Sa 23Sep 1972 Forest 1 - 1 Villa
1966/1967
DIV 1 Sa 15Apr 1967 Forest 3 - 0 Villa
DIV 1 Sa 19Nov 1966 Villa 1 - 1 Forest
1965/1966
DIV 1 Sa 15Jan 1966 Villa 3 - 0 Forest
DIV 1 Sa 23Oct 1965 Forest 1 - 2 Villa
1964/1965
DIV 1 Sa 20Mar 1965 Villa 2 - 1 Forest
DIV 1 Sa 07Nov 1964 Forest 4 - 2 Villa
1963/1964
DIV 1 Sa 14Dec 1963 Villa 3 - 0 Forest
DIV 1 Sa 24Aug 1963 Forest 0 - 1 Villa
1962/1963
DIV 1 Sa 04May 1963 Villa 0 - 2 Forest
DIV 1 Sa 22Sep 1962 Forest 3 - 1 Villa
1961/1962
DIV 1 Tu 24Apr 1962 Forest 2 - 0 Villa
DIV 1 Mo 23Apr 1962 Villa 5 - 1 Forest
1960/1961
DIV 1 Sa 01Apr 1961 Villa 1 - 2 Forest
DIV 1 Sa 10Dec 1960 Forest 2 - 0 Villa
1958/1959
DIV 1 Mo 20Apr 1959 Forest 2 - 0 Villa
FA CUP Sa 14Mar 1959 Forest 1 - 0 Villa
DIV 1 Sa 06Sep 1958 Villa 2 - 3 Forest
1957/1958
DIV 1 We 30Apr 1958 Villa 1 - 1 Forest
DIV 1 Sa 23Nov 1957 Forest 4 - 1 Villa
1937/1938
DIV 2 We 09Mar 1938 Villa 1 - 2 Forest
DIV 2 Sa 23Oct 1937 Forest 0 - 2 Villa
1936/1937
DIV 2 Mo 07Sep 1936 Villa 1 - 1 Forest
DIV 2 We 02Sep 1936 Forest 1 - 1 Villa
1924/1925
DIV 1 Sa 02May 1925 Villa 2 - 0 Forest
DIV 1 Th 02Oct 1924 Forest 0 - 2 Villa
1923/1924
DIV 1 Sa 19Apr 1924 Villa 2 - 0 Forest
DIV 1 Sa 12Apr 1924 Forest 0 - 0 Villa
1922/1923
DIV 1 Sa 27Jan 1923 Villa 4 - 0 Forest
DIV 1 Sa 20Jan 1923 Forest 3 - 1 Villa
1910/1911
DIV 1 Sa 11Feb 1911 Villa 3 - 1 Forest
DIV 1 Sa 08Oct 1910 Forest 3 - 1 Villa
1909/1910
DIV 1 Sa 01Jan 1910 Forest 1 - 4 Villa
DIV 1 Sa 25Sep 1909 Villa 0 - 0 Forest
1908/1909
FA CUP Sa 16Jan 1909 Forest 2 - 0 Villa
DIV 1 Sa 09Jan 1909 Villa 1 - 2 Forest
DIV 1 Sa 12Sep 1908 Forest 1 - 2 Villa
1907/1908
DIV 1 Th 26Dec 1907 Forest 2 - 2 Villa
DIV 1 We 25Dec 1907 Villa 4 - 0 Forest
1905/1906
DIV 1 Sa 17Feb 1906 Villa 3 - 1 Forest
DIV 1 Sa 14Oct 1905 Forest 2 - 2 Villa
1904/1905
DIV 1 Sa 14Jan 1905 Forest 1 - 1 Villa

DIV 1	Sa 17Sep 1904	Villa	2 - 0	Forest
1903/1904				
DIV 1	Sa 16Apr 1904	Villa	3 - 1	Forest
DIV 1	Sa 19Dec 1903	Forest	3 - 7	Villa
1902/1903				
DIV 1	Sa 10Jan 1903	Villa	3 - 1	Forest
DIV 1	Sa 13Sep 1902	Forest	2 - 0	Villa
1901/1902				
DIV 1	Tu 01Apr 1902	Forest	1 - 1	Villa
DIV 1	Sa 28Dec 1901	Villa	3 - 0	Forest
1900/1901				
DIV 1	Sa 20Apr 1901	Forest	3 - 1	Villa
FA CUP	We 27Feb 1901	Forest	1 - 3	Villa
FA CUP	Sa 23Feb 1901	Villa	0 - 0	Forest
DIV 1	Sa 15Dec 1900	Villa	2 - 1	Forest
1899/1900				
DIV 1	Sa 14Apr 1900	Forest	1 - 1	Villa
DIV 1	Sa 09Dec 1899	Villa	2 - 2	Forest
1898/1899				
DIV 1	Sa 18Feb 1899	Forest	1 - 0	Villa
FA CUP	Sa 28Jan 1899	Forest	2 - 1	Villa
DIV 1	Sa 22Oct 1898	Villa	3 - 0	Forest
1897/1898				
DIV 1	Sa 30Apr 1898	Villa	2 - 0	Forest
DIV 1	Sa 26Mar 1898	Forest	3 - 1	Villa
1896/1897				
DIV 1	Sa 06Mar 1897	Forest	2 - 4	Villa
DIV 1	Sa 19Dec 1896	Villa	3 - 2	Forest
1895/1896				
DIV 1	Fr 03Apr 1896	Forest	0 - 2	Villa
DIV 1	Sa 25Jan 1896	Villa	3 - 1	Forest
1894/1895				
FA CUP	Sa 02Mar 1895	Villa	6 - 2	Forest
DIV 1	Sa 24Nov 1894	Villa	4 - 1	Forest
DIV 1	Sa 06Oct 1894	Forest	2 - 1	Villa
1893/1894				
DIV 1	Sa 14Apr 1894	Villa	3 - 1	Forest
DIV 1	Sa 07Oct 1893	Forest	1 - 2	Villa
1892/1893				
DIV 1	Sa 12Nov 1892	Forest	4 - 5	Villa
DIV 1	Sa 15Oct 1892	Villa	1 - 0	Forest
1881/1882				
FA CUP	Sa 05Nov 1881	Villa	4 - 1	Forest
1880/1881				
FA CUP	Sa 04Dec 1880	Forest	1 - 2	Villa

ASTON VILLA VS. STOKE

	ASTON VILLA WINS	DRAWS	STOKE WINS
League	45	23	26
League Cup	1	0	0
FA Cup	3	4	3
Total	49	27	29

2010/2011		
FAPL	Sa 23Apr 2011	Aston Villa 1 - 1 Stoke
FAPL	Mo 13Sep 2010	Stoke 2 - 1 Aston Villa
2009/2010		
FAPL	Sa 13Mar 2010	Stoke 0 - 0 Aston Villa
FAPL	Sa 19Dec 2009	Aston Villa 1 - 0 Stoke
2008/2009		
FAPL	Su 01Mar 2009	Aston Villa 2 - 2 Stoke
FAPL	Sa 23Aug 2008	Stoke 3 - 2 Aston Villa
1987/1988		
DIV 2	Sa 26Mar 1988	Aston Villa 0 - 1 Stoke
DIV 2	Sa 24Oct 1987	Stoke 0 - 0 Aston Villa
1984/1985		
DIV 1	We 27Mar 1985	Aston Villa 2 - 0 Stoke
DIV 1	Mo 27Aug 1984	Stoke 1 - 3 Aston Villa
1983/1984		
DIV 1	Sa 10Mar 1984	Stoke 1 - 0 Aston Villa
DIV 1	Sa 12Nov 1983	Aston Villa 1 - 1 Stoke
1982/1983		
DIV 1	Sa 30Apr 1983	Aston Villa 4 - 0 Stoke
DIV 1	Sa 27Nov 1982	Stoke 0 - 3 Aston Villa
1981/1982		
DIV 1	We 05May 1982	Stoke 1 - 0 Aston Villa
DIV 1	We 23Sep 1981	Aston Villa 2 - 2 Stoke
1980/1981		
DIV 1	Mo 20Apr 1981	Stoke 1 - 1 Aston Villa
DIV 1	Fr 26Dec 1980	Aston Villa 1 - 0 Stoke
1979/1980		
DIV 1	Sa 29Mar 1980	Stoke 2 - 0 Aston Villa
DIV 1	Sa 17Nov 1979	Aston Villa 2 - 1 Stoke
1976/1977		
DIV 1	Mo 16May 1977	Aston Villa 1 - 0 Stoke
DIV 1	Sa 02Oct 1976	Stoke 1 - 0 Aston Villa
1975/1976		
DIV 1	Sa 27Mar 1976	Aston Villa 0 - 0 Stoke
DIV 1	Sa 06Dec 1975	Stoke 1 - 1 Aston Villa
1966/1967		
DIV 1	Sa 25Mar 1967	Aston Villa 2 - 1 Stoke
DIV 1	Sa 10Dec 1966	Stoke 6 - 1 Aston Villa
1965/1966		
DIV 1	Sa 09Apr 1966	Stoke 2 - 0 Aston Villa
DIV 1	Sa 13Nov 1965	Aston Villa 0 - 1 Stoke

1964/1965

DIV 1	Sa 27Mar 1965	Stoke 2 - 1 Aston Villa
DIV 1	Sa 14Nov 1964	Aston Villa 3 - 0 Stoke

1963/1964

DIV 1	We 04Sep 1963	Stoke 2 - 2 Aston Villa
DIV 1	Mo 26Aug 1963	Aston Villa 1 - 3 Stoke

1962/1963

LC	We 17Oct 1962	Aston Villa 3 - 1 Stoke

1959/1960

DIV 2	Mo 18Apr 1960	Aston Villa 2 - 1 Stoke
DIV 2	We 30Sep 1959	Stoke 3 - 3 Aston Villa

1957/1958

FA CUP	Mo 13Jan 1958	Stoke 2 - 0 Aston Villa
FA CUP	We 08Jan 1958	Aston Villa 3 - 3 Stoke
FA CUP	Sa 04Jan 1958	Stoke 1 - 1 Aston Villa

1952/1953

DIV 1	We 25Mar 1953	Aston Villa 1 - 1 Stoke
DIV 1	Sa 01Nov 1952	Stoke 1 - 4 Aston Villa

1951/1952

DIV 1	Sa 16Feb 1952	Aston Villa 2 - 3 Stoke
DIV 1	Sa 06Oct 1951	Stoke 4 - 1 Aston Villa

1950/1951

DIV 1	Sa 05May 1951	Aston Villa 6 - 2 Stoke
DIV 1	Sa 09Dec 1950	Stoke 1 - 0 Aston Villa

1949/1950

DIV 1	Sa 15Apr 1950	Stoke 1 - 0 Aston Villa
DIV 1	Sa 29Oct 1949	Aston Villa 1 - 1 Stoke

1948/1949

DIV 1	Sa 23Apr 1949	Aston Villa 2 - 1 Stoke
DIV 1	Sa 30Oct 1948	Stoke 4 - 2 Aston Villa

1947/1948

DIV 1	Sa 10Apr 1948	Aston Villa 1 - 0 Stoke
DIV 1	Sa 22Nov 1947	Stoke 1 - 2 Aston Villa

1946/1947

DIV 1	Mo 26May 1947	Aston Villa 0 - 1 Stoke
DIV 1	Sa 09Nov 1946	Stoke 0 - 0 Aston Villa

1938/1939

DIV 1	Sa 18Mar 1939	Aston Villa 3 - 0 Stoke
DIV 1	Sa 12Nov 1938	Stoke 3 - 1 Aston Villa

1935/1936

DIV 1	Sa 07Mar 1936	Stoke 2 - 3 Aston Villa
DIV 1	Sa 30Nov 1935	Aston Villa 4 - 0 Stoke

1934/1935

DIV 1	Sa 02Mar 1935	Aston Villa 4 - 1 Stoke
DIV 1	Sa 20Oct 1934	Stoke 4 - 1 Aston Villa

1933/1934

DIV 1	Sa 24Feb 1934	Aston Villa 1 - 2 Stoke
DIV 1	Sa 14Oct 1933	Stoke 1 - 1 Aston Villa

1922/1923

DIV 1	Sa 24Feb 1923	Stoke 1 - 1 Aston Villa
DIV 1	Sa 17Feb 1923	Aston Villa 6 - 0 Stoke

1921/1922

FA CUP	We 22Feb 1922	Aston Villa 4 - 0 Stoke
FA CUP	Sa 18Feb 1922	Stoke 0 - 0 Aston Villa

1913/1914

FA CUP	Sa 10Jan 1914	Aston Villa 4 - 0 Stoke

1906/1907

DIV 1	Mo 10Sep 1906	Aston Villa 1 - 0 Stoke
DIV 1	Mo 03Sep 1906	Stoke 0 - 2 Aston Villa

1905/1906

DIV 1	Sa 23Dec 1905	Aston Villa 3 - 0 Stoke
DIV 1	Mo 13Nov 1905	Stoke 0 - 1 Aston Villa

1904/1905

DIV 1	Sa 31Dec 1904	Stoke 1 - 4 Aston Villa
DIV 1	Sa 03Sep 1904	Aston Villa 3 - 0 Stoke

1903/1904

FA CUP	Sa 06Feb 1904	Stoke 2 - 3 Aston Villa
DIV 1	Sa 30Jan 1904	Aston Villa 3 - 1 Stoke
DIV 1	Sa 03Oct 1903	Stoke 2 - 0 Aston Villa

1902/1903

DIV 1	Mo 13Apr 1903	Aston Villa 2 - 0 Stoke
DIV 1	Sa 11Oct 1902	Stoke 1 - 0 Aston Villa

1901/1902

FA CUP	We 29Jan 1902	Aston Villa 1 - 2 Stoke
FA CUP	Sa 25Jan 1902	Stoke 2 - 2 Aston Villa
DIV 1	Sa 18Jan 1902	Aston Villa 0 - 0 Stoke
DIV 1	Sa 21Sep 1901	Stoke 1 - 0 Aston Villa

1900/1901

DIV 1	Sa 29Dec 1900	Stoke 0 - 0 Aston Villa
DIV 1	Sa 01Sep 1900	Aston Villa 2 - 0 Stoke

1899/1900

DIV 1	Sa 23Dec 1899	Aston Villa 4 - 1 Stoke
DIV 1	Mo 13Nov 1899	Stoke 0 - 2 Aston Villa

1898/1899

DIV 1	Sa 31Dec 1898	Stoke 3 - 0 Aston Villa
DIV 1	Sa 03Sep 1898	Aston Villa 3 - 1 Stoke

1897/1898

DIV 1	Sa 02Apr 1898	Aston Villa 1 - 1 Stoke
DIV 1	Sa 18Dec 1897	Stoke 0 - 0 Aston Villa

1896/1897

DIV 1	Sa 31Oct 1896	Stoke 0 - 2 Aston Villa
DIV 1	We 02Sep 1896	Aston Villa 2 - 1 Stoke

1895/1896

DIV 1	Sa 22Feb 1896	Aston Villa 5 - 2 Stoke
DIV 1	Sa 04Jan 1896	Stoke 1 - 2 Aston Villa

1894/1895

DIV 1	We 26Dec 1894	Aston Villa 6 - 0 Stoke
DIV 1	Sa 29Sep 1894	Stoke 4 - 1 Aston Villa

1893/1894

DIV 1	Mo 16Oct 1893	Stoke 3 - 3 Aston Villa

DIV 1 Mo 11Sep 1893 Aston Villa 5 - 1 Stoke

1892/1893

DIV 1 Mo 10Oct 1892 Aston Villa 3 - 2 Stoke

DIV 1 Mo 12Sep 1892 Stoke 0 - 1 Aston Villa

1891/1892

DIV 1 Sa 21Nov 1891 Aston Villa 2 - 1 Stoke

DIV 1 Sa 24Oct 1891 Stoke 2 - 3 Aston Villa

1890/1891

FA CUP Sa 31Jan 1891 Stoke 3 - 0 Aston Villa

1889/1890

DIV 1 Mo 17Mar 1890 Stoke 1 - 1 Aston Villa

DIV 1 Sa 07Dec 1889 Aston Villa 6 - 1 Stoke

1888/1889

DIV 1 Sa 03Nov 1888 Stoke 1 - 1 Aston Villa

DIV 1 Sa 15Sep 1888 Aston Villa 5 - 1 Stoke

ASTON VILLA VS. WALSALL

	VILLA WINS	DRAWS	WALSALL WINS
League	0	3	1
FA Cup	2	0	0
Total	2	3	1

1971/1972

DIV 3 `Sa 18Mar 1972 Aston Villa 0 - 0 Walsall

DIV 3 Sa 21Aug 1971 Walsall 1 - 1 Aston Villa

1970/1971

DIV 3 We 17Mar 1971 Aston Villa 0 - 0 Walsall

DIV 3 Sa 02Jan 1971 Walsall 3 - 0 Aston Villa

1929/1930

FA CUP Sa 25Jan 1930 Aston Villa 3 - 1 Walsall

1911/1912

FA CUP Sa 13Jan 1912 Aston Villa 6 - 0 Walsall

ASTON VILLA VS. WEST BROM

	VILLA WINS	DRAWS	WBA WINS
League	63	27	44
FA Cup	9	3	3
League Cup	2	1	4
Total	74	31	51

2010/2011

FAPL Sa 30Apr 2011 West Brom 2 - 1 Aston Villa

FAPL Sa 11Dec 2010 Aston Villa 2 - 1 West Brom

2008/2009

FAPL Sa 10Jan 2009 Aston Villa 2 - 1 West Brom

FAPL Su 21Sep 2008 West Brom 1 - 2 Aston Villa

2005/2006

FAPL Su 09Apr 2006 Aston Villa 0 - 0 West Brom

FAPL Mo 02Jan 2006 West Brom 1 - 2 Aston Villa

2004/2005

FAPL Su 10Apr 2005 Aston Villa 1 - 1 West Brom

FAPL Su 22Aug 2004 West Brom 1 - 1 Aston Villa

2002/2003

FAPL Sa 14Dec 2002 Aston Villa 2 - 1 West Brom

FAPL Sa 16Nov 2002 West Brom 0 - 0 Aston Villa

1997/1998

FA CUP Sa 24Jan 1998 Aston Villa 4 - 0 West Brom

1989/1990

FA CUP Sa 17Feb 1990 West Brom 0 - 2 Aston Villa

1987/1988

DIV 2 Fr 18Dec 1987 Aston Villa 0 - 0 West Brom

DIV 2 We 16Sep 1987 West Brom 0 - 2 Aston Villa

1985/1986

LC We 01Jan 1986 Aston Villa 2 - 2 West Brom

LC We 01Jan 1986 West Brom 1 - 2 Aston Villa

DIV 1 Sa 28Dec 1985 Aston Villa 1 - 1 West Brom

DIV 1 We 04Sep 1985 West Brom 0 - 3 Aston Villa

1984/1985

DIV 1 Mo 08Apr 1985 West Brom 1 - 0 Aston Villa

DIV 1 Tu 01Jan 1985 Aston Villa 3 - 1 West Brom

1983/1984

DIV 1 Sa 14Jan 1984 West Brom 3 - 1 Aston Villa

LC Su 01Jan 1984 West Brom 1 - 2 Aston Villa

DIV 1 Sa 27Aug 1983 Aston Villa 4 - 3 West Brom

1982/1983

DIV 1 Tu 19Apr 1983 Aston Villa 1 - 0 West Brom

DIV 1 Sa 02Oct 1982 West Brom 1 - 0 Aston Villa

1981/1982

DIV 1 Sa 08May 1982 West Brom 0 - 1 Aston Villa

DIV 1 Tu 30Mar 1982 Aston Villa 2 - 1 West Brom

LC Fr 01Jan 1982 Aston Villa 0 - 1 West Brom

1980/1981

DIV 1 We 08Apr 1981 Aston Villa 1 - 0 West Brom

DIV 1 Sa 08Nov 1980 West Brom 0 - 0 Aston Villa

1979/1980

DIV 1 Sa 23Feb 1980 West Brom 1 - 2 Aston Villa

DIV 1 Sa 13Oct 1979 Aston Villa 0 - 0 West Brom

1978/1979

DIV 1 Fr 11May 1979 Aston Villa 0 - 1 West Brom

DIV 1 Sa 25Nov 1978 West Brom 1 - 1 Aston Villa

1977/1978

DIV 1 Sa 22Apr 1978 West Brom 0 - 3 Aston Villa

DIV 1 Sa 10Dec 1977 Aston Villa 3 - 0 West Brom

1976/1977

DIV 1 Mo 23May 1977 Aston Villa 4 - 0 West Brom

DIV 1 We 10Nov 1976 West Brom 1 - 1 Aston Villa

1974/1975

DIV 2 Sa 29Mar 1975 Aston Villa 3 - 1 West Brom

DIV 2 Sa 21Dec 1974 West Brom 2 - 0 Aston Villa

1973/1974

DIV 2	Sa 02Mar 1974	Aston Villa 1 - 3 West Brom
DIV 2	We 26Dec 1973	West Brom 2 - 0 Aston Villa

1969/1970

LC	Th 01Jan 1970	Aston Villa 1 - 2 West Brom

1966/1967

LC	Su 01Jan 1967	West Brom 6 - 1 Aston Villa
DIV 1	Sa 05Nov 1966	Aston Villa 3 - 2 West Brom
DIV 1	Sa 15Oct 1966	West Brom 2 - 1 Aston Villa

1965/1966

DIV 1	Fr 11Feb 1966	West Brom 2 - 2 Aston Villa
LC	We 17Nov 1965	West Brom 3 - 1 Aston Villa
DIV 1	Sa 16Oct 1965	Aston Villa 1 - 1 West Brom

1964/1965

DIV 1	Sa 27Feb 1965	West Brom 3 - 1 Aston Villa
DIV 1	Sa 17Oct 1964	Aston Villa 0 - 1 West Brom

1963/1964

DIV 1	Sa 22Feb 1964	Aston Villa 1 - 0 West Brom
DIV 1	Sa 12Oct 1963	West Brom 4 - 3 Aston Villa

1962/1963

DIV 1	Sa 11May 1963	West Brom 1 - 0 Aston Villa
DIV 1	Sa 06Oct 1962	Aston Villa 2 - 0 West Brom

1961/1962

DIV 1	We 14Mar 1962	Aston Villa 1 - 0 West Brom
DIV 1	Sa 21Oct 1961	West Brom 1 - 1 Aston Villa

1960/1961

DIV 1	Tu 28Mar 1961	Aston Villa 0 - 1 West Brom
DIV 1	Sa 29Oct 1960	West Brom 0 - 2 Aston Villa

1958/1959

DIV 1	We 29Apr 1959	West Brom 1 - 1 Aston Villa
DIV 1	Sa 11Oct 1958	Aston Villa 1 - 4 West Brom

1957/1958

DIV 1	Sa 05Apr 1958	Aston Villa 2 - 1 West Brom
DIV 1	Sa 09Nov 1957	West Brom 3 - 2 Aston Villa

1956/1957

FA CUP	Th 28Mar 1957	Aston Villa 1 - 0 West Brom
FA CUP	Sa 23Mar 1957	Aston Villa 2 - 2 West Brom
DIV 1	Mo 27Aug 1956	Aston Villa 0 - 0 West Brom
DIV 1	We 22Aug 1956	West Brom 2 - 0 Aston Villa

1955/1956

DIV 1	Sa 28Apr 1956	Aston Villa 3 - 0 West Brom
DIV 1	Sa 08Oct 1955	West Brom 1 - 0 Aston Villa

1954/1955

DIV 1	Sa 19Mar 1955	Aston Villa 3 - 0 West Brom
DIV 1	Sa 30Oct 1954	West Brom 2 - 3 Aston Villa

1953/1954

DIV 1	Tu 20Apr 1954	Aston Villa 6 - 1 West Brom
DIV 1	Mo 19Apr 1954	West Brom 1 - 1 Aston Villa

1952/1953

DIV 1	Tu 07Apr 1953	Aston Villa 1 - 1 West Brom
DIV 1	Mo 06Apr 1953	West Brom 3 - 2 Aston Villa

1951/1952

DIV 1	Sa 19Apr 1952	Aston Villa 2 - 0 West Brom
DIV 1	Sa 01Dec 1951	West Brom 1 - 2 Aston Villa

1950/1951

DIV 1	Sa 16Dec 1950	West Brom 2 - 0 Aston Villa
DIV 1	Sa 19Aug 1950	Aston Villa 2 - 0 West Brom

1949/1950

DIV 1	Sa 25Feb 1950	Aston Villa 1 - 0 West Brom
DIV 1	Sa 08Oct 1949	West Brom 1 - 1 Aston Villa

1935/1936

DIV 1	We 01Apr 1936	West Brom 0 - 3 Aston Villa
DIV 1	Sa 19Oct 1935	Aston Villa 0 - 7 West Brom

1934/1935

DIV 1	We 03Apr 1935	Aston Villa 2 - 3 West Brom
DIV 1	Sa 03Nov 1934	West Brom 2 - 2 Aston Villa

1933/1934

DIV 1	Sa 28Apr 1934	Aston Villa 4 - 4 West Brom
DIV 1	Sa 16Dec 1933	West Brom 2 - 1 Aston Villa

1932/1933

DIV 1	Sa 11Mar 1933	Aston Villa 3 - 2 West Brom
DIV 1	Sa 29Oct 1932	West Brom 3 - 1 Aston Villa

1931/1932

DIV 1	Sa 26Mar 1932	Aston Villa 2 - 0 West Brom
FA CUP	Sa 09Jan 1932	West Brom 1 - 2 Aston Villa
DIV 1	Sa 14Nov 1931	West Brom 3 - 0 Aston Villa

1926/1927

DIV 1	Sa 12Mar 1927	West Brom 6 - 2 Aston Villa
DIV 1	Sa 23Oct 1926	Aston Villa 2 - 0 West Brom

1925/1926

DIV 1	Sa 13Feb 1926	Aston Villa 2 - 1 West Brom
FA CUP	Sa 30Jan 1926	West Brom 1 - 2 Aston Villa
DIV 1	Sa 03Oct 1925	West Brom 1 - 1 Aston Villa

1924/1925

DIV 1	Sa 28Feb 1925	West Brom 4 - 1 Aston Villa
FA CUP	We 25Feb 1925	Aston Villa 1 - 2 West Brom
FA CUP	Sa 21Feb 1925	West Brom 1 - 1 Aston Villa
DIV 1	Sa 25Oct 1924	Aston Villa 1 - 0 West Brom

1923/1924

FA CUP	Sa 08Mar 1924	West Brom 0 - 2 Aston Villa
DIV 1	Sa 27Oct 1923	Aston Villa 4 - 0 West Brom
DIV 1	Sa 20Oct 1923	West Brom 1 - 0 Aston Villa

1922/1923

DIV 1	Sa 16Sep 1922	West Brom 3 - 0 Aston Villa
DIV 1	Sa 09Sep 1922	Aston Villa 2 - 0 West Brom

1921/1922

DIV 1	Sa 15Oct 1921	Aston Villa 0 - 1 West Brom
DIV 1	Sa 08Oct 1921	West Brom 0 - 1 Aston Villa

1920/1921

DIV 1	Sa 13Nov 1920	West Brom 2 - 1 Aston Villa

DIV 1 Sa 06Nov 1920 Aston Villa 0 - 0 West Brom
1919/1920
DIV 1 Sa 15Nov 1919 Aston Villa 2 - 4 West Brom
DIV 1 Mo 10Nov 1919 West Brom 1 - 2 Aston Villa
1914/1915
DIV 1 Sa 23Jan 1915 West Brom 2 - 0 Aston Villa
DIV 1 Sa 19Sep 1914 Aston Villa 2 - 1 West Brom
1913/1914
FA CUP Sa 21Feb 1914 Aston Villa 2 - 1 West Brom
DIV 1 Sa 07Feb 1914 Aston Villa 2 - 0 West Brom
DIV 1 Sa 04Oct 1913 West Brom 1 - 0 Aston Villa
1912/1913
DIV 1 Sa 18Jan 1913 West Brom 2 - 2 Aston Villa
DIV 1 Sa 21Sep 1912 Aston Villa 2 - 4 West Brom
1911/1912
DIV 1 Sa 30Sep 1911 West Brom 2 - 2 Aston Villa
DIV 1 Mo 04Sep 1911 Aston Villa 0 - 3 West Brom
1903/1904
DIV 1 Sa 09Jan 1904 West Brom 1 - 3 Aston Villa
DIV 1 Sa 12Sep 1903 Aston Villa 3 - 1 West Brom
1902/1903
DIV 1 Sa 28Feb 1903 West Brom 1 - 2 Aston Villa
DIV 1 Sa 01Nov 1902 Aston Villa 0 - 3 West Brom
1900/1901
DIV 1 Sa 05Jan 1901 Aston Villa 0 - 1 West Brom
DIV 1 Sa 08Sep 1900 West Brom 0 - 1 Aston Villa
1899/1900
DIV 1 Sa 06Jan 1900 West Brom 0 - 2 Aston Villa
DIV 1 Sa 09Sep 1899 Aston Villa 0 - 2 West Brom
1898/1899
DIV 1 Mo 24Apr 1899 Aston Villa 7 - 1 West Brom
DIV 1 Sa 12Nov 1898 West Brom 0 - 1 Aston Villa
1897/1898
DIV 1 Sa 09Oct 1897 West Brom 1 - 1 Aston Villa
DIV 1 Sa 04Sep 1897 Aston Villa 4 - 3 West Brom
1896/1897
DIV 1 Sa 10Oct 1896 Aston Villa 2 - 0 West Brom
DIV 1 Sa 05Sep 1896 West Brom 3 - 1 Aston Villa
1895/1896
DIV 1 Sa 12Oct 1895 West Brom 1 - 1 Aston Villa
DIV 1 Mo 02Sep 1895 Aston Villa 1 - 0 West Brom
1894/1895
FA CUP Sa 20Apr 1895 Aston Villa 1 - 0 West Brom
DIV 1 Sa 17Nov 1894 West Brom 3 - 2 Aston Villa
DIV 1 Sa 13Oct 1894 Aston Villa 3 - 1 West Brom
1893/1894
DIV 1 Sa 21Oct 1893 West Brom 3 - 6 Aston Villa
DIV 1 Sa 02Sep 1893 Aston Villa 3 - 2 West Brom
1892/1893
DIV 1 Sa 05Nov 1892 Aston Villa 5 - 2 West Brom
DIV 1 Mo 19Sep 1892 West Brom 3 - 2 Aston Villa
1891/1892
FA CUP Sa 19Mar 1892 West Brom 3 - 0 Aston Villa
DIV 1 Sa 14Nov 1891 West Brom 0 - 3 Aston Villa
DIV 1 Sa 12Sep 1891 Aston Villa 5 - 1 West Brom
1890/1891
DIV 1 Sa 01Nov 1890 West Brom 0 - 3 Aston Villa
DIV 1 Sa 27Sep 1890 Aston Villa 0 - 4 West Brom
1889/1890
DIV 1 Sa 26Oct 1889 Aston Villa 1 - 0 West Brom
DIV 1 Sa 28Sep 1889 West Brom 3 - 0 Aston Villa
1888/1889
DIV 1 Sa 26Jan 1889 West Brom 3 - 3 Aston Villa
DIV 1 Sa 19Jan 1889 Aston Villa 2 - 0 West Brom
1886/1887
FA CUP Sa 02Apr 1887 Aston Villa 2 - 0 West Brom
1884/1885
FA CUP Sa 10Jan 1885 West Brom 3 - 0 Aston Villa
FA CUP Sa 03Jan 1885 Aston Villa 0 - 0 West Brom

ASTON VILLA VS. WOLVES

	VILLA WINS	DRAWS	WOLVES WINS
League	44	24	34
League Cup	4	1	0
FA Cup	4	5	3
Total	52	30	37

2010/2011
FAPL Sa 19Mar 2011 Aston Villa 0 - 1 Wolves
FAPL Su 26Sep 2010 Wolves 1 - 2 Aston Villa
2009/2010
FAPL Sa 20Mar 2010 Aston Villa 2 - 2 Wolves
FAPL Sa 24Oct 2009 Wolves 1 - 1 Aston Villa
2003/2004
FAPL Su 14Mar 2004 Wolves 0 - 4 Aston Villa
FAPL Su 14Dec 2003 Aston Villa 3 - 2 Wolves
1995/1996
LC We 10Jan 1996 Aston Villa 1 - 0 Wolves
1989/1990
LC We 04Oct 1989 Wolves 1 - 1 Aston Villa
LC We 20Sep 1989 Aston Villa 2 - 1 Wolves
1983/1984
DIV 1 Sa 25Feb 1984 Aston Villa 4 - 0 Wolves
DIV 1 Su 23Oct 1983 Wolves 1 - 1 Aston Villa
1982/1983
FA CUP Sa 29Jan 1983 Aston Villa 1 - 0 Wolves
1981/1982
DIV 1 Sa 13Mar 1982 Aston Villa 3 - 1 Wolves
LC Fr 01Jan 1982 Aston Villa 3 - 2 Wolves
LC Fr 01Jan 1982 Wolves 1 - 2 Aston Villa
DIV 1 Sa 24Oct 1981 Wolves 0 - 3 Aston Villa

1980/1981
DIV 1 Sa 28Feb 1981 Wolves 0 - 1 Aston Villa
DIV 1 Sa 20Sep 1980 Aston Villa 2 - 1 Wolves
1979/1980
DIV 1 Mo 10Mar 1980 Aston Villa 1 - 3 Wolves
DIV 1 Sa 27Oct 1979 Wolves 1 - 1 Aston Villa
1978/1979
DIV 1 Sa 11Nov 1978 Wolves 0 - 4 Aston Villa
DIV 1 Sa 19Aug 1978 Aston Villa 1 - 0 Wolves
1977/1978
DIV 1 Tu 02May 1978 Wolves 3 - 1 Aston Villa
DIV 1 Fr 23Sep 1977 Aston Villa 2 - 0 Wolves
1975/1976
DIV 1 Tu 24Feb 1976 Aston Villa 1 - 1 Wolves
DIV 1 Tu 23Sep 1975 Wolves 0 - 0 Aston Villa
1964/1965
DIV 1 Mo 22Mar 1965 Aston Villa 3 - 2 Wolves
FA CUP Mo 01Mar 1965 Aston Villa 1 - 3 Wolves
FA CUP We 24Feb 1965 Wolves 0 - 0 Aston Villa
FA CUP Sa 20Feb 1965 Aston Villa 1 - 1 Wolves
DIV 1 Sa 26Dec 1964 Wolves 0 - 1 Aston Villa
1963/1964
DIV 1 Sa 28Dec 1963 Aston Villa 2 - 2 Wolves
DIV 1 Th 26Dec 1963 Wolves 3 - 3 Aston Villa
1962/1963
DIV 1 Tu 16Apr 1963 Aston Villa 0 - 2 Wolves
DIV 1 Mo 15Apr 1963 Wolves 3 - 1 Aston Villa
1961/1962
DIV 1 Mo 02Oct 1961 Aston Villa 1 - 0 Wolves
DIV 1 Mo 28Aug 1961 Wolves 2 - 2 Aston Villa
1960/1961
DIV 1 Mo 26Dec 1960 Wolves 3 - 2 Aston Villa
DIV 1 Sa 24Dec 1960 Aston Villa 0 - 2 Wolves
1959/1960
FA CUP Sa 26Mar 1960 Wolves 1 - 0 Aston Villa
1958/1959
DIV 1 We 17Sep 1958 Wolves 4 - 0 Aston Villa
DIV 1 Mo 08Sep 1958 Aston Villa 1 - 3 Wolves
1957/1958
DIV 1 Mo 23Sep 1957 Aston Villa 2 - 3 Wolves
DIV 1 Mo 16Sep 1957 Wolves 2 - 1 Aston Villa
1956/1957
DIV 1 Tu 23Apr 1957 Wolves 3 - 0 Aston Villa
DIV 1 Mo 22Apr 1957 Aston Villa 4 - 0 Wolves
1955/1956
DIV 1 Tu 03Apr 1956 Aston Villa 0 - 0 Wolves
DIV 1 Mo 02Apr 1956 Wolves 0 - 0 Aston Villa
1954/1955
DIV 1 Tu 12Apr 1955 Aston Villa 4 - 2 Wolves
DIV 1 Mo 11Apr 1955 Wolves 1 - 0 Aston Villa
1953/1954
DIV 1 Sa 26Dec 1953 Aston Villa 1 - 2 Wolves
DIV 1 Th 24Dec 1953 Wolves 1 - 2 Aston Villa
1952/1953
DIV 1 Mo 15Sep 1952 Aston Villa 0 - 1 Wolves
DIV 1 Mo 08Sep 1952 Wolves 2 - 1 Aston Villa
1951/1952
DIV 1 We 26Dec 1951 Wolves 1 - 2 Aston Villa
DIV 1 Tu 25Dec 1951 Aston Villa 3 - 3 Wolves
1950/1951
DIV 1 Tu 27Mar 1951 Aston Villa 1 - 0 Wolves
DIV 1 Mo 26Mar 1951 Wolves 2 - 3 Aston Villa
FA CUP Sa 27Jan 1951 Wolves 3 - 1 Aston Villa
1949/1950
DIV 1 Tu 27Dec 1949 Aston Villa 1 - 4 Wolves
DIV 1 Mo 26Dec 1949 Wolves 2 - 3 Aston Villa
1948/1949
DIV 1 Mo 27Dec 1948 Aston Villa 5 - 1 Wolves
DIV 1 Sa 25Dec 1948 Wolves 4 - 0 Aston Villa
1947/1948
DIV 1 Sa 27Dec 1947 Wolves 4 - 1 Aston Villa
DIV 1 Fr 26Dec 1947 Aston Villa 1 - 2 Wolves
1946/1947
DIV 1 Mo 16Sep 1946 Aston Villa 3 - 0 Wolves
DIV 1 We 11Sep 1946 Wolves 1 - 2 Aston Villa
1938/1939
DIV 1 Tu 11Apr 1939 Aston Villa 2 - 2 Wolves
DIV 1 Mo 10Apr 1939 Wolves 2 - 1 Aston Villa
1935/1936
DIV 1 Mo 13Apr 1936 Wolves 2 - 2 Aston Villa
DIV 1 Fr 10Apr 1936 Aston Villa 4 - 2 Wolves
1934/1935
DIV 1 Mo 03Sep 1934 Wolves 5 - 2 Aston Villa
DIV 1 Mo 27Aug 1934 Aston Villa 2 - 1 Wolves
1933/1934
DIV 1 Tu 26Dec 1933 Wolves 4 - 3 Aston Villa
DIV 1 Mo 25Dec 1933 Aston Villa 6 - 2 Wolves
1932/1933
DIV 1 Tu 27Dec 1932 Wolves 2 - 4 Aston Villa
DIV 1 Mo 26Dec 1932 Aston Villa 1 - 3 Wolves
1905/1906
DIV 1 Sa 31Mar 1906 Wolves 4 - 1 Aston Villa
DIV 1 Sa 25Nov 1905 Aston Villa 6 - 0 Wolves
1904/1905
DIV 1 Th 27Apr 1905 Aston Villa 3 - 0 Wolves
DIV 1 Sa 17Dec 1904 Wolves 1 - 1 Aston Villa
1903/1904
DIV 1 Sa 12Mar 1904 Wolves 3 - 2 Aston Villa
DIV 1 Sa 14Nov 1903 Aston Villa 2 - 0 Wolves

1902/1903

DIV 1 Sa 04Apr 1903 Aston Villa 3 - 1 Wolves

DIV 1 Sa 06Dec 1902 Wolves 2 - 1 Aston Villa

1901/1902

DIV 1 Sa 22Mar 1902 Wolves 0 - 2 Aston Villa

DIV 1 Sa 23Nov 1901 Aston Villa 2 - 1 Wolves

1900/1901

DIV 1 Mo 08Apr 1901 Wolves 0 - 0 Aston Villa

DIV 1 Sa 27Oct 1900 Aston Villa 0 - 0 Wolves

1899/1900

DIV 1 Mo 16Apr 1900 Wolves 0 - 1 Aston Villa

DIV 1 Sa 11Nov 1899 Aston Villa 0 - 0 Wolves

1898/1899

DIV 1 Mo 03Apr 1899 Wolves 4 - 0 Aston Villa

DIV 1 Sa 10Dec 1898 Aston Villa 1 - 1 Wolves

1897/1898

DIV 1 Mo 11Apr 1898 Aston Villa 1 - 2 Wolves

DIV 1 Mo 27Dec 1897 Wolves 1 - 1 Aston Villa

1896/1897

DIV 1 Mo 19Apr 1897 Aston Villa 5 - 0 Wolves

DIV 1 Sa 26Dec 1896 Wolves 1 - 2 Aston Villa

1895/1896

DIV 1 Mo 06Apr 1896 Aston Villa 4 - 1 Wolves

DIV 1 Th 26Dec 1895 Wolves 1 - 2 Aston Villa

1894/1895

DIV 1 Mo 15Apr 1895 Aston Villa 2 - 2 Wolves

DIV 1 Sa 22Dec 1894 Wolves 0 - 4 Aston Villa

1893/1894

DIV 1 Mo 26Mar 1894 Aston Villa 1 - 1 Wolves

FA CUP Sa 27Jan 1894 Aston Villa 4 - 2 Wolves

DIV 1 Sa 23Dec 1893 Wolves 3 - 0 Aston Villa

1892/1893

DIV 1 Mo 03Apr 1893 Aston Villa 5 - 0 Wolves

DIV 1 Sa 08Oct 1892 Wolves 2 - 1 Aston Villa

1891/1892

DIV 1 Mo 18Apr 1892 Aston Villa 3 - 6 Wolves

FA CUP Sa 13Feb 1892 Wolves 1 - 3 Aston Villa

DIV 1 Sa 19Dec 1891 Wolves 2 - 0 Aston Villa

1890/1891

DIV 1 Sa 14Mar 1891 Aston Villa 6 - 2 Wolves

DIV 1 Sa 06Sep 1890 Wolves 2 - 1 Aston Villa

1889/1890

DIV 1 Sa 21Dec 1889 Wolves 1 - 1 Aston Villa

DIV 1 Sa 02Nov 1889 Aston Villa 2 - 1 Wolves

1888/1889

DIV 1 Sa 24Nov 1888 Aston Villa 2 - 1 Wolves

DIV 1 Sa 08Sep 1888 Wolves 1 - 1 Aston Villa

1886/1887

FA CUP Sa 29Jan 1887 Aston Villa 2 - 0 Wolves

FA CUP Sa 22Jan 1887 Wolves 3 - 3 Aston Villa

FA CUP Sa 11Dec 1886 Aston Villa 2 - 2 Wolves

FA CUP Mo 15Nov 1886 Wolves 1 - 1 Aston Villa

BIRMINGHAM V COVENTRY

	BIRMINGHAM WINS	DRAWS	COVENTRY WINS
League	20	13	14
FA Cup	2	0	1
League Cup	1	1	1
Total	23	14	16

2011/2012

CHAMP Sa 13Aug 2011 Birmingham 1 - 0 Coventry

2010/2011

FA Cup Sa 29Jan 2011 Birmingham 3 - 2 Coventry

2008/2009

CHAMP Sa 21Feb 2009 Coventry 1 - 0 Birmingham

CHAMP Mo 03Nov 2008 Birmingham 0 - 1 Coventry

2006/2007

CHAMP Su 01Apr 2007 Birmingham 3 - 0 Coventry

CHAMP Tu 31Oct 2006 Coventry 0 - 1 Birmingham

2001/2002

FL DIV 1 Su 24Mar 2002 Coventry 1 - 1 Birmingham

FL DIV 1 Su 25Nov 2001 Birmingham 2 - 0 Coventry

1996/1997

LC Tu 24Sep 1996 Birmingham 0 - 1 Coventry

LC We 18Sep 1996 Coventry 1 - 1 Birmingham

1985/1986

DIV 1 Su 16Feb 1986 Coventry 4 - 4 Birmingham

DIV 1 Sa 26Oct 1985 Birmingham 0 - 1 Coventry

1983/1984

DIV 1 Sa 03Mar 1984 Coventry 0 - 1 Birmingham

DIV 1 Sa 05Nov 1983 Birmingham 1 - 2 Coventry

1982/1983

DIV 1 Sa 16Apr 1983 Coventry 0 - 1 Birmingham

DIV 1 Sa 18Sep 1982 Birmingham 1 - 0 Coventry

1981/1982

DIV 1 Sa 15May 1982 Coventry 0 - 1 Birmingham

DIV 1 Tu 26Jan 1982 Birmingham 3 - 3 Coventry

1980/1981

FA Cup Th 01Jan 1981 Coventry 3 - 2 Birmingham

DIV 1 Sa 15Nov 1980 Coventry 2 - 1 Birmingham

DIV 1 Sa 16Aug 1980 Birmingham 3 - 1 Coventry

1978/1979

DIV 1 Sa 10Mar 1979 Birmingham 0 - 0 Coventry

DIV 1 Sa 28Oct 1978 Coventry 2 - 1 Birmingham

1977/1978

DIV 1 Sa 04Mar 1978 Coventry 4 - 0 Birmingham

DIV 1 Sa 08Oct 1977 Birmingham 1 - 1 Coventry

1976/1977

DIV 1 Sa 05Mar 1977 Birmingham 3 - 1 Coventry

DIV 1 Sa 25Sep 1976 Coventry 2 - 1 Birmingham
1975/1976
DIV 1 Sa 20Mar 1976 Birmingham 1 - 1 Coventry
DIV 1 Sa 29Nov 1975 Coventry 3 - 2 Birmingham
1974/1975
DIV 1 Sa 12Apr 1975 Coventry 1 - 0 Birmingham
DIV 1 Sa 05Oct 1974 Birmingham 1 - 2 Coventry
1973/1974
DIV 1 Sa 02Mar 1974 Coventry 0 - 1 Birmingham
DIV 1 We 26Dec 1973 Birmingham 1 - 0 Coventry
1972/1973
DIV 1 Sa 24Mar 1973 Birmingham 3 - 0 Coventry
LC Mo 01Jan 1973 Birmingham 2 - 1 Coventry
DIV 1 Sa 28Oct 1972 Coventry 0 - 0 Birmingham
1966/1967
DIV 2 Sa 07Jan 1967 Birmingham 1 - 1 Coventry
DIV 2 Sa 03Sep 1966 Coventry 1 - 1 Birmingham
1965/1966
DIV 2 Sa 16Apr 1966 Coventry 4 - 3 Birmingham
DIV 2 Sa 20Nov 1965 Birmingham 0 - 1 Coventry
1951/1952
DIV 2 Sa 01Mar 1952 Birmingham 3 - 1 Coventry
DIV 2 Sa 13Oct 1951 Coventry 1 - 1 Birmingham
1950/1951
DIV 2 Mo 11Sep 1950 Coventry 3 - 1 Birmingham
DIV 2 We 06Sep 1950 Birmingham 1 - 1 Coventry
1947/1948
DIV 2 We 03Sep 1947 Birmingham 1 - 1 Coventry
DIV 2 Mo 25Aug 1947 Coventry 0 - 1 Birmingham
1946/1947
DIV 2 Sa 15Feb 1947 Birmingham 2 - 0 Coventry
DIV 2 Sa 12Oct 1946 Coventry 0 - 0 Birmingham
1934/1935
FA Cup Sa 12Jan 1935 Birmingham 5 - 1 Coventry
1920/1921
DIV 2 Sa 11Dec 1920 Coventry 0 - 4 Birmingham
DIV 2 Sa 04Dec 1920 Birmingham 3 - 2 Coventry
1919/1920
DIV 2 Sa 20Sep 1919 Coventry 1 - 3 Birmingham
DIV 2 Sa 13Sep 1919 Birmingham 4 - 1 Coventry

BIRMINGHAM V DERBY

	BIRMINGHAM WINS	DRAWS	DERBY WINS
League	32	28	35
FA Cup	3	1	3
League Cup	3	0	1
Total	38	29	39

2011/2012
CHAMP Sa 06Aug 2011 Derby 2 - 1 Birmingham
2009/2010
FA CUP Sa 13Feb 2010 Derby 1 - 2 Birmingham
2008/2009
CHAMP Tu 27Jan 2009 Birmingham 1 - 0 Derby
CHAMP Tu 30Sep 2008 Derby 1 - 1 Birmingham
2007/2008
FAPL Sa 02Feb 2008 Birmingham 1 - 1 Derby
FAPL Sa 25Aug 2007 Derby 1 - 2 Birmingham
2006/2007
CHAMP Fr 09Mar 2007 Birmingham 1 - 0 Derby
CHAMP Sa 21Oct 2006 Derby 0 - 1 Birmingham
1995/1996
FL DIV 1 Sa 20Apr 1996 Derby 1 - 1 Birmingham
FL DIV 1 Tu 21Nov 1995 Birmingham 1 - 4 Derby
1993/1994
FL DIV 1 Sa 26Feb 1994 Derby 1 - 1 Birmingham
FL DIV 1 Sa 04Sep 1993 Birmingham 3 - 0 Derby
1992/1993
FL DIV 1 Tu 06Apr 1993 Birmingham 1 - 1 Derby
FL DIV 1 Sa 12Dec 1992 Derby 3 - 1 Birmingham
1986/1987
DIV 2 Sa 07Feb 1987 Derby 2 - 2 Birmingham
DIV 2 Sa 30Aug 1986 Birmingham 1 - 1 Derby
1983/1984
LC Su 01Jan 1984 Birmingham 4 - 0 Derby
LC Su 01Jan 1984 Derby 0 - 3 Birmingham
1982/1983
LC Sa 01Jan 1983 Birmingham 3 - 1 Derby
1978/1979
DIV 1 Sa 18Nov 1978 Derby 2 - 1 Birmingham
DIV 1 Sa 26Aug 1978 Birmingham 1 - 1 Derby
1977/1978
DIV 1 Sa 18Mar 1978 Derby 1 - 3 Birmingham
FA CUP Su 01Jan 1978 Derby 2 - 1 Birmingham
DIV 1 Sa 22Oct 1977 Birmingham 3 - 1 Derby
1976/1977
DIV 1 Sa 12Mar 1977 Derby 0 - 0 Birmingham
DIV 1 Sa 02Oct 1976 Birmingham 5 - 1 Derby
1975/1976
DIV 1 Sa 27Mar 1976 Derby 4 - 2 Birmingham
DIV 1 Sa 06Dec 1975 Birmingham 2 - 1 Derby
1974/1975
DIV 1 Th 26Dec 1974 Derby 2 - 1 Birmingham
DIV 1 Sa 14Sep 1974 Birmingham 3 - 2 Derby
1973/1974
DIV 1 Tu 01Jan 1974 Derby 1 - 1 Birmingham
DIV 1 Sa 01Sep 1973 Birmingham 0 - 0 Derby
1972/1973
DIV 1 Sa 10Feb 1973 Birmingham 2 - 0 Derby
DIV 1 Sa 16Sep 1972 Derby 1 - 0 Birmingham

1968/1969
DIV 2 Tu 14Jan 1969 Birmingham 1 - 1 Derby
DIV 2 Sa 26Oct 1968 Derby 1 - 0 Birmingham
1967/1968
DIV 2 Tu 02Apr 1968 Birmingham 3 - 1 Derby
LC Mo 01Jan 1968 Derby 3 - 1 Birmingham
DIV 2 Sa 04Nov 1967 Derby 2 - 2 Birmingham
1966/1967
DIV 2 Sa 15Apr 1967 Birmingham 2 - 0 Derby
DIV 2 Sa 19Nov 1966 Derby 1 - 2 Birmingham
1965/1966
DIV 2 Sa 09Apr 1966 Birmingham 5 - 5 Derby
DIV 2 Sa 30Oct 1965 Derby 5 - 3 Birmingham
1954/1955
DIV 2 Sa 19Mar 1955 Derby 0 - 0 Birmingham
DIV 2 Sa 30Oct 1954 Birmingham 1 - 1 Derby
1953/1954
DIV 2 Sa 20Mar 1954 Birmingham 3 - 0 Derby
DIV 2 Sa 31Oct 1953 Derby 2 - 4 Birmingham
1950/1951
FA CUP Sa 27Jan 1951 Derby 1 - 3 Birmingham
1949/1950
DIV 1 Tu 27Dec 1949 Derby 4 - 1 Birmingham
DIV 1 Mo 26Dec 1949 Birmingham 2 - 2 Derby
1948/1949
DIV 1 Sa 23Apr 1949 Derby 1 - 0 Birmingham
DIV 1 Sa 30Oct 1948 Birmingham 0 - 1 Derby
1945/1946
FA CUP We 27Mar 1946 Derby 4 - 0 Birmingham
FA CUP Sa 23Mar 1946 Derby 1 - 1 Birmingham
1938/1939
DIV 1 Sa 18Feb 1939 Derby 0 - 1 Birmingham
DIV 1 Sa 15Oct 1938 Birmingham 3 - 0 Derby
1937/1938
DIV 1 Sa 05Mar 1938 Derby 0 - 0 Birmingham
DIV 1 Sa 23Oct 1937 Birmingham 1 - 0 Derby
1936/1937
DIV 1 Sa 17Apr 1937 Derby 3 - 1 Birmingham
DIV 1 Sa 12Dec 1936 Birmingham 0 - 1 Derby
1935/1936
DIV 1 Sa 21Mar 1936 Birmingham 2 - 3 Derby
DIV 1 Sa 16Nov 1935 Derby 2 - 2 Birmingham
1934/1935
DIV 1 Sa 23Mar 1935 Birmingham 3 - 2 Derby
DIV 1 Sa 10Nov 1934 Derby 1 - 1 Birmingham
1933/1934
DIV 1 We 21Feb 1934 Birmingham 2 - 1 Derby
DIV 1 Sa 07Oct 1933 Derby 4 - 0 Birmingham
1932/1933
DIV 1 We 01Feb 1933 Birmingham 3 - 1 Derby
DIV 1 Sa 17Sep 1932 Derby 2 - 2 Birmingham
1931/1932
DIV 1 Sa 20Feb 1932 Birmingham 1 - 1 Derby
DIV 1 Sa 10Oct 1931 Derby 2 - 1 Birmingham
1930/1931
DIV 1 Sa 03Jan 1931 Birmingham 1 - 2 Derby
DIV 1 Sa 06Sep 1930 Derby 0 - 0 Birmingham
1929/1930
DIV 1 Sa 05Apr 1930 Birmingham 2 - 4 Derby
DIV 1 Sa 30Nov 1929 Derby 3 - 1 Birmingham
1928/1929
DIV 1 Sa 16Feb 1929 Derby 2 - 2 Birmingham
DIV 1 Sa 06Oct 1928 Birmingham 1 - 4 Derby
1927/1928
DIV 1 Sa 05May 1928 Birmingham 2 - 1 Derby
DIV 1 Sa 24Dec 1927 Derby 4 - 1 Birmingham
1926/1927
DIV 1 Sa 05Mar 1927 Derby 4 - 1 Birmingham
DIV 1 Sa 16Oct 1926 Birmingham 1 - 0 Derby
1914/1915
DIV 2 Sa 20Mar 1915 Birmingham 0 - 2 Derby
DIV 2 Sa 14Nov 1914 Derby 1 - 0 Birmingham
1911/1912
DIV 2 We 21Feb 1912 Derby 0 - 1 Birmingham
DIV 2 Sa 16Sep 1911 Birmingham 0 - 4 Derby
1910/1911
DIV 2 Sa 18Feb 1911 Birmingham 2 - 0 Derby
DIV 2 Sa 15Oct 1910 Derby 1 - 0 Birmingham
1909/1910
DIV 2 Sa 23Apr 1910 Derby 3 - 1 Birmingham
DIV 2 Sa 11Dec 1909 Birmingham 1 - 3 Derby
1908/1909
DIV 2 Sa 03Apr 1909 Birmingham 1 - 1 Derby
DIV 2 Sa 28Nov 1908 Derby 1 - 2 Birmingham
1906/1907
DIV 1 Sa 30Mar 1907 Derby 1 - 1 Birmingham
DIV 1 Sa 24Nov 1906 Birmingham 2 - 1 Derby
1905/1906
DIV 1 Sa 07Apr 1906 Derby 0 - 0 Birmingham
DIV 1 Sa 02Dec 1905 Birmingham 3 - 1 Derby
1904/1905
DIV 1 Sa 08Apr 1905 Birmingham 2 - 0 Derby
DIV 1 Sa 10Dec 1904 Derby 3 - 0 Birmingham
1903/1904
DIV 1 Sa 09Apr 1904 Birmingham 1 - 0 Derby
DIV 1 Tu 01Sep 1903 Derby 4 - 1 Birmingham
1902/1903
FA CUP Sa 07Feb 1903 Derby 2 - 1 Birmingham
1901/1902
DIV 1 Sa 12Apr 1902 Birmingham 5 - 1 Derby

DIV 1 Mo 31Mar 1902 Derby 0 - 0 Birmingham
1895/1896
DIV 1 Sa 04Jan 1896 Birmingham 1 - 3 Derby
DIV 1 Sa 30Nov 1895 Derby 8 - 0 Birmingham
1894/1895
DIV 1 Sa 30Mar 1895 Derby 4 - 1 Birmingham
DIV 1 Sa 16Mar 1895 Birmingham 3 - 5 Derby
1885/1886
FA CUP Sa 12Dec 1885 Birmingham 4 - 2 Derby

BIRMINGHAM V LEICESTER

	BIRMINGHAM WINS	DRAWS	LEICESTER WINS
League	49	21	48
FA Cup	0	3	6
Total	49	24	54

2006/2007
CHAMP Tu 17Apr 2007 Leicester 1 - 2 Birmingham
CHAMP Sa 30Sep 2006 Birmingham 1 - 1 Leicester
2003/2004
PREMIERSHIP Sa 13Mar 2004 Birmingham 0 - 1 Leicester
PREMIERSHIP Sa 13Dec 2003 Leicester 0 - 2 Birmingham
1998/1999
FA CUP Sa 02Jan 1999 Leicester 4 - 2 Birmingham
1995/1996
FL DIV 1 Sa 27Apr 1996 Leicester 3 - 0 Birmingham
FL DIV 1 Su 26Nov 1995 Birmingham 2 - 2 Leicester
1993/1994
FL DIV 1 Tu 15Mar 1994 Birmingham 0 - 3 Leicester
FL DIV 1 Su 12Sep 1993 Leicester 1 - 1 Birmingham
1992/1993
FL DIV 1 Su 28Feb 1993 Leicester 2 - 1 Birmingham
FL DIV 1 Sa 10Oct 1992 Birmingham 0 - 2 Leicester
1988/1989
DIV 2 Sa 25Mar 1989 Leicester 2 - 0 Birmingham
DIV 2 Sa 03Sep 1988 Birmingham 2 - 3 Leicester
1987/1988
DIV 2 Tu 05Apr 1988 Leicester 2 - 0 Birmingham
DIV 2 Sa 14Nov 1987 Birmingham 2 - 2 Leicester
1985/1986
DIV 1 We 12Mar 1986 Leicester 4 - 2 Birmingham
DIV 1 Sa 21Sep 1985 Birmingham 2 - 1 Leicester
1983/1984
DIV 1 Sa 04Feb 1984 Leicester 2 - 3 Birmingham
DIV 1 Sa 01Oct 1983 Birmingham 2 - 1 Leicester
1980/1981
DIV 1 Sa 25Apr 1981 Leicester 1 - 0 Birmingham
DIV 1 Sa 06Dec 1980 Birmingham 1 - 2 Leicester
1979/1980
DIV 2 Sa 12Apr 1980 Leicester 2 - 1 Birmingham
DIV 2 Sa 01Dec 1979 Birmingham 1 - 2 Leicester
1977/1978
DIV 1 Sa 15Apr 1978 Leicester 1 - 4 Birmingham
DIV 1 Sa 19Nov 1977 Birmingham 1 - 1 Leicester
1976/1977
DIV 1 Sa 30Apr 1977 Birmingham 1 - 1 Leicester
DIV 1 Sa 04Dec 1976 Leicester 2 - 6 Birmingham
1975/1976
DIV 1 Sa 20Dec 1975 Birmingham 2 - 1 Leicester
DIV 1 Sa 16Aug 1975 Leicester 3 - 3 Birmingham
1974/1975
DIV 1 We 28Aug 1974 Leicester 1 - 1 Birmingham
DIV 1 Tu 20Aug 1974 Birmingham 3 - 4 Leicester
1973/1974
DIV 1 Sa 06Apr 1974 Leicester 3 - 3 Birmingham
DIV 1 Sa 24Nov 1973 Birmingham 3 - 0 Leicester
1972/1973
DIV 1 Sa 14Apr 1973 Leicester 0 - 1 Birmingham
DIV 1 Sa 09Dec 1972 Birmingham 1 - 1 Leicester
1970/1971
DIV 2 Sa 16Jan 1971 Leicester 1 - 4 Birmingham
DIV 2 Tu 20Oct 1970 Birmingham 0 - 0 Leicester
1969/1970
DIV 2 Sa 14Feb 1970 Birmingham 0 - 1 Leicester
DIV 2 Sa 09Aug 1969 Leicester 3 - 1 Birmingham
1965/1966
FA CUP Sa 12Feb 1966 Birmingham 1 - 2 Leicester
1964/1965
DIV 1 Sa 10Apr 1965 Birmingham 2 - 0 Leicester
DIV 1 Sa 28Nov 1964 Leicester 4 - 4 Birmingham
1963/1964
DIV 1 We 04Sep 1963 Birmingham 2 - 0 Leicester
DIV 1 We 28Aug 1963 Leicester 3 - 0 Birmingham
1962/1963
DIV 1 Sa 18May 1963 Birmingham 3 - 2 Leicester
DIV 1 Sa 29Sep 1962 Leicester 3 - 0 Birmingham
1961/1962
DIV 1 Sa 13Jan 1962 Leicester 1 - 2 Birmingham
DIV 1 Sa 02Sep 1961 Birmingham 1 - 5 Leicester
1960/1961
DIV 1 Sa 29Apr 1961 Leicester 3 - 2 Birmingham
FA CUP We 22Feb 1961 Leicester 2 - 1 Birmingham
FA CUP Sa 18Feb 1961 Birmingham 1 - 1 Leicester
DIV 1 Sa 26Nov 1960 Birmingham 0 - 2 Leicester
1959/1960
DIV 1 Sa 06Feb 1960 Leicester 1 - 3 Birmingham
DIV 1 Sa 19Sep 1959 Birmingham 3 - 4 Leicester
1958/1959

DIV 1 We 18Mar 1959 Leicester 2 - 4 Birmingham
DIV 1 Sa 27Sep 1958 Birmingham 4 - 2 Leicester
1957/1958
DIV 1 Sa 26Apr 1958 Birmingham 0 - 1 Leicester
DIV 1 Sa 14Dec 1957 Leicester 2 - 2 Birmingham
1953/1954
DIV 2 Sa 16Jan 1954 Leicester 3 - 4 Birmingham
DIV 2 Sa 05Sep 1953 Birmingham 1 - 2 Leicester
1952/1953
DIV 2 Sa 24Jan 1953 Leicester 3 - 4 Birmingham
DIV 2 Sa 13Sep 1952 Birmingham 3 - 1 Leicester
1951/1952
DIV 2 Sa 22Dec 1951 Birmingham 2 - 0 Leicester
DIV 2 Sa 25Aug 1951 Leicester 4 - 0 Birmingham
1950/1951
DIV 2 Mo 28Aug 1950 Leicester 1 - 3 Birmingham
DIV 2 We 23Aug 1950 Birmingham 2 - 0 Leicester
1948/1949
FA CUP Mo 17Jan 1949 Leicester 2 - 1 Birmingham
FA CUP Sa 15Jan 1949 Birmingham 1 - 1 Leicester
FA CUP Sa 08Jan 1949 Leicester 1 - 1 Birmingham
1947/1948
DIV 2 Mo 19Apr 1948 Leicester 0 - 0 Birmingham
DIV 2 Sa 20Sep 1947 Birmingham 1 - 0 Leicester
1946/1947
DIV 2 Th 12Sep 1946 Leicester 2 - 1 Birmingham
DIV 2 We 04Sep 1946 Birmingham 4 - 0 Leicester
1938/1939
DIV 1 Mo 12Sep 1938 Leicester 2 - 1 Birmingham
DIV 1 We 07Sep 1938 Birmingham 2 - 1 Leicester
1937/1938
DIV 1 Sa 07May 1938 Leicester 1 - 4 Birmingham
DIV 1 We 15Sep 1937 Birmingham 4 - 1 Leicester
1934/1935
DIV 1 Sa 16Mar 1935 Leicester 2 - 1 Birmingham
DIV 1 Sa 03Nov 1934 Birmingham 2 - 3 Leicester
1933/1934
DIV 1 Sa 28Apr 1934 Leicester 3 - 7 Birmingham
DIV 1 We 28Mar 1934 Birmingham 3 - 0 Leicester
FA CUP Sa 17Feb 1934 Birmingham 1 - 2 Leicester
1932/1933
DIV 1 Sa 29Apr 1933 Birmingham 0 - 4 Leicester
DIV 1 Sa 17Dec 1932 Leicester 2 - 2 Birmingham
1931/1932
DIV 1 Sa 26Mar 1932 Leicester 3 - 1 Birmingham
DIV 1 Sa 14Nov 1931 Birmingham 2 - 0 Leicester
1930/1931
DIV 1 Sa 02May 1931 Birmingham 2 - 1 Leicester
DIV 1 Mo 01Sep 1930 Leicester 2 - 1 Birmingham
1929/1930
DIV 1 Sa 03May 1930 Birmingham 3 - 0 Leicester
DIV 1 Th 17Oct 1929 Leicester 2 - 1 Birmingham
1928/1929
DIV 1 Mo 10Sep 1928 Birmingham 1 - 0 Leicester
DIV 1 Mo 27Aug 1928 Leicester 5 - 3 Birmingham
1927/1928
DIV 1 Sa 14Apr 1928 Leicester 3 - 0 Birmingham
DIV 1 Sa 03Dec 1927 Birmingham 0 - 2 Leicester
1926/1927
DIV 1 Sa 01Jan 1927 Birmingham 2 - 1 Leicester
DIV 1 Mo 30Aug 1926 Leicester 5 - 2 Birmingham
1925/1926
DIV 1 Sa 06Mar 1926 Leicester 1 - 0 Birmingham
DIV 1 Sa 24Oct 1925 Birmingham 1 - 1 Leicester
1920/1921
DIV 2 Sa 02Oct 1920 Birmingham 5 - 0 Leicester
DIV 2 Sa 25Sep 1920 Leicester 3 - 0 Birmingham
1919/1920
DIV 2 Fr 26Dec 1919 Birmingham 0 - 1 Leicester
DIV 2 Th 25Dec 1919 Leicester 1 - 0 Birmingham
1914/1915
DIV 2 Sa 02Jan 1915 Birmingham 2 - 0 Leicester
DIV 2 Sa 05Sep 1914 Leicester 1 - 0 Birmingham
1913/1914
DIV 2 Sa 17Jan 1914 Leicester 0 - 0 Birmingham
DIV 2 Sa 20Sep 1913 Birmingham 1 - 0 Leicester
1912/1913
DIV 2 Sa 18Jan 1913 Birmingham 5 - 1 Leicester
DIV 2 Sa 21Sep 1912 Leicester 1 - 2 Birmingham
1911/1912
DIV 2 Sa 17Feb 1912 Leicester 5 - 2 Birmingham
DIV 2 Sa 14Oct 1911 Birmingham 4 - 0 Leicester
1910/1911
DIV 2 Sa 04Mar 1911 Birmingham 1 - 0 Leicester
DIV 2 Sa 29Oct 1910 Leicester 2 - 0 Birmingham
1909/1910
DIV 2 Sa 19Mar 1910 Birmingham 2 - 1 Leicester
FA CUP Sa 15Jan 1910 Birmingham 1 - 4 Leicester
DIV 2 Sa 06Nov 1909 Leicester 3 - 1 Birmingham
1902/1903
DIV 2 Sa 03Jan 1903 Birmingham 4 - 3 Leicester
DIV 2 Sa 06Sep 1902 Leicester 1 - 3 Birmingham
1900/1901
DIV 2 Sa 05Jan 1901 Leicester 1 - 1 Birmingham
DIV 2 Sa 08Sep 1900 Birmingham 0 - 0 Leicester
1899/1900
DIV 2 Tu 17Apr 1900 Leicester 2 - 0 Birmingham
DIV 2 Sa 14Apr 1900 Birmingham 4 - 1 Leicester
1898/1899

DIV 2 Sa 29Apr 1899 Leicester 0 - 0 Birmingham
DIV 2 Sa 18Mar 1899 Birmingham 0 - 3 Leicester

1897/1898

DIV 2 Sa 26Mar 1898 Leicester 2 - 0 Birmingham
DIV 2 Sa 11Sep 1897 Birmingham 2 - 1 Leicester

1896/1897

DIV 2 Fr 16Apr 1897 Birmingham 2 - 2 Leicester
DIV 2 Sa 27Mar 1897 Leicester 0 - 1 Birmingham

BIRMINGHAM V NOTTM FOREST

	BIRMINGHAM WINS	DRAWS	NOTTM FOREST WINS
League	30	24	33
FA Cup	3	4	2
League Cup	2	1	2
Total	35	29	37

2011/2012

CHAMP Su 02Oct 2011 Forest 1 - 3 Birmingham

2009/2010

FA Cup Tu 12Jan 2010 Birmingham 1 - 0 Forest
FA Cup Sa 02Jan 2010 Forest 0 - 0 Birmingham

2008/2009

CHAMP Sa 14Feb 2009 Birmingham 2 - 0 Forest
CHAMP Sa 08Nov 2008 Forest 1 - 1 Birmingham

2001/2002

FL DIV 1 Tu 01Jan 2002 Birmingham 1 - 1 Forest
FL DIV 1 We 17Oct 2001 Forest 0 - 0 Birmingham

2000/2001

FL DIV 1 Mo 01Jan 2001 Birmingham 0 - 2 Forest
FL DIV 1 Sa 26Aug 2000 Forest 1 - 2 Birmingham

1999/2000

FL DIV 1 Sa 15Apr 2000 Birmingham 0 - 1 Forest
FL DIV 1 Tu 28Dec 1999 Forest 1 - 0 Birmingham

1997/1998

FL DIV 1 Sa 21Mar 1998 Birmingham 1 - 2 Forest
FL DIV 1 Sa 15Nov 1997 Forest 1 - 0 Birmingham

1993/1994

FL DIV 1 Sa 04Dec 1993 Forest 1 - 0 Birmingham
FL DIV 1 Sa 06Nov 1993 Birmingham 0 - 3 Forest

1987/1988

FA Cup Sa 20Feb 1988 Birmingham 0 - 1 Forest

1985/1986

DIV 1 Mo 31Mar 1986 Forest 3 - 0 Birmingham
DIV 1 Th 26Dec 1985 Birmingham 0 - 1 Forest

1983/1984

DIV 1 Sa 21Apr 1984 Forest 5 - 1 Birmingham
DIV 1 Mo 26Dec 1983 Birmingham 1 - 2 Forest

1982/1983

DIV 1 Sa 26Feb 1983 Birmingham 1 - 1 Forest
DIV 1 Sa 16Oct 1982 Forest 1 - 1 Birmingham

1981/1982

DIV 1 Sa 09Jan 1982 Forest 2 - 1 Birmingham
LC Fr 01Jan 1982 Birmingham 2 - 3 Forest
LC Fr 01Jan 1982 Forest 2 - 1 Birmingham
DIV 1 Sa 05Sep 1981 Birmingham 4 - 3 Forest

1980/1981

DIV 1 Tu 11Nov 1980 Birmingham 2 - 0 Forest
DIV 1 We 20Aug 1980 Forest 2 - 1 Birmingham

1978/1979

DIV 1 Sa 21Apr 1979 Birmingham 0 - 2 Forest
DIV 1 Sa 16Dec 1978 Forest 1 - 0 Birmingham

1977/1978

DIV 1 Sa 29Apr 1978 Forest 0 - 0 Birmingham
DIV 1 Sa 03Dec 1977 Birmingham 0 - 2 Forest

1970/1971

LC Fr 01Jan 1971 Birmingham 2 - 1 Forest

1966/1967

LC Su 01Jan 1967 Birmingham 2 - 1 Forest
LC Su 01Jan 1967 Forest 1 - 1 Birmingham

1964/1965

DIV 1 Sa 12Dec 1964 Birmingham 1 - 1 Forest
DIV 1 Sa 22Aug 1964 Forest 4 - 3 Birmingham

1963/1964

DIV 1 Sa 04Apr 1964 Forest 4 - 0 Birmingham
DIV 1 Sa 23Nov 1963 Birmingham 3 - 3 Forest

1962/1963

DIV 1 Sa 13Apr 1963 Forest 0 - 2 Birmingham
DIV 1 Sa 10Nov 1962 Birmingham 2 - 2 Forest

1961/1962

DIV 1 We 30Aug 1961 Birmingham 1 - 1 Forest
DIV 1 Tu 22Aug 1961 Forest 2 - 1 Birmingham

1960/1961

DIV 1 Sa 11Feb 1961 Forest 1 - 0 Birmingham
FA Cup Sa 07Jan 1961 Forest 0 - 2 Birmingham
DIV 1 Sa 24Sep 1960 Birmingham 3 - 1 Forest

1959/1960

DIV 1 Sa 05Mar 1960 Birmingham 4 - 1 Forest
DIV 1 Sa 17Oct 1959 Forest 0 - 2 Birmingham

1958/1959

DIV 1 Sa 07Mar 1959 Forest 1 - 7 Birmingham
FA Cup Mo 23Feb 1959 Forest 5 - 0 Birmingham
FA Cup We 18Feb 1959 Forest 1 - 1 Birmingham
FA Cup Sa 14Feb 1959 Birmingham 1 - 1 Forest
DIV 1 Sa 18Oct 1958 Birmingham 0 - 3 Forest

1957/1958

DIV 1 We 04Sep 1957 Birmingham 0 - 2 Forest
DIV 1 We 28Aug 1957 Forest 1 - 1 Birmingham

1956/1957

FA Cup Th 07Mar 1957 Forest 0 - 1 Birmingham

FA Cup Sa 02Mar 1957 Birmingham 0 - 0 Forest

1954/1955

DIV 2 Mo 27Dec 1954 Forest 0 - 2 Birmingham

DIV 2 Sa 25Dec 1954 Birmingham 0 - 1 Forest

1953/1954

DIV 2 Mo 19Apr 1954 Birmingham 2 - 2 Forest

DIV 2 Fr 16Apr 1954 Forest 1 - 1 Birmingham

1952/1953

DIV 2 Sa 18Apr 1953 Forest 0 - 2 Birmingham

DIV 2 Sa 29Nov 1952 Birmingham 0 - 5 Forest

1951/1952

DIV 2 Sa 29Dec 1951 Forest 0 - 1 Birmingham

DIV 2 Sa 01Sep 1951 Birmingham 0 - 2 Forest

1947/1948

DIV 2 Sa 03Apr 1948 Birmingham 2 - 1 Forest

DIV 2 Sa 15Nov 1947 Forest 0 - 2 Birmingham

1946/1947

DIV 2 Sa 10May 1947 Forest 1 - 1 Birmingham

DIV 2 Sa 05Oct 1946 Birmingham 4 - 0 Forest

1924/1925

DIV 1 Sa 11Apr 1925 Birmingham 1 - 1 Forest

DIV 1 Sa 06Dec 1924 Forest 1 - 1 Birmingham

1923/1924

DIV 1 Sa 26Jan 1924 Forest 1 - 1 Birmingham

DIV 1 Sa 19Jan 1924 Birmingham 0 - 2 Forest

1922/1923

DIV 1 Sa 25Nov 1922 Forest 1 - 1 Birmingham

DIV 1 Sa 18Nov 1922 Birmingham 2 - 0 Forest

1920/1921

DIV 2 Sa 16Apr 1921 Forest 1 - 1 Birmingham

DIV 2 Sa 09Apr 1921 Birmingham 3 - 0 Forest

1919/1920

DIV 2 We 10Mar 1920 Birmingham 8 - 0 Forest

DIV 2 Sa 28Feb 1920 Forest 1 - 2 Birmingham

1914/1915

DIV 2 Mo 28Dec 1914 Birmingham 3 - 0 Forest

DIV 2 We 02Sep 1914 Forest 1 - 1 Birmingham

1913/1914

DIV 2 Sa 21Mar 1914 Forest 3 - 1 Birmingham

DIV 2 Sa 15Nov 1913 Birmingham 2 - 0 Forest

1912/1913

DIV 2 Sa 22Mar 1913 Birmingham 2 - 0 Forest

DIV 2 Sa 16Nov 1912 Forest 3 - 1 Birmingham

1911/1912

DIV 2 Sa 09Mar 1912 Birmingham 4 - 2 Forest

DIV 2 Sa 04Nov 1911 Forest 0 - 1 Birmingham

1907/1908

DIV 1 Mo 30Mar 1908 Birmingham 1 - 0 Forest

DIV 1 Sa 26Oct 1907 Forest 1 - 1 Birmingham

1905/1906

DIV 1 Sa 21Apr 1906 Forest 2 - 1 Birmingham

DIV 1 Sa 16Dec 1905 Birmingham 5 - 0 Forest

1904/1905

DIV 1 Sa 11Mar 1905 Birmingham 1 - 2 Forest

DIV 1 Sa 12Nov 1904 Forest 0 - 2 Birmingham

1903/1904

DIV 1 Sa 24Oct 1903 Forest 0 - 1 Birmingham

DIV 1 Mo 07Sep 1903 Birmingham 3 - 3 Forest

1901/1902

DIV 1 Sa 05Apr 1902 Birmingham 1 - 1 Forest

DIV 1 Sa 26Oct 1901 Forest 1 - 1 Birmingham

1895/1896

DIV 1 Sa 09Nov 1895 Birmingham 1 - 0 Forest

DIV 1 Sa 21Sep 1895 Forest 3 - 0 Birmingham

1894/1895

DIV 1 Sa 26Jan 1895 Forest 2 - 0 Birmingham

DIV 1 Sa 22Dec 1894 Birmingham 1 - 2 Forest

BIRMINGHAM V STOKE

	BLUES WINS	DRAWS	STOKE WINS
League	29	19	38
FA Cup	3	3	2
Total	32	22	40

2010/2011

FAPL Sa 12Feb 2011 Birmingham 1 - 0 Stoke

FAPL Tu 09Nov 2010 Stoke 3 - 2 Birmingham

2009/2010

FAPL Mo 28Dec 2009 Stoke 0 - 1 Birmingham

FAPL Sa 22Aug 2009 Birmingham 0 - 0 Stoke

2006/2007

CHAMP Su 11Feb 2007 Birmingham 1 - 0 Stoke

CHAMP Sa 12Aug 2006 Stoke 0 - 0 Birmingham

2005/2006

FA CUP Su 19Feb 2006 Stoke 0 - 1 Birmingham

1997/1998

FL DIV 1 Sa 10Jan 1998 Stoke 0 - 7 Birmingham

FL DIV 1 Sa 09Aug 1997 Birmingham 2 - 0 Stoke

1996/1997

FL DIV 1 Fr 10Jan 1997 Stoke 1 - 0 Birmingham

FL DIV 1 Sa 14Sep 1996 Birmingham 3 - 1 Stoke

1995/1996

FL DIV 1 Sa 17Feb 1996 Stoke 1 - 0 Birmingham

FL DIV 1 Tu 12Sep 1995 Birmingham 1 - 1 Stoke

1993/1994

FL DIV 1 Sa 02Apr 1994 Birmingham 3 - 1 Stoke

FL DIV 1 Su 26Dec 1993 Stoke 2 - 1 Birmingham

1991/1992

DIV 3 Sa 29Feb 1992 Birmingham 1 - 1 Stoke

DIV 3 Sa 04Jan 1992 Stoke 2 - 1 Birmingham

1990/1991		
DIV 3	Tu 16Apr 1991	Birmingham 2 - 1 Stoke
DIV 3	Sa 08Sep 1990	Stoke 0 - 1 Birmingham
1988/1989		
DIV 2	Tu 28Feb 1989	Stoke 1 - 0 Birmingham
DIV 2	Tu 25Oct 1988	Birmingham 0 - 1 Stoke
1987/1988		
DIV 2	Sa 16Jan 1988	Stoke 3 - 1 Birmingham
DIV 2	Sa 15Aug 1987	Birmingham 2 - 0 Stoke
1986/1987		
DIV 2	Sa 24Jan 1987	Birmingham 0 - 0 Stoke
DIV 2	Sa 23Aug 1986	Stoke 0 - 2 Birmingham
1983/1984		
DIV 1	Sa 17Mar 1984	Stoke 2 - 1 Birmingham
DIV 1	Tu 06Sep 1983	Birmingham 1 - 0 Stoke
1982/1983		
DIV 1	Mo 03Jan 1983	Stoke 1 - 1 Birmingham
DIV 1	Sa 04Sep 1982	Birmingham 1 - 4 Stoke
1981/1982		
DIV 1	Sa 13Mar 1982	Birmingham 2 - 1 Stoke
DIV 1	Sa 24Oct 1981	Stoke 1 - 0 Birmingham
1980/1981		
DIV 1	Sa 28Mar 1981	Stoke 0 - 0 Birmingham
DIV 1	Sa 25Oct 1980	Birmingham 1 - 1 Stoke
1976/1977		
DIV 1	Sa 16Apr 1977	Birmingham 2 - 0 Stoke
DIV 1	Sa 20Nov 1976	Stoke 1 - 0 Birmingham
1975/1976		
DIV 1	Mo 19Apr 1976	Stoke 1 - 0 Birmingham
DIV 1	Sa 27Dec 1975	Birmingham 1 - 1 Stoke
1974/1975		
DIV 1	Sa 11Jan 1975	Stoke 0 - 0 Birmingham
DIV 1	Sa 07Dec 1974	Birmingham 0 - 3 Stoke
1973/1974		
DIV 1	Sa 13Apr 1974	Birmingham 0 - 0 Stoke
DIV 1	Sa 17Nov 1973	Stoke 5 - 2 Birmingham
1972/1973		
DIV 1	Sa 21Apr 1973	Birmingham 3 - 1 Stoke
DIV 1	Sa 18Nov 1972	Stoke 1 - 2 Birmingham
1971/1972		
FA CUP	Sa 05Aug 1972	Birmingham 0 - 0 Stoke
1964/1965		
DIV 1	We 17Mar 1965	Stoke 2 - 1 Birmingham
DIV 1	Sa 29Aug 1964	Birmingham 1 - 2 Stoke
1963/1964		
DIV 1	Sa 11Apr 1964	Birmingham 0 - 1 Stoke
DIV 1	Sa 30Nov 1963	Stoke 4 - 1 Birmingham
1954/1955		
DIV 2	Sa 18Dec 1954	Birmingham 2 - 0 Stoke
DIV 2	Sa 21Aug 1954	Stoke 2 - 1 Birmingham
1953/1954		
DIV 2	Sa 23Jan 1954	Birmingham 1 - 0 Stoke
DIV 2	Sa 12Sep 1953	Stoke 3 - 2 Birmingham
1949/1950		
DIV 1	Sa 24Dec 1949	Birmingham 1 - 0 Stoke
DIV 1	Sa 27Aug 1949	Stoke 3 - 1 Birmingham
1948/1949		
DIV 1	Sa 19Feb 1949	Stoke 2 - 1 Birmingham
DIV 1	Sa 25Sep 1948	Birmingham 2 - 1 Stoke
1938/1939		
DIV 1	Sa 14Jan 1939	Stoke 6 - 3 Birmingham
DIV 1	Sa 10Sep 1938	Birmingham 1 - 2 Stoke
1937/1938		
DIV 1	Sa 01Jan 1938	Birmingham 1 - 1 Stoke
DIV 1	Sa 28Aug 1937	Stoke 2 - 2 Birmingham
1936/1937		
FA CUP	Sa 16Jan 1937	Stoke 4 - 1 Birmingham
DIV 1	Sa 09Jan 1937	Stoke 2 - 0 Birmingham
DIV 1	Sa 12Sep 1936	Birmingham 2 - 4 Stoke
1935/1936		
DIV 1	Mo 03Feb 1936	Stoke 3 - 1 Birmingham
DIV 1	Sa 21Sep 1935	Birmingham 0 - 5 Stoke
1934/1935		
DIV 1	Sa 05Jan 1935	Birmingham 0 - 0 Stoke
DIV 1	Sa 01Sep 1934	Stoke 2 - 0 Birmingham
1933/1934		
DIV 1	Sa 10Mar 1934	Birmingham 0 - 1 Stoke
DIV 1	Sa 28Oct 1933	Stoke 1 - 1 Birmingham
1922/1923		
DIV 1	Mo 02Apr 1923	Stoke 0 - 0 Birmingham
DIV 1	We 13Sep 1922	Birmingham 2 - 0 Stoke
1920/1921		
DIV 2	Sa 27Nov 1920	Birmingham 3 - 0 Stoke
DIV 2	Sa 20Nov 1920	Stoke 1 - 2 Birmingham
1919/1920		
DIV 2	Sa 13Dec 1919	Birmingham 2 - 1 Stoke
DIV 2	Sa 06Dec 1919	Stoke 0 - 1 Birmingham
1906/1907		
DIV 1	Sa 09Mar 1907	Stoke 3 - 0 Birmingham
DIV 1	Sa 03Nov 1906	Birmingham 2 - 1 Stoke
1905/1906		
DIV 1	Sa 17Feb 1906	Stoke 2 - 2 Birmingham
FA CUP	Sa 03Feb 1906	Stoke 0 - 1 Birmingham
DIV 1	Sa 14Oct 1905	Birmingham 2 - 0 Stoke
1904/1905		
DIV 1	Sa 29Apr 1905	Stoke 1 - 0 Birmingham
DIV 1	Sa 22Apr 1905	Birmingham 0 - 1 Stoke
1903/1904		
DIV 1	Sa 02Apr 1904	Stoke 1 - 0 Birmingham
DIV 1	Sa 05Dec 1903	Birmingham 1 - 0 Stoke

1901/1902
DIV 1 Sa 15Mar 1902 Stoke 1 - 0 Birmingham
DIV 1 Mo 17Feb 1902 Birmingham 1 - 1 Stoke
1900/1901
FA CUP We 13Feb 1901 Birmingham 2 - 1 Stoke
FA CUP Sa 09Feb 1901 Stoke 1 - 1 Birmingham
1898/1899
FA CUP We 15Feb 1899 Birmingham 1 - 2 Stoke
FA CUP Sa 11Feb 1899 Stoke 2 - 2 Birmingham
1895/1896
DIV 1 Sa 19Oct 1895 Stoke 6 - 1 Birmingham
DIV 1 Sa 14Sep 1895 Birmingham 1 - 2 Stoke
1894/1895
DIV 1 Sa 17Nov 1894 Birmingham 4 - 2 Stoke
DIV 1 Sa 27Oct 1894 Stoke 2 - 2 Birmingham

BIRMINGHAM VS. WALSALL

	BLUES WINS	DRAWS	WALSALL WINS
League	16	2	4
FA Cup	2	1	1
Total	18	3	5

2001/2002
FL DIV 1 Sa 22Dec 2001 Birmingham 1 - 0 Walsall
FL DIV 1 Sa 25Aug 2001 Walsall 1 - 2 Birmingham
1999/2000
FL DIV 1 Mo 24Apr 2000 Birmingham 2 - 0 Walsall
FL DIV 1 Fr 08Oct 1999 Walsall 1 - 0 Birmingham
1989/1990
DIV 3 Sa 10Mar 1990 Walsall 0 - 1 Birmingham
DIV 3 Tu 26Sep 1989 Birmingham 2 - 0 Walsall
1988/1989
DIV 2 Sa 18Mar 1989 Birmingham 1 - 0 Walsall
DIV 2 Tu 20Sep 1988 Walsall 5 - 0 Birmingham
1986/1987
FA CUP Sa 31Jan 1987 Walsall 1 - 0 Birmingham
1982/1983
FA CUP Sa 01Jan 1983 Birmingham 1 - 0 Walsall
FA CUP Sa 01Jan 1983 Walsall 0 - 0 Birmingham
1974/1975
FA CUP We 01Jan 1975 Birmingham 2 - 1 Walsall
1900/1901
DIV 2 Mo 08Apr 1901 Birmingham 2 - 1 Walsall
DIV 2 Sa 29Sep 1900 Walsall 2 - 2 Birmingham
1899/1900
DIV 2 Sa 30Dec 1899 Walsall 1 - 0 Birmingham
DIV 2 Sa 02Sep 1899 Birmingham 3 - 2 Walsall
1898/1899
DIV 2 Sa 22Apr 1899 Walsall 2 - 0 Birmingham
DIV 2 Sa 24Dec 1898 Birmingham 2 - 1 Walsall
1897/1898
DIV 2 Sa 18Dec 1897 Walsall 1 - 2 Birmingham
DIV 2 Sa 04Dec 1897 Birmingham 6 - 0 Walsall
1896/1897
DIV 2 Fr 25Dec 1896 Birmingham 3 - 3 Walsall
DIV 2 Sa 24Oct 1896 Walsall 1 - 6 Birmingham
1893/1894
DIV 2 Sa 16Sep 1893 Birmingham 4 - 0 Walsall
DIV 2 Sa 02Sep 1893 Walsall 1 - 3 Birmingham
1892/1893
DIV 2 Sa 17Dec 1892 Birmingham 12 - 0 Walsall
DIV 2 Sa 10Sep 1892 Walsall 1 - 3 Birmingham

BIRMINGHAM VS. WBA

	BLUES WINS	DRAWS	WBA WINS
League	34	33	49
League Cup	0	1	1
FA Cup	1	1	6
Total	35	35	56

2010/2011
FAPL Sa 05Mar 2011 Birmingham 1 - 3 West Brom
FAPL Sa 18Sep 2010 West Brom 3 - 1 Birmingham
2006/2007
CHAMP. Su 18Mar 2007 West Brom 1 - 1 Birmingham
CHAMP. Sa 28Oct 2006 Birmingham 2 - 0 West Brom
2005/2006
FAPL Sa 11Mar 2006 Birmingham 1 - 1 West Brom
FAPL Sa 27Aug 2005 West Brom 2 - 3 Birmingham
2004/2005
FAPL Su 06Mar 2005 West Brom 2 - 0 Birmingham
FAPL Sa 18Dec 2004 Birmingham 4 - 0 West Brom
2002/2003
FAPL Sa 22Mar 2003 Birmingham 1 - 0 West Brom
FAPL Sa 19Oct 2002 West Brom 1 - 1 Birmingham
2001/2002
FL DIV 1 Tu 29Jan 2002 West Brom 1 - 0 Birmingham
FL DIV 1 We 07Nov 2001 Birmingham 0 - 1 West Brom
2000/2001
FL DIV 1 Sa 17Feb 2001 Birmingham 2 - 1 West Brom
FL DIV 1 Su 17Sep 2000 West Brom 1 - 1 Birmingham
1999/2000
FL DIV 1 Sa 04Mar 2000 West Brom 0 - 3 Birmingham
FL DIV 1 Sa 11Sep 1999 Birmingham 1 - 1 West Brom
1998/1999
FL DIV 1 Sa 13Mar 1999 Birmingham 4 - 0 West Brom
FL DIV 1 Sa 07Nov 1998 West Brom 1 - 3 Birmingham
1997/1998
FL DIV 1 Sa 28Mar 1998 Birmingham 1 - 0 West Brom
FL DIV 1 Su 23Nov 1997 West Brom 1 - 0 Birmingham

1996/1997
FL DIV 1 Su 16Mar 1997 West Brom 2 - 0 Birmingham
FL DIV 1 Tu 04Feb 1997 Birmingham 2 - 3 West Brom
1995/1996
FL DIV 1 We 20Mar 1996 Birmingham 1 - 1 West Brom
FL DIV 1 Su 17Sep 1995 West Brom 1 - 0 Birmingham
1993/1994
FL DIV 1 We 27Apr 1994 West Brom 2 - 4 Birmingham
FL DIV 1 Tu 28Dec 1993 Birmingham 2 - 0 West Brom
1991/1992
DIV 3 Sa 08Feb 1992 Birmingham 0 - 3 West Brom
DIV 3 Sa 26Oct 1991 West Brom 0 - 1 Birmingham
1988/1989
DIV 2 Sa 25Feb 1989 West Brom 0 - 0 Birmingham
DIV 2 Sa 15Oct 1988 Birmingham 1 - 4 West Brom
1987/1988
DIV 2 Tu 08Mar 1988 Birmingham 0 - 1 West Brom
DIV 2 We 30Sep 1987 West Brom 3 - 1 Birmingham
1986/1987
DIV 2 Su 12Apr 1987 Birmingham 0 - 1 West Brom
DIV 2 Sa 01Nov 1986 West Brom 3 - 2 Birmingham
1985/1986
DIV 1 Sa 08Feb 1986 Birmingham 0 - 1 West Brom
DIV 1 Sa 19Oct 1985 West Brom 2 - 1 Birmingham
1984/1985
LC We 07Nov 1984 West Brom 3 - 1 Birmingham
LC Tu 30Oct 1984 Birmingham 0 - 0 West Brom
1983/1984
DIV 1 Tu 28Feb 1984 Birmingham 2 - 1 West Brom
DIV 1 Sa 29Oct 1983 West Brom 1 - 2 Birmingham
1982/1983
DIV 1 Sa 19Mar 1983 West Brom 2 - 0 Birmingham
DIV 1 Sa 06Nov 1982 Birmingham 2 - 1 West Brom
1981/1982
DIV 1 Sa 20Mar 1982 West Brom 1 - 1 Birmingham
DIV 1 Sa 31Oct 1981 Birmingham 3 - 3 West Brom
1980/1981
DIV 1 Sa 28Feb 1981 West Brom 2 - 2 Birmingham
DIV 1 Sa 20Sep 1980 Birmingham 1 - 1 West Brom
1978/1979
DIV 1 Tu 24Apr 1979 Birmingham 1 - 1 West Brom
DIV 1 Sa 04Nov 1978 West Brom 1 - 0 Birmingham
1977/1978
DIV 1 Tu 28Feb 1978 Birmingham 1 - 2 West Brom
DIV 1 Sa 24Sep 1977 West Brom 3 - 1 Birmingham
1976/1977
DIV 1 Mo 28Feb 1977 West Brom 2 - 1 Birmingham
DIV 1 Sa 11Sep 1976 Birmingham 0 - 1 West Brom
1972/1973
DIV 1 Sa 28Apr 1973 Birmingham 3 - 2 West Brom
DIV 1 We 30Aug 1972 West Brom 2 - 2 Birmingham
1967/1968
FA CUP Sa 27Apr 1968 West Brom 2 - 0 Birmingham
1964/1965
DIV 1 We 16Sep 1964 West Brom 0 - 2 Birmingham
DIV 1 We 09Sep 1964 Birmingham 1 - 1 West Brom
1963/1964
DIV 1 We 18Sep 1963 West Brom 3 - 1 Birmingham
DIV 1 We 11Sep 1963 Birmingham 0 - 1 West Brom
1962/1963
DIV 1 We 19Sep 1962 Birmingham 0 - 0 West Brom
DIV 1 We 12Sep 1962 West Brom 1 - 0 Birmingham
1961/1962
DIV 1 We 20Sep 1961 Birmingham 1 - 2 West Brom
DIV 1 We 06Sep 1961 West Brom 0 - 0 Birmingham
1960/1961
DIV 1 We 31Aug 1960 Birmingham 3 - 1 West Brom
DIV 1 We 24Aug 1960 West Brom 1 - 2 Birmingham
1959/1960
DIV 1 Tu 19Apr 1960 West Brom 1 - 1 Birmingham
DIV 1 Mo 18Apr 1960 Birmingham 1 - 7 West Brom
1958/1959
DIV 1 We 03Sep 1958 Birmingham 0 - 6 West Brom
DIV 1 We 27Aug 1958 West Brom 2 - 2 Birmingham
1957/1958
DIV 1 Th 26Dec 1957 Birmingham 3 - 5 West Brom
DIV 1 Tu 01Oct 1957 West Brom 0 - 0 Birmingham
1956/1957
DIV 1 Tu 23Apr 1957 Birmingham 2 - 0 West Brom
DIV 1 Mo 22Apr 1957 West Brom 0 - 0 Birmingham
1955/1956
DIV 1 Tu 03Apr 1956 West Brom 0 - 2 Birmingham
DIV 1 Mo 02Apr 1956 Birmingham 2 - 0 West Brom
FA CUP Sa 18Feb 1956 West Brom 0 - 1 Birmingham
1949/1950
DIV 1 We 31Aug 1949 West Brom 3 - 0 Birmingham
DIV 1 We 24Aug 1949 Birmingham 2 - 0 West Brom
1947/1948
DIV 2 Tu 30Mar 1948 West Brom 1 - 1 Birmingham
DIV 2 Mo 29Mar 1948 Birmingham 4 - 0 West Brom
1946/1947
DIV 2 We 25Sep 1946 Birmingham 1 - 0 West Brom
DIV 2 We 18Sep 1946 West Brom 3 - 0 Birmingham
1937/1938
DIV 1 Mo 18Apr 1938 West Brom 4 - 3 Birmingham
DIV 1 Fr 15Apr 1938 Birmingham 2 - 1 West Brom
1936/1937
DIV 1 We 09Sep 1936 Birmingham 1 - 1 West Brom
DIV 1 We 02Sep 1936 West Brom 3 - 2 Birmingham

1935/1936

DIV 1 Sa 02May 1936 Birmingham 1 - 3 West Brom
DIV 1 We 18Sep 1935 West Brom 0 - 0 Birmingham

1934/1935

DIV 1 Mo 03Sep 1934 Birmingham 1 - 2 West Brom
DIV 1 We 29Aug 1934 West Brom 1 - 2 Birmingham

1933/1934

DIV 1 Sa 24Feb 1934 West Brom 1 - 2 Birmingham
DIV 1 Sa 14Oct 1933 Birmingham 0 - 1 West Brom

1932/1933

DIV 1 We 26Apr 1933 Birmingham 1 - 1 West Brom
DIV 1 Sa 15Oct 1932 West Brom 1 - 0 Birmingham

1931/1932

DIV 1 Sa 26Dec 1931 Birmingham 1 - 0 West Brom
DIV 1 Fr 25Dec 1931 West Brom 0 - 1 Birmingham

1930/1931

FA CUP Sa 25Apr 1931 West Brom 2 - 1 Birmingham

1926/1927

DIV 1 Sa 05Feb 1927 Birmingham 1 - 0 West Brom
DIV 1 Sa 18Sep 1926 West Brom 1 - 2 Birmingham

1925/1926

DIV 1 Sa 06Feb 1926 West Brom 5 - 1 Birmingham
DIV 1 Sa 26Sep 1925 Birmingham 3 - 0 West Brom

1924/1925

DIV 1 Mo 16Mar 1925 Birmingham 0 - 0 West Brom
DIV 1 Sa 18Oct 1924 West Brom 1 - 1 Birmingham

1923/1924

DIV 1 Sa 22Dec 1923 Birmingham 0 - 0 West Brom
DIV 1 Sa 15Dec 1923 West Brom 0 - 0 Birmingham

1922/1923

DIV 1 Sa 27Jan 1923 West Brom 1 - 0 Birmingham
DIV 1 Sa 20Jan 1923 Birmingham 0 - 2 West Brom

1921/1922

DIV 1 Tu 27Dec 1921 Birmingham 0 - 2 West Brom
DIV 1 Mo 26Dec 1921 West Brom 1 - 0 Birmingham

1910/1911

DIV 2 Mo 17Apr 1911 West Brom 1 - 0 Birmingham
DIV 2 Tu 27Dec 1910 Birmingham 1 - 1 West Brom

1909/1910

DIV 2 Sa 01Jan 1910 Birmingham 0 - 1 West Brom
DIV 2 Mo 27Dec 1909 West Brom 3 - 1 Birmingham

1908/1909

DIV 2 Mo 28Dec 1908 Birmingham 0 - 0 West Brom
DIV 2 Sa 26Dec 1908 West Brom 1 - 1 Birmingham

1907/1908

FA CUP We 15Jan 1908 Birmingham 1 - 2 West Brom
FA CUP Sa 11Jan 1908 West Brom 1 - 1 Birmingham

1903/1904

DIV 1 Sa 12Mar 1904 West Brom 0 - 1 Birmingham
DIV 1 Sa 14Nov 1903 Birmingham 0 - 1 West Brom

1895/1896

DIV 1 Mo 06Apr 1896 West Brom 0 - 0 Birmingham
DIV 1 Sa 21Dec 1895 Birmingham 2 - 2 West Brom

1894/1895

DIV 1 Sa 23Feb 1895 Birmingham 1 - 2 West Brom
FA CUP Sa 02Feb 1895 Birmingham 1 - 2 West Brom
DIV 1 Sa 10Nov 1894 West Brom 4 - 1 Birmingham

1888/1889

FA CUP Sa 02Feb 1889 Birmingham 2 - 3 West Brom

1885/1886

FA CUP Sa 06Mar 1886 West Brom 4 - 0 Birmingham

BIRMINGHAM V WOLVES

	BLUES WINS	DRAWS	WOLVES WINS
League	36	28	56
FA Cup	1	1	3
League Cup	1	0	2
Total	38	29	61

2010/2011

FAPL Su 01May 2011 Birmingham 1 - 1 Wolves
FAPL Su 12Dec 2010 Wolves 1 - 0 Birmingham

2009/2010

FAPL Su 07Feb 2010 Birmingham 2 - 1 Wolves
FAPL Su 29Nov 2009 Wolves 0 - 1 Birmingham

2008/2009

CHAMP Mo 06Apr 2009 Birmingham 2 - 0 Wolves
FA CUP Tu 13Jan 2009 Birmingham 0 - 2 Wolves
CHAMP Sa 29Nov 2008 Wolves 1 - 1 Birmingham

2006/2007

CHAMP Su 22Apr 2007 Wolves 2 - 3 Birmingham
CHAMP Sa 18Nov 2006 Birmingham 1 - 1 Wolves

2003/2004

FAPL Su 25Apr 2004 Birmingham 2 - 2 Wolves
FAPL Sa 08Nov 2003 Wolves 1 - 1 Birmingham

2001/2002

FL DIV 1 Sa 09Mar 2002 Birmingham 2 - 2 Wolves
FL DIV 1 Su 16Dec 2001 Wolves 2 - 1 Birmingham

2000/2001

FL DIV 1 Su 01Apr 2001 Birmingham 0 - 1 Wolves
FL DIV 1 Su 17Dec 2000 Wolves 0 - 1 Birmingham

1999/2000

FL DIV 1 Sa 01Apr 2000 Birmingham 1 - 0 Wolves
FL DIV 1 Fr 17Dec 1999 Wolves 2 - 1 Birmingham

1998/1999

FL DIV 1 Sa 17Apr 1999 Birmingham 0 - 1 Wolves
FL DIV 1 Su 22Nov 1998 Wolves 3 - 1 Birmingham

1997/1998

FL DIV 1 Sa 28Feb 1998 Wolves 1 - 3 Birmingham
FL DIV 1 Su 12Oct 1997 Birmingham 1 - 0 Wolves

1996/1997
FL DIV 1 Tu 04Mar 1997 Birmingham 1 - 2 Wolves
FL DIV 1 Su 17Nov 1996 Wolves 1 - 2 Birmingham
1995/1996
FL DIV 1 Sa 23Mar 1996 Wolves 3 - 2 Birmingham
FL DIV 1 Tu 05Mar 1996 Birmingham 2 - 0 Wolves
FA CUP We 17Jan 1996 Wolves 2 - 1 Birmingham
FA CUP Sa 06Jan 1996 Birmingham 1 - 1 Wolves
1993/1994
FL DIV 1 Tu 22Feb 1994 Wolves 3 - 0 Birmingham
FL DIV 1 Su 22Aug 1993 Birmingham 2 - 2 Wolves
1992/1993
FL DIV 1 Su 17Jan 1993 Wolves 2 - 1 Birmingham
FL DIV 1 Su 27Sep 1992 Birmingham 0 - 4 Wolves
1988/1989
LC Tu 06Sep 1988 Birmingham 1 - 0 Wolves
LC Tu 30Aug 1988 Wolves 3 - 2 Birmingham
1984/1985
DIV 2 Sa 30Mar 1985 Birmingham 1 - 0 Wolves
DIV 2 Sa 22Sep 1984 Wolves 0 - 2 Birmingham
1983/1984
DIV 1 Sa 11Feb 1984 Birmingham 0 - 0 Wolves
DIV 1 Sa 10Sep 1983 Wolves 1 - 1 Birmingham
1981/1982
DIV 1 Sa 17Apr 1982 Wolves 1 - 1 Birmingham
DIV 1 Sa 21Nov 1981 Birmingham 0 - 3 Wolves
1980/1981
DIV 1 Tu 17Mar 1981 Birmingham 1 - 0 Wolves
DIV 1 Sa 04Oct 1980 Wolves 1 - 0 Birmingham
1978/1979
DIV 1 Sa 14Apr 1979 Birmingham 1 - 1 Wolves
DIV 1 Tu 26Dec 1978 Wolves 2 - 1 Birmingham
1977/1978
DIV 1 Sa 01Apr 1978 Wolves 0 - 1 Birmingham
DIV 1 Sa 05Nov 1977 Birmingham 2 - 1 Wolves
1975/1976
DIV 1 Sa 10Jan 1976 Birmingham 0 - 1 Wolves
LC Th 01Jan 1976 Birmingham 0 - 2 Wolves
DIV 1 Sa 13Sep 1975 Wolves 2 - 0 Birmingham
1974/1975
DIV 1 Sa 01Mar 1975 Wolves 0 - 1 Birmingham
DIV 1 Sa 31Aug 1974 Birmingham 1 - 1 Wolves
1973/1974
DIV 1 Sa 16Feb 1974 Wolves 1 - 0 Birmingham
DIV 1 Sa 13Oct 1973 Birmingham 2 - 1 Wolves
1972/1973
DIV 1 Tu 27Feb 1973 Birmingham 0 - 1 Wolves
DIV 1 Sa 02Sep 1972 Wolves 3 - 2 Birmingham
1966/1967
DIV 2 Sa 17Dec 1966 Birmingham 3 - 2 Wolves
DIV 2 Sa 20Aug 1966 Wolves 1 - 2 Birmingham
1965/1966
DIV 2 Tu 12Apr 1966 Wolves 2 - 0 Birmingham
DIV 2 Mo 11Apr 1966 Birmingham 2 - 2 Wolves
1964/1965
DIV 1 Sa 13Mar 1965 Birmingham 0 - 1 Wolves
DIV 1 We 30Sep 1964 Wolves 0 - 2 Birmingham
1963/1964
DIV 1 Sa 07Mar 1964 Wolves 5 - 1 Birmingham
DIV 1 Sa 26Oct 1963 Birmingham 2 - 2 Wolves
1962/1963
DIV 1 Sa 09Mar 1963 Birmingham 3 - 4 Wolves
DIV 1 We 24Oct 1962 Wolves 0 - 2 Birmingham
1961/1962
DIV 1 Sa 24Feb 1962 Wolves 2 - 1 Birmingham
DIV 1 Sa 07Oct 1961 Birmingham 3 - 6 Wolves
1960/1961
DIV 1 Sa 18Mar 1961 Wolves 5 - 1 Birmingham
DIV 1 Sa 29Oct 1960 Birmingham 1 - 2 Wolves
1959/1960
DIV 1 Sa 19Dec 1959 Wolves 2 - 0 Birmingham
DIV 1 Sa 22Aug 1959 Birmingham 0 - 1 Wolves
1958/1959
DIV 1 Sa 14Mar 1959 Birmingham 0 - 3 Wolves
DIV 1 Sa 25Oct 1958 Wolves 3 - 1 Birmingham
1957/1958
DIV 1 Sa 22Feb 1958 Wolves 5 - 1 Birmingham
DIV 1 Sa 12Oct 1957 Birmingham 1 - 5 Wolves
1956/1957
DIV 1 Sa 09Feb 1957 Birmingham 2 - 2 Wolves
DIV 1 Sa 29Sep 1956 Wolves 3 - 0 Birmingham
1955/1956
DIV 1 Sa 10Mar 1956 Birmingham 0 - 0 Wolves
DIV 1 Sa 29Oct 1955 Wolves 1 - 0 Birmingham
1953/1954
FA CUP Sa 09Jan 1954 Wolves 1 - 2 Birmingham
1949/1950
DIV 1 Sa 06May 1950 Wolves 6 - 1 Birmingham
DIV 1 We 14Sep 1949 Birmingham 1 - 1 Wolves
1948/1949
DIV 1 Sa 18Dec 1948 Birmingham 0 - 1 Wolves
DIV 1 Sa 21Aug 1948 Wolves 2 - 2 Birmingham
1938/1939
DIV 1 Sa 11Mar 1939 Birmingham 3 - 2 Wolves
DIV 1 Sa 05Nov 1938 Wolves 2 - 1 Birmingham
1937/1938
DIV 1 Sa 02Apr 1938 Wolves 3 - 2 Birmingham
DIV 1 Sa 20Nov 1937 Birmingham 2 - 0 Wolves
1936/1937
DIV 1 Sa 24Apr 1937 Birmingham 1 - 0 Wolves

DIV 1 Sa 19Dec 1936 Wolves 2 - 1 Birmingham
1935/1936
DIV 1 Sa 28Dec 1935 Birmingham 0 - 0 Wolves
DIV 1 Sa 31Aug 1935 Wolves 3 - 1 Birmingham
1934/1935
DIV 1 Sa 09Mar 1935 Birmingham 1 - 1 Wolves
DIV 1 Sa 27Oct 1934 Wolves 3 - 1 Birmingham
1933/1934
DIV 1 Sa 03Mar 1934 Wolves 2 - 0 Birmingham
DIV 1 Sa 21Oct 1933 Birmingham 0 - 0 Wolves
1932/1933
DIV 1 Sa 08Apr 1933 Wolves 1 - 0 Birmingham
DIV 1 Sa 26Nov 1932 Birmingham 0 - 0 Wolves
1920/1921
DIV 2 Sa 13Nov 1920 Birmingham 4 - 1 Wolves
DIV 2 Sa 06Nov 1920 Wolves 0 - 3 Birmingham
1919/1920
DIV 2 Sa 15Nov 1919 Wolves 0 - 2 Birmingham
DIV 2 Sa 08Nov 1919 Birmingham 2 - 0 Wolves
1914/1915
DIV 2 Mo 19Apr 1915 Wolves 0 - 0 Birmingham
DIV 2 Sa 26Sep 1914 Birmingham 1 - 2 Wolves
1913/1914
DIV 2 Sa 24Jan 1914 Birmingham 4 - 1 Wolves
DIV 2 Sa 27Sep 1913 Wolves 1 - 0 Birmingham
1912/1913
DIV 2 Sa 04Jan 1913 Wolves 2 - 2 Birmingham
DIV 2 Sa 14Sep 1912 Birmingham 0 - 0 Wolves
1911/1912
DIV 2 Sa 10Feb 1912 Birmingham 3 - 1 Wolves
DIV 2 Sa 07Oct 1911 Wolves 1 - 0 Birmingham
1910/1911
DIV 2 Sa 11Mar 1911 Wolves 3 - 1 Birmingham
DIV 2 Sa 05Nov 1910 Birmingham 1 - 3 Wolves
1909/1910
DIV 2 Sa 19Feb 1910 Birmingham 1 - 0 Wolves
DIV 2 Sa 09Oct 1909 Wolves 4 - 2 Birmingham
1908/1909
DIV 2 Sa 13Feb 1909 Wolves 2 - 0 Birmingham
DIV 2 Sa 10Oct 1908 Birmingham 1 - 1 Wolves
1905/1906
DIV 1 Sa 24Mar 1906 Birmingham 3 - 3 Wolves
DIV 1 Sa 18Nov 1905 Wolves 0 - 0 Birmingham
1904/1905
DIV 1 Sa 11Feb 1905 Birmingham 4 - 1 Wolves
DIV 1 Sa 15Oct 1904 Wolves 0 - 1 Birmingham
1903/1904
DIV 1 Sa 19Mar 1904 Birmingham 3 - 0 Wolves
DIV 1 Sa 21Nov 1903 Wolves 1 - 0 Birmingham
1901/1902
DIV 1 Sa 18Jan 1902 Wolves 2 - 1 Birmingham
DIV 1 Sa 21Sep 1901 Birmingham 1 - 2 Wolves
1895/1896
DIV 1 Sa 25Jan 1896 Wolves 7 - 2 Birmingham
DIV 1 Sa 18Jan 1896 Birmingham 3 - 2 Wolves
1894/1895
DIV 1 Sa 06Oct 1894 Birmingham 4 - 3 Wolves
DIV 1 Sa 15Sep 1894 Wolves 2 - 1 Birmingham
1889/1890
FA CUP Sa 01Feb 1890 Wolves 2 - 1 Birmingham

COVENTRY V LEICESTER

	COVENTRY WINS	DRAWS	LEICESTER WINS
League	23	23	35
FA Cup	2	1	0
League Cup	0	0	1
Total	25	24	36

2011/2012
CHAMP Sa 06Aug 2011 Coventry 0 - 1 Leicester
2010/2011
CHAMP Sa 26Feb 2011 Leicester 1 - 1 Coventry
CHAMP Sa 11Sep 2010 Coventry 1 - 1 Leicester
2009/2010
CHAMP Su 21Mar 2010 Leicester 2 - 2 Coventry
CHAMP Sa 03Oct 2009 Coventry 1 - 1 Leicester
2007/2008
CHAMP Sa 23Feb 2008 Coventry 2 - 0 Leicester
CHAMP Sa 12Jan 2008 Leicester 2 - 0 Coventry
2006/2007
CHAMP Sa 17Feb 2007 Leicester 3 - 0 Coventry
CHAMP Fr 18Aug 2006 Coventry 0 - 0 Leicester
2005/2006
CHAMP Mo 17Apr 2006 Coventry 1 - 1 Leicester
CHAMP Su 23Oct 2005 Leicester 2 - 1 Coventry
2004/2005
CHAMP Mo 08Nov 2004 Leicester 3 - 0 Coventry
CHAMP Sa 16Oct 2004 Coventry 1 - 1 Leicester
2002/2003
FL DIV 1 Sa 22Mar 2003 Coventry 1 - 2 Leicester
FL DIV 1 Tu 29Oct 2002 Leicester 2 - 1 Coventry
2000/2001
FAPL Sa 07Apr 2001 Leicester 1 - 3 Coventry
FAPL Su 10Dec 2000 Coventry 1 - 0 Leicester
1999/2000
FAPL Sa 27Nov 1999 Coventry 0 - 1 Leicester
FAPL We 11Aug 1999 Leicester 1 - 0 Coventry
1998/1999
FAPL Sa 24Apr 1999 Leicester 1 - 0 Coventry
FA Cup Sa 23Jan 1999 Leicester 0 - 3 Coventry

FAPL Sa 28Nov 1998 Coventry 1 - 1 Leicester
1997/1998
FAPL Sa 04Apr 1998 Leicester 1 - 1 Coventry
FAPL Sa 29Nov 1997 Coventry 0 - 2 Leicester
1996/1997
FAPL Sa 08Mar 1997 Coventry 0 - 0 Leicester
FAPL Sa 21Dec 1996 Leicester 0 - 2 Coventry
1994/1995
FAPL Sa 25Feb 1995 Coventry 4 - 2 Leicester
FAPL Mo 03Oct 1994 Leicester 2 - 2 Coventry
1986/1987
DIV 1 Mo 04May 1987 Leicester 1 - 1 Coventry
DIV 1 Sa 06Dec 1986 Coventry 1 - 0 Leicester
1985/1986
DIV 1 Sa 08Mar 1986 Leicester 2 - 1 Coventry
DIV 1 Su 06Oct 1985 Coventry 3 - 0 Leicester
1984/1985
DIV 1 Su 23Dec 1984 Leicester 5 - 1 Coventry
DIV 1 Sa 01Sep 1984 Coventry 2 - 0 Leicester
1983/1984
DIV 1 Sa 21Jan 1984 Leicester 1 - 1 Coventry
DIV 1 Sa 17Sep 1983 Coventry 2 - 1 Leicester
1980/1981
DIV 1 Sa 14Mar 1981 Coventry 4 - 1 Leicester
DIV 1 Sa 11Oct 1980 Leicester 1 - 3 Coventry
1977/1978
DIV 1 Sa 11Mar 1978 Coventry 1 - 0 Leicester
DIV 1 Sa 15Oct 1977 Leicester 1 - 2 Coventry
1976/1977
DIV 1 Sa 12Mar 1977 Leicester 3 - 1 Coventry
DIV 1 Sa 02Oct 1976 Coventry 1 - 1 Leicester
1975/1976
DIV 1 Sa 03Apr 1976 Coventry 0 - 2 Leicester
DIV 1 Sa 27Sep 1975 Leicester 0 - 3 Coventry
1974/1975
DIV 1 Sa 15Mar 1975 Coventry 2 - 2 Leicester
DIV 1 Sa 28Sep 1974 Leicester 0 - 1 Coventry
1973/1974
DIV 1 Sa 22Dec 1973 Coventry 1 - 2 Leicester
DIV 1 Sa 29Sep 1973 Leicester 0 - 2 Coventry
1972/1973
DIV 1 Sa 06Jan 1973 Coventry 3 - 2 Leicester
DIV 1 Sa 26Aug 1972 Leicester 0 - 0 Coventry
1971/1972
DIV 1 Sa 22Apr 1972 Leicester 1 - 0 Coventry
DIV 1 Sa 04Dec 1971 Coventry 1 - 1 Leicester
1968/1969
DIV 1 Tu 01Apr 1969 Coventry 1 - 0 Leicester
DIV 1 Sa 28Sep 1968 Leicester 1 - 1 Coventry
1967/1968
DIV 1 Sa 27Apr 1968 Coventry 0 - 1 Leicester
DIV 1 Sa 02Dec 1967 Leicester 0 - 0 Coventry
1964/1965
LC Fr 01Jan 1965 Coventry 1 - 8 Leicester
1951/1952
DIV 2 Sa 08Mar 1952 Coventry 1 - 3 Leicester
FA Cup Mo 14Jan 1952 Coventry 4 - 1 Leicester
FA Cup Sa 12Jan 1952 Leicester 1 - 1 Coventry
DIV 2 Sa 20Oct 1951 Leicester 3 - 1 Coventry
1950/1951
DIV 2 Sa 03Feb 1951 Leicester 3 - 0 Coventry
DIV 2 Sa 23Sep 1950 Coventry 2 - 1 Leicester
1949/1950
DIV 2 Tu 27Dec 1949 Coventry 1 - 2 Leicester
DIV 2 Mo 26Dec 1949 Leicester 1 - 0 Coventry
1948/1949
DIV 2 Sa 01Jan 1949 Leicester 3 - 1 Coventry
DIV 2 Sa 28Aug 1948 Coventry 1 - 2 Leicester
1947/1948
DIV 2 Sa 17Jan 1948 Leicester 2 - 2 Coventry
DIV 2 Sa 06Sep 1947 Coventry 0 - 1 Leicester
1946/1947
DIV 2 Sa 10May 1947 Coventry 2 - 1 Leicester
DIV 2 Sa 19Oct 1946 Leicester 1 - 0 Coventry
1936/1937
DIV 2 Th 25Feb 1937 Coventry 0 - 2 Leicester
DIV 2 Sa 17Oct 1936 Leicester 1 - 0 Coventry
1924/1925
DIV 2 Sa 24Jan 1925 Leicester 5 - 1 Coventry
DIV 2 Sa 20Sep 1924 Coventry 4 - 2 Leicester
1923/1924
DIV 2 Sa 23Feb 1924 Leicester 2 - 0 Coventry
DIV 2 Sa 16Feb 1924 Coventry 2 - 4 Leicester
1922/1923
DIV 2 Sa 24Mar 1923 Coventry 1 - 1 Leicester
DIV 2 Sa 17Mar 1923 Leicester 2 - 1 Coventry
1921/1922
DIV 2 Sa 26Nov 1921 Leicester 1 - 1 Coventry
DIV 2 Sa 19Nov 1921 Coventry 0 - 0 Leicester
1920/1921
DIV 2 Tu 29Mar 1921 Coventry 1 - 0 Leicester
DIV 2 Mo 28Mar 1921 Leicester 0 - 1 Coventry
1919/1920
DIV 2 Sa 04Oct 1919 Coventry 1 - 2 Leicester
DIV 2 Sa 27Sep 1919 Leicester 1 - 0 Coventry

COVENTRY V DERBY

	COVENTRY WINS	DRAWS	DERBY WINS
League	24	18	29
FA Cup	2	1	1
League Cup	2	0	0
Total	28	19	30

2011/2012				
CHAMP	Sa 10Sep 2011	Coventry	2 - 0	Derby
2010/2011				
CHAMP	Sa 09Apr 2011	Derby	2 - 2	Coventry
CHAMP	Sa 21Aug 2010	Coventry	2 - 1	Derby
2009/2010				
CHAMP	Sa 03Apr 2010	Coventry	0 - 1	Derby
CHAMP	Fr 06Nov 2009	Derby	2 - 1	Coventry
2008/2009				
CHAMP	Sa 31Jan 2009	Derby	2 - 1	Coventry
CHAMP	Sa 25Oct 2008	Coventry	1 - 1	Derby
2006/2007				
CHAMP	Mo 09Apr 2007	Derby	1 - 1	Coventry
CHAMP	Sa 11Nov 2006	Coventry	1 - 2	Derby
2005/2006				
CHAMP	Sa 21Jan 2006	Coventry	6 - 1	Derby
CHAMP	We 14Sep 2005	Derby	1 - 1	Coventry
2004/2005				
CHAMP	Sa 30Apr 2005	Coventry	6 - 2	Derby
CHAMP	Sa 04Dec 2004	Derby	2 - 2	Coventry
2003/2004				
FL DIV 1	Sa 28Feb 2004	Coventry	2 - 0	Derby
FL DIV 1	Sa 25Oct 2003	Derby	1 - 3	Coventry
2002/2003				
FL DIV 1	Sa 19Apr 2003	Derby	1 - 0	Coventry
FL DIV 1	Sa 21Dec 2002	Coventry	3 - 0	Derby
2000/2001				
FAPL	Sa 31Mar 2001	Coventry	2 - 0	Derby
FAPL	Sa 16Dec 2000	Derby	1 - 0	Coventry
1999/2000				
FAPL	Sa 22Jan 2000	Derby	0 - 0	Coventry
FAPL	Sa 21Aug 1999	Coventry	2 - 0	Derby
1998/1999				
FAPL	Sa 08May 1999	Derby	0 - 0	Coventry
FAPL	Sa 19Dec 1998	Coventry	1 - 1	Derby
1997/1998				
FAPL	Sa 28Mar 1998	Coventry	1 - 0	Derby
FA CUP	Sa 24Jan 1998	Coventry	2 - 0	Derby
FAPL	Sa 22Nov 1997	Derby	3 - 1	Coventry
1996/1997				
FAPL	Sa 03May 1997	Coventry	1 - 2	Derby
FA CUP	We 26Feb 1997	Derby	3 - 2	Coventry
FAPL	Sa 30Nov 1996	Derby	2 - 1	Coventry
1990/1991				
DIV 1	Sa 13Apr 1991	Coventry	3 - 0	Derby
DIV 1	Tu 01Jan 1991	Derby	1 - 1	Coventry
1989/1990				
DIV 1	Sa 07Apr 1990	Coventry	1 - 0	Derby
DIV 1	Sa 30Dec 1989	Derby	4 - 1	Coventry
1988/1989				
DIV 1	Sa 01Apr 1989	Derby	1 - 0	Coventry
DIV 1	Sa 17Dec 1988	Coventry	0 - 2	Derby
1987/1988				
DIV 1	Sa 19Mar 1988	Coventry	0 - 3	Derby
DIV 1	Sa 31Oct 1987	Derby	2 - 0	Coventry
1979/1980				
DIV 1	Mo 07Apr 1980	Coventry	2 - 1	Derby
DIV 1	We 26Dec 1979	Derby	1 - 2	Coventry
1978/1979				
DIV 1	Tu 21Nov 1978	Coventry	4 - 2	Derby
DIV 1	Sa 02Sep 1978	Derby	0 - 2	Coventry
1977/1978				
DIV 1	Mo 02Jan 1978	Derby	4 - 2	Coventry
DIV 1	Sa 20Aug 1977	Coventry	3 - 1	Derby
1976/1977				
DIV 1	Mo 25Apr 1977	Coventry	2 - 0	Derby
DIV 1	We 09Mar 1977	Derby	1 - 1	Coventry
1975/1976				
DIV 1	Sa 31Jan 1976	Derby	2 - 0	Coventry
DIV 1	Tu 19Aug 1975	Coventry	1 - 1	Derby
1974/1975				
DIV 1	Tu 27Aug 1974	Coventry	1 - 1	Derby
DIV 1	We 21Aug 1974	Derby	1 - 1	Coventry
1973/1974				
DIV 1	Mo 15Apr 1974	Derby	1 - 0	Coventry
FA CUP	We 30Jan 1974	Derby	0 - 1	Coventry
FA CUP	Su 27Jan 1974	Coventry	0 - 0	Derby
DIV 1	Tu 18Sep 1973	Coventry	1 - 0	Derby
1972/1973				
DIV 1	Sa 14Apr 1973	Coventry	0 - 2	Derby
DIV 1	Sa 09Dec 1972	Derby	2 - 0	Coventry
1971/1972				
DIV 1	Sa 29Jan 1972	Derby	1 - 0	Coventry
DIV 1	Tu 24Aug 1971	Coventry	2 - 2	Derby
1970/1971				
DIV 1	Tu 27Apr 1971	Coventry	0 - 0	Derby
LC	Tu 27Oct 1970	Coventry	1 - 0	Derby
DIV 1	We 02Sep 1970	Derby	3 - 4	Coventry
1969/1970				
DIV 1	We 08Oct 1969	Derby	1 - 3	Coventry
DIV 1	Sa 16Aug 1969	Coventry	1 - 1	Derby
1966/1967				
DIV 2	Sa 01Apr 1967	Coventry	2 - 2	Derby
LC	Su 01Jan 1967	Coventry	2 - 1	Derby

DIV 2	Sa 05Nov 1966	Derby	1 - 2	Coventry

1965/1966

DIV 2	Tu 12Apr 1966	Coventry	3 - 2	Derby
DIV 2	Mo 11Apr 1966	Derby	1 - 0	Coventry

1964/1965

DIV 2	Tu 15Sep 1964	Coventry	0 - 2	Derby
DIV 2	We 09Sep 1964	Derby	2 - 1	Coventry

1924/1925

DIV 2	Sa 25Apr 1925	Coventry	0 - 0	Derby
DIV 2	Sa 20Dec 1924	Derby	5 - 1	Coventry

1923/1924

DIV 2	Tu 22Apr 1924	Coventry	0 - 1	Derby
DIV 2	Mo 21Apr 1924	Derby	1 - 0	Coventry

1922/1923

DIV 2	Sa 28Oct 1922	Derby	4 - 0	Coventry
DIV 2	Sa 21Oct 1922	Coventry	1 - 0	Derby

1921/1922

DIV 2	Th 17Nov 1921	Coventry	1 - 2	Derby
DIV 2	Sa 05Nov 1921	Derby	1 - 0	Coventry

COVENTRY V NOTTM FOREST

	COVENTRY WINS	DRAWS	NOTTM FOREST WINS
League	15	27	42
League Cup	2	1	2
FA Cup	1	0	0
Total	18	28	44

2010/2011

CHAMP	Tu 01Feb 2011	Coventry	1 - 2	Forest
CHAMP	Tu 09Nov 2010	Forest	2 - 1	Coventry

2009/2010

CHAMP	Tu 09Feb 2010	Coventry	1 - 0	Forest
CHAMP	Mo 28Dec 2009	Forest	2 - 0	Coventry

2008/2009

CHAMP	Sa 18Apr 2009	Forest	1 - 0	Coventry
CHAMP	Sa 06Dec 2008	Coventry	2 - 2	Forest

2004/2005

CHAMP	We 06Apr 2005	Coventry	2 - 0	Forest
CHAMP	Sa 28Aug 2004	Forest	1 - 4	Coventry

2003/2004

FL DIV 1	Sa 07Feb 2004	Forest	0 - 1	Coventry
FL DIV 1	We 27Aug 2003	Coventry	1 - 3	Forest

2002/2003

FL DIV 1	Sa 18Jan 2003	Forest	1 - 1	Coventry
FL DIV 1	Sa 31Aug 2002	Coventry	0 - 1	Forest

2001/2002

FL DIV 1	Sa 29Dec 2001	Forest	2 - 1	Coventry
FL DIV 1	Mo 27Aug 2001	Coventry	0 - 0	Forest

1998/1999

FAPL	Sa 09Jan 1999	Coventry	4 - 0	Forest
FAPL	Sa 22Aug 1998	Forest	1 - 0	Coventry

1996/1997

FAPL	We 29Jan 1997	Forest	0 - 1	Coventry
FAPL	Sa 17Aug 1996	Coventry	0 - 3	Forest

1995/1996

FAPL	We 17Apr 1996	Forest	0 - 0	Coventry
FAPL	Sa 09Sep 1995	Coventry	1 - 1	Forest

1994/1995

FAPL	Mo 17Apr 1995	Forest	2 - 0	Coventry
FAPL	Mo 26Dec 1994	Coventry	0 - 0	Forest

1992/1993

FAPL	Sa 09Jan 1993	Coventry	0 - 1	Forest
FAPL	Mo 21Sep 1992	Forest	1 - 1	Coventry

1991/1992

DIV 1	We 11Mar 1992	Coventry	0 - 2	Forest
DIV 1	Sa 16Nov 1991	Forest	1 - 0	Coventry

1990/1991

DIV 1	Sa 12Jan 1991	Forest	3 - 0	Coventry
LC	We 28Nov 1990	Coventry	5 - 4	Forest
DIV 1	Sa 01Sep 1990	Coventry	2 - 2	Forest

1989/1990

DIV 1	Sa 10Mar 1990	Forest	2 - 4	Coventry
LC	Su 25Feb 1990	Coventry	0 - 0	Forest
LC	Su 11Feb 1990	Forest	2 - 1	Coventry
DIV 1	Sa 14Oct 1989	Coventry	0 - 2	Forest

1988/1989

DIV 1	Mo 15May 1989	Coventry	2 - 2	Forest
DIV 1	Sa 19Nov 1988	Forest	0 - 0	Coventry
LC	We 02Nov 1988	Forest	3 - 2	Coventry

1987/1988

DIV 1	Mo 28Dec 1987	Forest	4 - 1	Coventry
DIV 1	Sa 19Sep 1987	Coventry	0 - 3	Forest

1986/1987

DIV 1	Sa 04Apr 1987	Forest	0 - 0	Coventry
DIV 1	Sa 08Nov 1986	Coventry	1 - 0	Forest

1985/1986

DIV 1	Sa 29Mar 1986	Coventry	0 - 0	Forest
DIV 1	We 01Jan 1986	Forest	5 - 2	Coventry

1984/1985

DIV 1	Sa 20Apr 1985	Forest	2 - 0	Coventry
DIV 1	Sa 17Nov 1984	Coventry	1 - 3	Forest

1983/1984

DIV 1	Tu 17Apr 1984	Coventry	2 - 1	Forest
DIV 1	We 28Dec 1983	Forest	3 - 0	Coventry

1982/1983

DIV 1	Tu 05Apr 1983	Coventry	1 - 2	Forest
DIV 1	Mo 27Dec 1982	Forest	4 - 2	Coventry

1981/1982

DIV 1	Tu 09Mar 1982	Coventry	0 - 1	Forest
DIV 1	Sa 17Oct 1981	Forest	2 - 1	Coventry

1980/1981

DIV 1	Sa 02May 1981	Forest	1 - 1	Coventry
DIV 1	Sa 29Nov 1980	Coventry	1 - 1	Forest

1979/1980

DIV 1	Sa 29Dec 1979	Coventry	0 - 3	Forest
DIV 1	Sa 25Aug 1979	Forest	4 - 1	Coventry

1978/1979

DIV 1	Sa 24Mar 1979	Forest	3 - 0	Coventry
DIV 1	Tu 22Aug 1978	Coventry	0 - 0	Forest

1977/1978

DIV 1	Sa 22Apr 1978	Coventry	0 - 0	Forest
DIV 1	Sa 10Dec 1977	Forest	2 - 1	Coventry

1976/1977

LC	Sa 01Jan 1977	Forest	0 - 3	Coventry

1971/1972

DIV 1	Sa 25Mar 1972	Forest	4 - 0	Coventry
DIV 1	Sa 11Sep 1971	Coventry	1 - 1	Forest

1970/1971

DIV 1	Sa 17Oct 1970	Coventry	2 - 0	Forest
DIV 1	Sa 15Aug 1970	Forest	2 - 0	Coventry

1969/1970

DIV 1	Tu 07Apr 1970	Forest	1 - 4	Coventry
DIV 1	Tu 16Sep 1969	Coventry	3 - 2	Forest

1968/1969

DIV 1	Sa 19Apr 1969	Coventry	1 - 1	Forest
DIV 1	Sa 14Sep 1968	Forest	0 - 0	Coventry

1967/1968

DIV 1	Tu 29Aug 1967	Coventry	1 - 3	Forest
DIV 1	Tu 22Aug 1967	Forest	3 - 3	Coventry

1951/1952

DIV 2	Sa 15Mar 1952	Forest	3 - 1	Coventry
DIV 2	Sa 27Oct 1951	Coventry	3 - 3	Forest

1948/1949

DIV 2	Sa 26Mar 1949	Forest	3 - 0	Coventry
DIV 2	Sa 30Oct 1948	Coventry	1 - 2	Forest

1947/1948

DIV 2	Sa 20Mar 1948	Coventry	1 - 1	Forest
DIV 2	Sa 01Nov 1947	Forest	4 - 0	Coventry

1946/1947

DIV 2	Sa 01Feb 1947	Coventry	1 - 1	Forest
DIV 2	Sa 28Sep 1946	Forest	1 - 0	Coventry

1938/1939

DIV 2	Sa 28Jan 1939	Coventry	5 - 1	Forest
DIV 2	Sa 24Sep 1938	Forest	3 - 0	Coventry

1937/1938

DIV 2	Sa 05Feb 1938	Forest	2 - 1	Coventry
DIV 2	Sa 25Sep 1937	Coventry	1 - 1	Forest

1936/1937

DIV 2	Sa 23Jan 1937	Coventry	2 - 2	Forest
DIV 2	Sa 19Sep 1936	Forest	1 - 1	Coventry

1921/1922

DIV 2	Sa 17Sep 1921	Forest	1 - 0	Coventry
DIV 2	Sa 10Sep 1921	Coventry	0 - 1	Forest

1920/1921

DIV 2	Sa 07May 1921	Forest	0 - 2	Coventry
DIV 2	Mo 02May 1921	Coventry	0 - 0	Forest

1919/1920

DIV 2	Sa 10Apr 1920	Coventry	4 - 2	Forest
DIV 2	Sa 03Apr 1920	Forest	2 - 1	Coventry

1909/1910

FA CUP	Sa 19Feb 1910	Coventry	3 - 1	Forest

COVENTRY V STOKE

	COVENTRY WINS	DRAWS	STOKE WINS
League	21	8	25
FA Cup	1	0	0
League Cup	1	0	0
Total	23	8	25

2007/2008

CHAMP	Sa 12Apr 2008	Coventry	1 - 2	Stoke
CHAMP	Sa 03Nov 2007	Stoke	1 - 3	Coventry

2006/2007

CHAMP	Sa 02Dec 2006	Coventry	0 - 0	Stoke
CHAMP	Mo 06Nov 2006	Stoke	1 - 0	Coventry

2005/2006

CHAMP	Sa 22Apr 2006	Stoke	0 - 1	Coventry
CHAMP	We 02Nov 2005	Coventry	1 - 2	Stoke

2004/2005

CHAMP	Sa 26Feb 2005	Coventry	0 - 0	Stoke
CHAMP	Sa 11Dec 2004	Stoke	1 - 0	Coventry

2003/2004

FL DIV 1	Sa 03Apr 2004	Stoke	1 - 0	Coventry
FL DIV 1	Sa 13Sep 2003	Coventry	4 - 2	Stoke

2002/2003

FL DIV 1	Mo 21Apr 2003	Coventry	0 - 1	Stoke
FL DIV 1	Sa 07Dec 2002	Stoke	1 - 2	Coventry

1986/1987

FA CUP	Sa 21Feb 1987	Stoke	0 - 1	Coventry

1984/1985

DIV 1	Fr 17May 1985	Stoke	0 - 1	Coventry
DIV 1	Tu 01Jan 1985	Coventry	4 - 0	Stoke

1983/1984

DIV 1	Sa 18Feb 1984	Coventry	2 - 3	Stoke
DIV 1	Sa 29Oct 1983	Stoke	1 - 3	Coventry

1982/1983

DIV 1	Sa 07May 1983	Stoke	0 - 3	Coventry
DIV 1	Sa 18Dec 1982	Coventry	2 - 0	Stoke

1981/1982

DIV 1 Tu 24Nov 1981 Coventry 3 - 0 Stoke

DIV 1 We 02Sep 1981 Stoke 4 - 0 Coventry

1980/1981

DIV 1 Sa 18Apr 1981 Coventry 2 - 2 Stoke

DIV 1 Sa 27Dec 1980 Stoke 2 - 2 Coventry

1979/1980

DIV 1 Sa 03Nov 1979 Coventry 1 - 3 Stoke

DIV 1 Sa 18Aug 1979 Stoke 3 - 2 Coventry

1976/1977

DIV 1 Sa 30Apr 1977 Coventry 5 - 2 Stoke

DIV 1 We 16Feb 1977 Stoke 2 - 0 Coventry

1975/1976

DIV 1 Sa 10Apr 1976 Stoke 0 - 1 Coventry

DIV 1 Sa 20Sep 1975 Coventry 0 - 3 Stoke

1974/1975

DIV 1 Th 26Dec 1974 Coventry 2 - 0 Stoke

DIV 1 Sa 14Sep 1974 Stoke 2 - 0 Coventry

1973/1974

DIV 1 Sa 09Mar 1974 Coventry 2 - 0 Stoke

ENGLISH LEAGUE CUP Tu 01Jan 1974 Coventry
2 - 1 Stoke

DIV 1 Sa 27Oct 1973 Stoke 3 - 0 Coventry

1972/1973

DIV 1 Mo 26Mar 1973 Stoke 2 - 1 Coventry

DIV 1 Sa 02Sep 1972 Coventry 2 - 1 Stoke

1971/1972

DIV 1 Sa 16Oct 1971 Stoke 1 - 0 Coventry

DIV 1 Sa 14Aug 1971 Coventry 1 - 1 Stoke

1970/1971

DIV 1 Sa 06Feb 1971 Stoke 2 - 1 Coventry

DIV 1 Sa 05Dec 1970 Coventry 1 - 0 Stoke

1969/1970

DIV 1 Sa 04Apr 1970 Coventry 0 - 3 Stoke

DIV 1 We 27Aug 1969 Stoke 2 - 0 Coventry

1968/1969

DIV 1 Tu 18Mar 1969 Coventry 1 - 1 Stoke

DIV 1 Sa 09Nov 1968 Stoke 0 - 3 Coventry

1967/1968

DIV 1 Tu 16Apr 1968 Stoke 3 - 3 Coventry

DIV 1 Mo 15Apr 1968 Coventry 2 - 0 Stoke

1924/1925

DIV 2 Sa 31Jan 1925 Coventry 3 - 1 Stoke

DIV 2 Sa 27Sep 1924 Stoke 4 - 1 Coventry

1923/1924

DIV 2 Sa 22Dec 1923 Stoke 2 - 1 Coventry

DIV 2 Sa 15Dec 1923 Coventry 1 - 2 Stoke

1921/1922

DIV 2 Sa 11Mar 1922 Coventry 0 - 1 Stoke

DIV 2 Sa 04Mar 1922 Stoke 2 - 2 Coventry

1920/1921

DIV 2 Sa 30Oct 1920 Coventry 1 - 0 Stoke

DIV 2 Sa 23Oct 1920 Stoke 4 - 1 Coventry

1919/1920

DIV 2 Fr 26Dec 1919 Stoke 6 - 1 Coventry

DIV 2 Th 25Dec 1919 Coventry 3 - 2 Stoke

COVENTRY V WALSALL

	COVENTRY WINS	DRAWS	WALSALL WINS
League	14	11	9
League Cup	1	0	1
FA Cup	1	0	0
Total	16	11	10

2003/2004

FL DIV 1 Sa 17Jan 2004 Walsall 1 - 6 Coventry

FL DIV 1 Sa 16Aug 2003 Coventry 0 - 0 Walsall

2002/2003

FL DIV 1 Tu 15Apr 2003 Walsall 0 - 0 Coventry

FL DIV 1 Sa 26Oct 2002 Coventry 0 - 0 Walsall

2001/2002

FL DIV 1 Tu 19Feb 2002 Coventry 2 - 1 Walsall

FL DIV 1 Su 14Oct 2001 Walsall 0 - 1 Coventry

1984/1985

LC Tu 09Oct 1984 Coventry 0 - 3 Walsall

LC Tu 25Sep 1984 Walsall 1 - 2 Coventry

1963/1964

DIV 3 Sa 21Dec 1963 Coventry 1 - 0 Walsall

DIV 3 Sa 31Aug 1963 Walsall 0 - 3 Coventry

1960/1961

DIV 3 Sa 18Mar 1961 Coventry 1 - 2 Walsall

DIV 3 Fr 28Oct 1960 Walsall 1 - 1 Coventry

1958/1959

DIV 4 Tu 31Mar 1959 Coventry 0 - 0 Walsall

DIV 4 Mo 30Mar 1959 Walsall 3 - 0 Coventry

1957/1958

DIV 3 (S) Mo 24Mar 1958 Coventry 4 - 1 Walsall

DIV 3 (S) Mo 10Mar 1958 Walsall 4 - 1 Coventry

1956/1957

DIV 3 (S) Sa 09Mar 1957 Walsall 1 - 1 Coventry

DIV 3 (S) Sa 08Dec 1956 Coventry 2 - 2 Walsall

1955/1956

DIV 3 (S) Sa 07Apr 1956 Walsall 2 - 0 Coventry

DIV 3 (S) Sa 26Nov 1955 Coventry 1 - 0 Walsall

1954/1955

DIV 3 (S) Sa 12Feb 1955 Coventry 5 - 3 Walsall

DIV 3 (S) Sa 25Sep 1954 Walsall 1 - 1 Coventry

1953/1954

DIV 3 (S) Sa 03Apr 1954 Walsall 1 - 0 Coventry

DIV 3 (S) Sa 14Nov 1953 Coventry 2 - 0 Walsall

1952/1953

DIV 3 (S) Sa 24Jan 1953 Coventry 3 - 1 Walsall
DIV 3 (S) Sa 13Sep 1952 Walsall 1 - 1 Coventry
1947/1948
FA CUP Sa 10Jan 1948 Coventry 2 - 1 Walsall
1930/1931
DIV 3 (S) Sa 07Feb 1931 Coventry 2 - 1 Walsall
DIV 3 (S) Sa 04Oct 1930 Walsall 1 - 2 Coventry
1929/1930
DIV 3 (S) Sa 22Feb 1930 Coventry 4 - 0 Walsall
DIV 3 (S) Sa 19Oct 1929 Walsall 3 - 2 Coventry
1928/1929
DIV 3 (S) Sa 02Mar 1929 Coventry 1 - 1 Walsall
DIV 3 (S) Sa 20Oct 1928 Walsall 0 - 0 Coventry
1927/1928
DIV 3 (S) Sa 11Feb 1928 Walsall 7 - 0 Coventry
DIV 3 (S) Sa 01Oct 1927 Coventry 0 - 1 Walsall
1925/1926
DIV 3 (N) Sa 03Apr 1926 Walsall 4 - 1 Coventry
DIV 3 (N) Sa 21Nov 1925 Coventry 2 - 0 Walsall

COVENTRY V WEST BROM

	COVENTRY WINS	DRAWS	WBA WINS
League	14	12	24
FA Cup	2	2	4
League Cup	0	2	3
Total	16	16	31

2009/2010
CHAMP We 24Mar 2010 WBA 1 - 0 Coventry
CHAMP Sa 24Oct 2009 Coventry 0 - 0 WBA
2007/2008
FA CUP Sa 16Feb 2008 Coventry 0 - 5 WBA
CHAMP Tu 04Dec 2007 WBA 2 - 4 Coventry
CHAMP Mo 12Nov 2007 Coventry 0 - 4 WBA
2006/2007
CHAMP Sa 28Apr 2007 Coventry 0 - 1 WBA
CHAMP Sa 16Dec 2006 WBA 5 - 0 Coventry
2003/2004
FL DIV 1 Sa 06Mar 2004 WBA 3 - 0 Coventry
FL DIV 1 Sa 20Dec 2003 Coventry 1 - 0 WBA
2001/2002
FL DIV 1 Mo 01Apr 2002 Coventry 0 - 1 WBA
FL DIV 1 We 12Dec 2001 WBA 1 - 0 Coventry
1994/1995
FA CUP We 18Jan 1995 WBA 1 - 2 Coventry
FA CUP Sa 07Jan 1995 Coventry 1 - 1 WBA
1985/1986
DIV 1 We 19Mar 1986 WBA 0 - 0 Coventry
LC We 06Nov 1985 WBA 4 - 3 Coventry
LC Tu 29Oct 1985 Coventry 0 - 0 WBA
DIV 1 Sa 28Sep 1985 Coventry 3 - 0 WBA
1984/1985
DIV 1 Sa 27Apr 1985 Coventry 2 - 1 WBA
DIV 1 Sa 24Nov 1984 WBA 5 - 2 Coventry
1983/1984
DIV 1 Sa 25Feb 1984 WBA 1 - 1 Coventry
DIV 1 Sa 22Oct 1983 Coventry 1 - 2 WBA
1982/1983
DIV 1 Sa 30Apr 1983 Coventry 0 - 1 WBA
DIV 1 Sa 27Nov 1982 WBA 2 - 0 Coventry
1981/1982
DIV 1 Sa 10Apr 1982 WBA 1 - 2 Coventry
FA CUP Fr 01Jan 1982 WBA 2 - 0 Coventry
DIV 1 Sa 26Dec 1981 Coventry 0 - 2 WBA
1980/1981
DIV 1 Sa 13Dec 1980 Coventry 3 - 0 WBA
DIV 1 We 08Oct 1980 WBA 1 - 0 Coventry
1979/1980
DIV 1 Sa 08Mar 1980 Coventry 0 - 2 WBA
LC Tu 01Jan 1980 WBA 2 - 1 Coventry
DIV 1 Sa 27Oct 1979 WBA 4 - 1 Coventry
1978/1979
DIV 1 Sa 03Mar 1979 Coventry 1 - 3 WBA
FA CUP Mo 01Jan 1979 WBA 4 - 0 Coventry
FA CUP Mo 01Jan 1979 Coventry 2 - 2 WBA
DIV 1 Sa 21Oct 1978 WBA 7 - 1 Coventry
1977/1978
DIV 1 Sa 25Feb 1978 WBA 3 - 3 Coventry
DIV 1 Sa 01Oct 1977 Coventry 1 - 2 WBA
1976/1977
DIV 1 Tu 19Apr 1977 Coventry 1 - 1 WBA
DIV 1 Fr 17Sep 1976 WBA 1 - 1 Coventry
1972/1973
DIV 1 Tu 26Dec 1972 Coventry 0 - 0 WBA
DIV 1 Sa 23Sep 1972 WBA 1 - 0 Coventry
1971/1972
DIV 1 Fr 17Mar 1972 Coventry 0 - 2 WBA
FA CUP Sa 01Jan 1972 WBA 1 - 2 Coventry
DIV 1 Sa 21Aug 1971 WBA 1 - 1 Coventry
1970/1971
DIV 1 Sa 10Apr 1971 WBA 0 - 0 Coventry
DIV 1 Sa 26Dec 1970 Coventry 1 - 1 WBA
1969/1970
DIV 1 We 20Aug 1969 WBA 0 - 1 Coventry
DIV 1 Tu 12Aug 1969 Coventry 3 - 1 WBA
1968/1969
DIV 1 We 09Oct 1968 WBA 6 - 1 Coventry
DIV 1 Tu 27Aug 1968 Coventry 4 - 2 WBA
1967/1968
DIV 1 Sa 03Feb 1968 WBA 0 - 1 Coventry
DIV 1 Sa 23Sep 1967 Coventry 4 - 2 WBA

1965/1966				
LC	We 10Nov 1965	WBA	6 - 1	Coventry
LC	We 03Nov 1965	Coventry	1 - 1	WBA
1948/1949				
DIV 2	Tu 19Apr 1949	Coventry	1 - 0	WBA
DIV 2	Mo 18Apr 1949	WBA	1 - 0	Coventry
1947/1948				
DIV 2	Mo 15Sep 1947	Coventry	1 - 0	WBA
DIV 2	We 10Sep 1947	WBA	3 - 1	Coventry
1946/1947				
DIV 2	Sa 03May 1947	WBA	1 - 1	Coventry
DIV 2	Mo 02Sep 1946	Coventry	3 - 2	WBA
1938/1939				
DIV 2	Sa 11Feb 1939	Coventry	1 - 1	WBA
DIV 2	Sa 08Oct 1938	WBA	3 - 1	Coventry
1936/1937				
FA CUP	Sa 20Feb 1937	Coventry	2 - 3	WBA

COVENTRY V WOLVES

	COVENTRY WINS	DRAWS	WOLVES WINS
League	27	12	19
League Cup	0	0	1
FA Cup	1	2	1
Total	28	14	21

2008/2009				
CHAMP	Sa 07Feb 2009	Coventry	2 - 1	Wolves
CHAMP	Sa 18Oct 2008	Wolves	2 - 1	Coventry
2007/2008				
CHAMP	Sa 26Apr 2008	Coventry	1 - 1	Wolves
CHAMP	Sa 06Oct 2007	Wolves	1 - 0	Coventry
2006/2007				
CHAMP	Tu 13Mar 2007	Coventry	2 - 1	Wolves
CHAMP	Tu 17Oct 2006	Wolves	1 - 0	Coventry
2005/2006				
CHAMP	Sa 08Apr 2006	Wolves	2 - 2	Coventry
CHAMP	Mo 02Jan 2006	Coventry	2 - 0	Wolves
2004/2005				
CHAMP	Sa 16Apr 2005	Coventry	2 - 2	Wolves
CHAMP	Sa 20Nov 2004	Wolves	0 - 1	Coventry
2002/2003				
FL DIV 1	Sa 14Dec 2002	Wolves	0 - 2	Coventry
FL DIV 1	Sa 16Nov 2002	Coventry	0 - 2	Wolves
2001/2002				
FL DIV 1	Su 13Jan 2002	Wolves	3 - 1	Coventry
FL DIV 1	Su 19Aug 2001	Coventry	0 - 1	Wolves
1995/1996				
LC	We 29Nov 1995	Wolves	2 - 1	Coventry
1983/1984				
DIV 1	Sa 14Apr 1984	Coventry	2 - 1	Wolves
FA Cup	Mo 16Jan 1984	Coventry	3 - 0	Wolves
FA Cup	Tu 10Jan 1984	Wolves	1 - 1	Coventry
FA Cup	Sa 07Jan 1984	Coventry	1 - 1	Wolves
DIV 1	Sa 19Nov 1983	Wolves	0 - 0	Coventry
1981/1982				
DIV 1	Sa 27Mar 1982	Coventry	0 - 0	Wolves
DIV 1	Sa 07Nov 1981	Wolves	1 - 0	Coventry
1980/1981				
DIV 1	Sa 07Feb 1981	Coventry	2 - 2	Wolves
DIV 1	Sa 13Sep 1980	Wolves	0 - 1	Coventry
1979/1980				
DIV 1	Sa 29Mar 1980	Coventry	1 - 3	Wolves
DIV 1	Sa 17Nov 1979	Wolves	0 - 3	Coventry
1978/1979				
DIV 1	Sa 05May 1979	Coventry	3 - 0	Wolves
DIV 1	Sa 30Dec 1978	Wolves	1 - 1	Coventry
1977/1978				
DIV 1	Tu 28Mar 1978	Coventry	4 - 0	Wolves
DIV 1	Sa 29Oct 1977	Wolves	1 - 3	Coventry
1975/1976				
DIV 1	Sa 17Apr 1976	Coventry	3 - 1	Wolves
DIV 1	Fr 26Dec 1975	Wolves	0 - 1	Coventry
1974/1975				
DIV 1	Sa 11Jan 1975	Coventry	2 - 1	Wolves
DIV 1	Sa 07Dec 1974	Wolves	2 - 0	Coventry
1973/1974				
DIV 1	Sa 20Apr 1974	Wolves	1 - 1	Coventry
DIV 1	Sa 08Dec 1973	Coventry	1 - 0	Wolves
1972/1973				
DIV 1	Sa 28Apr 1973	Wolves	3 - 0	Coventry
FA Cup	Mo 01Jan 1973	Wolves	2 - 0	Coventry
DIV 1	Tu 29Aug 1972	Coventry	0 - 1	Wolves
1971/1972				
DIV 1	Sa 19Feb 1972	Coventry	0 - 0	Wolves
DIV 1	Sa 30Oct 1971	Wolves	1 - 1	Coventry
1970/1971				
DIV 1	Sa 16Jan 1971	Wolves	0 - 0	Coventry
DIV 1	Tu 25Aug 1970	Coventry	0 - 1	Wolves
1969/1970				
DIV 1	Fr 10Apr 1970	Wolves	0 - 1	Coventry
DIV 1	Sa 30Aug 1969	Coventry	1 - 0	Wolves
1968/1969				
DIV 1	Tu 15Apr 1969	Wolves	1 - 1	Coventry
DIV 1	Sa 05Oct 1968	Coventry	0 - 1	Wolves
1967/1968				
DIV 1	Sa 30Mar 1968	Coventry	1 - 0	Wolves
DIV 1	Sa 04Nov 1967	Wolves	2 - 0	Coventry
1966/1967				
DIV 2	Sa 29Apr 1967	Coventry	3 - 1	Wolves
DIV 2	Sa 03Dec 1966	Wolves	1 - 3	Coventry

1965/1966				
DIV 2	Sa 29Jan 1966	Wolves	0 - 1	Coventry
DIV 2	Sa 21Aug 1965	Coventry	2 - 1	Wolves
1924/1925				
DIV 2	Sa 21Mar 1925	Wolves	3 - 1	Coventry
DIV 2	Sa 15Nov 1924	Coventry	2 - 4	Wolves
1922/1923				
DIV 2	Tu 26Dec 1922	Wolves	1 - 2	Coventry
DIV 2	Mo 25Dec 1922	Coventry	7 - 1	Wolves
1921/1922				
DIV 2	Sa 01Oct 1921	Wolves	1 - 0	Coventry
DIV 2	Sa 24Sep 1921	Coventry	3 - 1	Wolves
1920/1921				
DIV 2	Th 24Feb 1921	Coventry	4 - 0	Wolves
DIV 2	Sa 12Feb 1921	Wolves	1 - 0	Coventry
1919/1920				
DIV 2	Sa 14Feb 1920	Wolves	2 - 0	Coventry
DIV 2	Sa 07Feb 1920	Coventry	1 - 0	Wolves

DERBY V LEICESTER

	DERBY WINS	DRAWS	LEICESTER WINS
League	41	25	27
Cup	0	0	1
League Cup	2	1	0
FA Cup	2	1	0
Total	45	27	28

2011/2012				
CHAMP	Sa 01Oct 2011	Leicester	4 - 0	Derby
2010/2011				
CHAMP	Sa 12Feb 2011	Derby	0 - 2	Leicester
CHAMP	Sa 13Nov 2010	Leicester	2 - 0	Derby
2009/2010				
CHAMP	Sa 27Mar 2010	Derby	1 - 0	Leicester
CHAMP	Sa 17Oct 2009	Leicester	0 - 0	Derby
2006/2007				
CHAMP	Fr 06Apr 2007	Leicester	1 - 1	Derby
CHAMP	Sa 25Nov 2006	Derby	1 - 0	Leicester
2005/2006				
CHAMP	Tu 14Feb 2006	Leicester	2 - 2	Derby
CHAMP	Sa 01Oct 2005	Derby	1 - 1	Leicester
2004/2005				
CHAMP	Tu 26Apr 2005	Leicester	1 - 0	Derby
CHAMP	We 11Aug 2004	Derby	1 - 2	Leicester
2002/2003				
FL DIV 1	Sa 01Mar 2003	Derby	1 - 1	Leicester
FL DIV 1	Sa 14Sep 2002	Leicester	3 - 1	Derby
2001/2002				
FAPL	Sa 23Feb 2002	Leicester	0 - 3	Derby
FAPL	Sa 15Sep 2001	Derby	2 - 3	Leicester
2000/2001				
FAPL	Mo 16Apr 2001	Derby	2 - 0	Leicester
FAPL	Sa 28Oct 2000	Leicester	2 - 1	Derby
1999/2000				
FAPL	Su 02Apr 2000	Derby	3 - 0	Leicester
FAPL	Sa 18Dec 1999	Leicester	0 - 1	Derby
1998/1999				
FAPL	We 05May 1999	Leicester	1 - 2	Derby
FAPL	Sa 19Sep 1998	Derby	2 - 0	Leicester
1997/1998				
FAPL	Su 26Apr 1998	Derby	0 - 4	Leicester
FAPL	Mo 06Oct 1997	Leicester	1 - 2	Derby
1996/1997				
FAPL	Sa 22Feb 1997	Leicester	4 - 2	Derby
FAPL	Sa 02Nov 1996	Derby	2 - 0	Leicester
1995/1996				
FL DIV 1	We 28Feb 1996	Leicester	0 - 0	Derby
FL DIV 1	Su 10Sep 1995	Derby	0 - 1	Leicester
1993/1994				
PLAY-OFF	Mo 30May 1994	Leicester	2 - 1	Derby
FL DIV 1	Tu 05Apr 1994	Leicester	3 - 3	Derby
FL DIV 1	Tu 28Dec 1993	Derby	3 - 2	Leicester
1992/1993				
FL DIV 1	We 24Feb 1993	Derby	2 - 0	Leicester
FL DIV 1	We 26Aug 1992	Leicester	3 - 2	Derby
1991/1992				
DIV 2	Sa 22Feb 1992	Leicester	1 - 2	Derby
DIV 2	Sa 30Nov 1991	Derby	1 - 2	Leicester
1985/1986				
LC	We 01Jan 1986	Leicester	1 - 1	Derby
LC	We 25Sep 1985	Derby	2 - 0	Leicester
1982/1983				
DIV 2	Sa 05Mar 1983	Leicester	1 - 1	Derby
DIV 2	Sa 23Oct 1982	Derby	0 - 4	Leicester
1981/1982				
DIV 2	Sa 06Feb 1982	Leicester	2 - 1	Derby
DIV 2	Sa 12Sep 1981	Derby	3 - 1	Leicester
1978/1979				
LC	Mo 01Jan 1979	Leicester	0 - 1	Derby
1977/1978				
DIV 1	Sa 22Apr 1978	Derby	4 - 1	Leicester
DIV 1	Sa 10Dec 1977	Leicester	1 - 1	Derby
1976/1977				
DIV 1	Tu 12Apr 1977	Leicester	1 - 1	Derby
DIV 1	Mo 27Dec 1976	Derby	1 - 0	Leicester
1975/1976				
DIV 1	Sa 17Apr 1976	Derby	2 - 2	Leicester
DIV 1	Fr 26Dec 1975	Leicester	2 - 1	Derby
1974/1975				
DIV 1	Sa 19Apr 1975	Leicester	0 - 0	Derby

DIV 1 Sa 12Oct 1974 Derby 1 - 0 Leicester

1973/1974

DIV 1 Sa 16Mar 1974 Leicester 0 - 1 Derby

DIV 1 Sa 20Oct 1973 Derby 2 - 1 Leicester

1972/1973

DIV 1 Sa 10Mar 1973 Leicester 0 - 0 Derby

DIV 1 Sa 14Oct 1972 Derby 2 - 1 Leicester

1971/1972

DIV 1 Sa 18Mar 1972 Derby 3 - 0 Leicester

DIV 1 Sa 21Aug 1971 Leicester 0 - 2 Derby

1953/1954

DIV 2 Sa 12Dec 1953 Derby 2 - 1 Leicester

DIV 2 We 19Aug 1953 Leicester 2 - 2 Derby

1938/1939

DIV 1 Sa 15Apr 1939 Derby 1 - 1 Leicester

DIV 1 Sa 10Dec 1938 Leicester 2 - 3 Derby

1937/1938

DIV 1 Sa 01Jan 1938 Derby 0 - 1 Leicester

DIV 1 Sa 28Aug 1937 Leicester 0 - 0 Derby

1934/1935

DIV 1 Th 31Jan 1935 Leicester 0 - 1 Derby

DIV 1 Sa 15Sep 1934 Derby 1 - 1 Leicester

1933/1934

DIV 1 Th 19Apr 1934 Leicester 2 - 0 Derby

DIV 1 Sa 04Nov 1933 Derby 2 - 1 Leicester

1932/1933

DIV 1 Sa 08Apr 1933 Leicester 4 - 0 Derby

DIV 1 Sa 26Nov 1932 Derby 3 - 2 Leicester

1931/1932

DIV 1 Sa 27Feb 1932 Leicester 1 - 1 Derby

DIV 1 Sa 17Oct 1931 Derby 1 - 1 Leicester

1930/1931

DIV 1 Sa 27Dec 1930 Derby 1 - 0 Leicester

DIV 1 Sa 30Aug 1930 Leicester 1 - 1 Derby

1929/1930

DIV 1 Sa 12Apr 1930 Derby 2 - 2 Leicester

DIV 1 Sa 07Dec 1929 Leicester 0 - 0 Derby

1928/1929

DIV 1 Sa 23Mar 1929 Leicester 1 - 0 Derby

DIV 1 Sa 10Nov 1928 Derby 5 - 2 Leicester

1927/1928

DIV 1 Sa 21Jan 1928 Leicester 4 - 0 Derby

DIV 1 Sa 10Sep 1927 Derby 2 - 1 Leicester

1926/1927

DIV 1 Sa 26Mar 1927 Leicester 1 - 1 Derby

DIV 1 Sa 06Nov 1926 Derby 4 - 1 Leicester

1924/1925

DIV 2 Sa 11Apr 1925 Leicester 0 - 0 Derby

DIV 2 Sa 06Dec 1924 Derby 0 - 3 Leicester

1923/1924

DIV 2 Sa 03May 1924 Derby 4 - 0 Leicester

DIV 2 Sa 26Apr 1924 Leicester 3 - 0 Derby

1922/1923

DIV 2 Sa 23Dec 1922 Leicester 0 - 1 Derby

DIV 2 Sa 16Dec 1922 Derby 2 - 0 Leicester

1921/1922

DIV 2 Sa 10Dec 1921 Leicester 1 - 1 Derby

DIV 2 Sa 03Dec 1921 Derby 0 - 1 Leicester

1914/1915

DIV 2 Mo 05Apr 1915 Derby 1 - 0 Leicester

DIV 2 Mo 28Dec 1914 Leicester 0 - 6 Derby

1911/1912

DIV 2 Sa 13Apr 1912 Leicester 0 - 1 Derby

DIV 2 Sa 09Dec 1911 Derby 5 - 0 Leicester

1910/1911

DIV 2 Mo 17Apr 1911 Leicester 1 - 2 Derby

DIV 2 Mo 26Dec 1910 Derby 3 - 0 Leicester

1909/1910

DIV 2 Sa 26Feb 1910 Leicester 6 - 0 Derby

DIV 2 Sa 16Oct 1909 Derby 0 - 1 Leicester

1908/1909

DIV 1 Sa 06Feb 1909 Leicester 0 - 2 Derby

1907/1908

DIV 2 Sa 22Feb 1908 Derby 1 - 2 Leicester

DIV 2 Sa 23Nov 1907 Leicester 1 - 3 Derby

1893/1894

DIV 1 Sa 17Feb 1894 Derby 3 - 0 Leicester

DIV 1 Sa 10Feb 1894 Leicester 0 - 0 Derby

DERBY VS FOREST

	DERBY WINS	DRAWS	FOREST WINS
League	26	19	33
FA Cup	4	2	2
League Cup	0	0	1
Total	30	21	36

2010/2011

CHAMP Sa 22Jan 2011 Derby 0 - 1 Nottm Forest

CHAMP We 29Dec 2010 Nottm Forest 5 - 2 Derby

2009/2010

CHAMP Sa 30Jan 2010 Derby 1 - 0 Nottm Forest

CHAMP Sa 29Aug 2009 Nottm Forest 3 - 2 Derby

2008/2009

CHAMP Sa 21Feb 2009 Nottm Forest 1 - 3 Derby

FA CUP We 04Feb 2009 Nottm Forest 2 - 3 Derby

FA CUP Fr 23Jan 2009 Derby 1 - 1 Nottm Forest

CHAMP Su 02Nov 2008 Derby 1 - 1 Nottm Forest

2004/2005

CHAMP Sa 26Feb 2005 Nottm Forest 2 - 2 Derby

CHAMP Sa 11Dec 2004 Derby 3 - 0 Nottm Forest
2003/2004
FL DIV 1 Sa 20Mar 2004 Derby 4 - 2 Nottm Forest
FL DIV 1 Sa 27Sep 2003 Nottm Forest 1 - 1 Derby
2002/2003
FL DIV 1 We 19Mar 2003 Nottm Forest 3 - 0 Derby
FL DIV 1 Su 20Oct 2002 Derby 0 - 0 Nottm Forest
1998/1999
FAPL Sa 10Apr 1999 Derby 1 - 0 Nottm Forest
FAPL Mo 16Nov 1998 Nottm Forest 2 - 2 Derby
1996/1997
FAPL We 23Apr 1997 Derby 0 - 0 Nottm Forest
FAPL Sa 19Oct 1996 Nottm Forest 1 - 1 Derby
1993/1994
FL DIV 1 We 27Apr 1994 Derby 0 - 2 Nottm Forest
FL DIV 1 We 18Aug 1993 Nottm Forest 1 - 1 Derby
1990/1991
DIV 1 We 10Apr 1991 Nottm Forest 1 - 0 Derby
DIV 1 Sa 24Nov 1990 Derby 2 - 1 Nottm Forest
1989/1990
DIV 1 Sa 20Jan 1990 Derby 0 - 2 Nottm Forest
DIV 1 We 30Aug 1989 Nottm Forest 2 - 1 Derby
1988/1989
DIV 1 Sa 25Mar 1989 Derby 0 - 2 Nottm Forest
DIV 1 Sa 17Sep 1988 Nottm Forest 1 - 1 Derby
1987/1988
DIV 1 We 30Mar 1988 Nottm Forest 2 - 1 Derby
DIV 1 Sa 10Oct 1987 Derby 0 - 1 Nottm Forest
1985/1986
LC We 30Oct 1985 Derby 1 - 2 Nottm Forest
1982/1983
FA CUP Sa 08Jan 1983 Derby 2 - 0 Nottm Forest
1979/1980
DIV 1 Sa 19Apr 1980 Nottm Forest 1 - 0 Derby
DIV 1 Sa 24Nov 1979 Derby 4 - 1 Nottm Forest
1978/1979
DIV 1 Sa 14Apr 1979 Derby 1 - 2 Nottm Forest
DIV 1 Tu 26Dec 1978 Nottm Forest 1 - 1 Derby
1977/1978
DIV 1 Sa 14Jan 1978 Derby 0 - 0 Nottm Forest
DIV 1 Sa 27Aug 1977 Nottm Forest 3 - 0 Derby
1971/1972
DIV 1 Sa 19Feb 1972 Derby 4 - 0 Nottm Forest
DIV 1 Sa 30Oct 1971 Nottm Forest 0 - 2 Derby
1970/1971
DIV 1 We 31Mar 1971 Derby 1 - 2 Nottm Forest
DIV 1 Sa 28Nov 1970 Nottm Forest 2 - 4 Derby
1969/1970
DIV 1 Sa 14Mar 1970 Nottm Forest 1 - 3 Derby
DIV 1 Sa 29Nov 1969 Derby 0 - 2 Nottm Forest
1954/1955
DIV 2 Sa 02Apr 1955 Derby 1 - 2 Nottm Forest
DIV 2 Sa 13Nov 1954 Nottm Forest 3 - 0 Derby
1953/1954
DIV 2 Sa 10Apr 1954 Derby 1 - 2 Nottm Forest
DIV 2 Sa 07Nov 1953 Nottm Forest 4 - 2 Derby
1935/1936
FA CUP Sa 25Jan 1936 Derby 2 - 0 Nottm Forest
1927/1928
FA CUP We 01Feb 1928 Nottm Forest 2 - 0 Derby
FA CUP Sa 28Jan 1928 Derby 0 - 0 Nottm Forest
1925/1926
DIV 2 Sa 06Feb 1926 Derby 2 - 0 Nottm Forest
DIV 2 Sa 26Sep 1925 Nottm Forest 1 - 2 Derby
1921/1922
DIV 2 Sa 01Oct 1921 Nottm Forest 3 - 0 Derby
DIV 2 Sa 24Sep 1921 Derby 1 - 2 Nottm Forest
1914/1915
DIV 2 Sa 26Dec 1914 Derby 1 - 0 Nottm Forest
DIV 2 Fr 25Dec 1914 Nottm Forest 2 - 2 Derby
1911/1912
DIV 2 Tu 09Apr 1912 Derby 1 - 0 Nottm Forest
DIV 2 Tu 26Dec 1911 Nottm Forest 1 - 3 Derby
1908/1909
FA CUP Sa 13Mar 1909 Derby 3 - 0 Nottm Forest
1905/1906
DIV 1 Tu 17Apr 1906 Nottm Forest 0 - 0 Derby
DIV 1 Tu 26Dec 1905 Derby 2 - 2 Nottm Forest
1904/1905
DIV 1 Sa 25Feb 1905 Derby 3 - 2 Nottm Forest
DIV 1 Sa 29Oct 1904 Nottm Forest 0 - 1 Derby
1903/1904
DIV 1 Sa 12Mar 1904 Nottm Forest 5 - 1 Derby
DIV 1 Sa 14Nov 1903 Derby 2 - 6 Nottm Forest
1902/1903
DIV 1 Sa 17Jan 1903 Derby 0 - 1 Nottm Forest
DIV 1 Sa 20Sep 1902 Nottm Forest 2 - 3 Derby
1901/1902
DIV 1 Sa 01Mar 1902 Nottm Forest 3 - 1 Derby
DIV 1 Sa 02Nov 1901 Derby 1 - 1 Nottm Forest
1900/1901
DIV 1 Sa 16Mar 1901 Derby 0 - 0 Nottm Forest
DIV 1 Sa 10Nov 1900 Nottm Forest 1 - 0 Derby
1899/1900
DIV 1 Sa 03Mar 1900 Nottm Forest 4 - 1 Derby
DIV 1 Sa 28Oct 1899 Derby 2 - 2 Nottm Forest
1898/1899
DIV 1 Th 20Apr 1899 Derby 2 - 0 Nottm Forest
DIV 1 Sa 17Dec 1898 Nottm Forest 3 - 3 Derby

1897/1898

FA CUP Sa 16Apr 1898 Nottm Forest 3 - 1 Derby
DIV 1 Mo 11Apr 1898 Derby 5 - 0 Nottm Forest
DIV 1 Sa 30Oct 1897 Nottm Forest 3 - 4 Derby

1896/1897

DIV 1 We 18Nov 1896 Nottm Forest 1 - 2 Derby
DIV 1 Sa 05Sep 1896 Derby 1 - 1 Nottm Forest

1895/1896

DIV 1 Sa 07Dec 1895 Derby 4 - 0 Nottm Forest
DIV 1 Sa 05Oct 1895 Nottm Forest 2 - 5 Derby

1894/1895

DIV 1 Sa 03Nov 1894 Nottm Forest 2 - 1 Derby
DIV 1 Sa 08Sep 1894 Derby 4 - 2 Nottm Forest

1893/1894

DIV 1 Sa 30Dec 1893 Nottm Forest 4 - 2 Derby
DIV 1 Sa 09Dec 1893 Derby 3 - 4 Nottm Forest

1892/1893

DIV 1 Sa 28Jan 1893 Nottm Forest 1 - 0 Derby
DIV 1 Sa 01Oct 1892 Derby 2 - 3 Nottm Forest

DERBY V STOKE

	DERBY WINS	DRAWS	STOKE WINS
League Cup	1	0	0
League	48	37	39
FA Cup	2	0	1
Total	51	37	40

2008/2009

CARLING CUP Tu 02Dec 2008 Stoke 0 - 1 Derby

2006/2007

CHAMP	We 21Feb 2007	Derby	0 - 2	Stoke
CHAMP	Tu 08Aug 2006	Stoke	2 - 0	Derby
2005/2006				
CHAMP	Tu 22Nov 2005	Stoke	1 - 2	Derby
CHAMP	Sa 15Oct 2005	Derby	2 - 1	Stoke
2004/2005				
CHAMP	Sa 09Apr 2005	Derby	3 - 1	Stoke
CHAMP	Mo 30Aug 2004	Stoke	1 - 0	Derby
2003/2004				
FL DIV 1	Sa 10Jan 2004	Stoke	2 - 1	Derby
FL DIV 1	Sa 09Aug 2003	Derby	0 - 3	Stoke
2002/2003				
FL DIV 1	Sa 18Jan 2003	Stoke	1 - 3	Derby
FL DIV 1	Sa 31Aug 2002	Derby	2 - 0	Stoke
1995/1996				
FL DIV 1	Sa 30Mar 1996	Derby	3 - 1	Stoke
FL DIV 1	Su 22Oct 1995	Stoke	1 - 1	Derby
1994/1995				
FL DIV 1	Sa 04Mar 1995	Stoke	0 - 0	Derby
FL DIV 1	Su 25Sep 1994	Derby	3 - 0	Stoke
1993/1994				
FL DIV 1	Sa 09Apr 1994	Derby	4 - 2	Stoke
FL DIV 1	Sa 01Jan 1994	Stoke	2 - 1	Derby
1986/1987				
DIV 2	Sa 11Apr 1987	Derby	0 - 0	Stoke
DIV 2	Sa 01Nov 1986	Stoke	0 - 2	Derby
1979/1980				
DIV 1	Sa 08Mar 1980	Derby	2 - 2	Stoke
DIV 1	Sa 27Oct 1979	Stoke	3 - 2	Derby
1976/1977				
DIV 1	Sa 02Apr 1977	Derby	2 - 0	Stoke
DIV 1	Sa 23Oct 1976	Stoke	1 - 0	Derby
1975/1976				
DIV 1	We 24Mar 1976	Derby	1 - 1	Stoke
DIV 1	Sa 27Sep 1975	Stoke	1 - 0	Derby
1974/1975				
DIV 1	Sa 15Mar 1975	Derby	1 - 2	Stoke
DIV 1	Sa 28Sep 1974	Stoke	1 - 1	Derby
1973/1974				
DIV 1	Sa 02Mar 1974	Derby	1 - 1	Stoke
DIV 1	We 26Dec 1973	Stoke	0 - 0	Derby
1972/1973				
DIV 1	We 14Feb 1973	Derby	0 - 3	Stoke
DIV 1	Sa 23Dec 1972	Stoke	4 - 0	Derby
1971/1972				
DIV 1	Sa 25Mar 1972	Stoke	1 - 1	Derby
DIV 1	Sa 11Sep 1971	Derby	4 - 0	Stoke
1970/1971				
DIV 1	Sa 19Dec 1970	Stoke	1 - 0	Derby
DIV 1	Sa 22Aug 1970	Derby	2 - 0	Stoke
1969/1970				
DIV 1	Fr 26Dec 1969	Stoke	1 - 0	Derby
DIV 1	Sa 23Aug 1969	Derby	0 - 0	Stoke
1962/1963				
DIV 2	We 29Aug 1962	Stoke	3 - 3	Derby
DIV 2	We 22Aug 1962	Derby	1 - 1	Stoke
1961/1962				
DIV 2	Sa 13Jan 1962	Derby	2 - 0	Stoke
DIV 2	Sa 02Sep 1961	Stoke	1 - 1	Derby
1960/1961				
DIV 2	Mo 20Mar 1961	Stoke	2 - 1	Derby
DIV 2	Sa 17Sep 1960	Derby	1 - 1	Stoke
1959/1960				
DIV 2	Sa 16Jan 1960	Derby	2 - 0	Stoke
DIV 2	Sa 05Sep 1959	Stoke	2 - 1	Derby
1958/1959				
DIV 2	Mo 30Mar 1959	Derby	3 - 0	Stoke
DIV 2	We 22Oct 1958	Stoke	2 - 1	Derby
1957/1958				
DIV 2	Sa 26Apr 1958	Stoke	2 - 1	Derby

DIV 2 Sa 14Dec 1957 Derby 0 - 0 Stoke

1954/1955

DIV 2 Sa 16Apr 1955 Derby 1 - 2 Stoke

DIV 2 Sa 27Nov 1954 Stoke 3 - 1 Derby

1953/1954

DIV 2 We 02Sep 1953 Derby 1 - 1 Stoke

DIV 2 Mo 24Aug 1953 Stoke 2 - 2 Derby

1952/1953

DIV 1 Sa 25Apr 1953 Stoke 1 - 2 Derby

DIV 1 Sa 06Dec 1952 Derby 4 - 0 Stoke

1951/1952

DIV 1 Sa 29Dec 1951 Stoke 3 - 1 Derby

DIV 1 Sa 01Sep 1951 Derby 4 - 2 Stoke

1950/1951

DIV 1 Sa 30Dec 1950 Derby 1 - 1 Stoke

DIV 1 Sa 02Sep 1950 Stoke 4 - 1 Derby

1949/1950

DIV 1 Sa 31Dec 1949 Stoke 1 - 3 Derby

DIV 1 Sa 03Sep 1949 Derby 2 - 3 Stoke

1948/1949

DIV 1 Sa 07May 1949 Derby 4 - 1 Stoke

DIV 1 Sa 11Dec 1948 Stoke 4 - 2 Derby

1947/1948

DIV 1 Sa 01May 1948 Stoke 1 - 0 Derby

DIV 1 Sa 13Dec 1947 Derby 1 - 1 Stoke

1946/1947

DIV 1 Sa 18Jan 1947 Derby 3 - 0 Stoke

DIV 1 Sa 14Sep 1946 Stoke 3 - 2 Derby

1938/1939

DIV 1 Sa 28Jan 1939 Stoke 3 - 0 Derby

DIV 1 Sa 24Sep 1938 Derby 5 - 0 Stoke

1937/1938

DIV 1 We 02Feb 1938 Derby 4 - 1 Stoke

FA CUP Sa 08Jan 1938 Derby 1 - 2 Stoke

DIV 1 Sa 11Sep 1937 Stoke 8 - 1 Derby

1936/1937

DIV 1 Sa 13Mar 1937 Stoke 1 - 2 Derby

DIV 1 Sa 07Nov 1936 Derby 2 - 2 Stoke

1935/1936

DIV 1 Sa 14Mar 1936 Derby 0 - 1 Stoke

DIV 1 Sa 26Oct 1935 Stoke 0 - 0 Derby

1934/1935

DIV 1 Sa 19Jan 1935 Stoke 1 - 1 Derby

DIV 1 Sa 08Sep 1934 Derby 0 - 2 Stoke

1933/1934

DIV 1 Sa 03Feb 1934 Derby 5 - 1 Stoke

DIV 1 Sa 23Sep 1933 Stoke 0 - 4 Derby

1925/1926

DIV 2 Sa 06Mar 1926 Stoke 0 - 1 Derby

DIV 2 Sa 24Oct 1925 Derby 7 - 3 Stoke

1924/1925

DIV 2 Sa 18Apr 1925 Derby 1 - 2 Stoke

DIV 2 Sa 13Dec 1924 Stoke 1 - 1 Derby

1923/1924

DIV 2 Sa 10Nov 1923 Derby 1 - 1 Stoke

DIV 2 Sa 03Nov 1923 Stoke 1 - 1 Derby

1921/1922

DIV 2 Mo 06Mar 1922 Stoke 1 - 1 Derby

DIV 2 Sa 25Feb 1922 Derby 2 - 4 Stoke

1907/1908

DIV 2 Sa 04Apr 1908 Derby 3 - 0 Stoke

DIV 2 Sa 07Dec 1907 Stoke 0 - 3 Derby

1906/1907

DIV 1 Sa 16Feb 1907 Derby 2 - 1 Stoke

DIV 1 Sa 13Oct 1906 Stoke 2 - 1 Derby

1905/1906

DIV 1 Sa 03Mar 1906 Stoke 2 - 2 Derby

DIV 1 Sa 28Oct 1905 Derby 1 - 0 Stoke

1904/1905

DIV 1 Sa 26Nov 1904 Derby 3 - 0 Stoke

DIV 1 Th 01Sep 1904 Stoke 1 - 2 Derby

1903/1904

DIV 1 Sa 23Apr 1904 Stoke 1 - 1 Derby

DIV 1 Sa 26Dec 1903 Derby 5 - 0 Stoke

1902/1903

DIV 1 Sa 14Mar 1903 Derby 2 - 0 Stoke

FA CUP Sa 07Mar 1903 Derby 3 - 0 Stoke

DIV 1 Sa 15Nov 1902 Stoke 2 - 0 Derby

1901/1902

DIV 1 Sa 22Mar 1902 Derby 1 - 0 Stoke

DIV 1 Sa 23Nov 1901 Stoke 1 - 1 Derby

1900/1901

DIV 1 Sa 30Mar 1901 Derby 4 - 1 Stoke

DIV 1 Sa 24Nov 1900 Stoke 0 - 1 Derby

1899/1900

DIV 1 Sa 17Mar 1900 Stoke 1 - 1 Derby

DIV 1 Sa 11Nov 1899 Derby 2 - 0 Stoke

1898/1899

FA CUP Sa 18Mar 1899 Derby 3 - 1 Stoke

DIV 1 Sa 29Oct 1898 Derby 1 - 1 Stoke

DIV 1 Th 01Sep 1898 Stoke 0 - 0 Derby

1897/1898

DIV 1 Sa 06Nov 1897 Derby 4 - 1 Stoke

DIV 1 Sa 02Oct 1897 Stoke 2 - 1 Derby

1896/1897

DIV 1 Sa 05Dec 1896 Stoke 2 - 2 Derby

DIV 1 Sa 07Nov 1896 Derby 5 - 1 Stoke

1895/1896

DIV 1 Sa 12Oct 1895 Derby 2 - 1 Stoke

DIV 1 Sa 07Sep 1895 Stoke 2 - 1 Derby

1894/1895

DIV 1	Sa 23Mar 1895	Stoke	4 - 1	Derby
DIV 1	Sa 19Jan 1895	Derby	1 - 1	Stoke

1893/1894

DIV 1	Sa 23Dec 1893	Derby	5 - 2	Stoke
DIV 1	Sa 23Sep 1893	Stoke	3 - 1	Derby

1892/1893

DIV 1	Sa 24Dec 1892	Derby	1 - 0	Stoke
DIV 1	Sa 03Sep 1892	Stoke	1 - 3	Derby

1891/1892

DIV 1	Sa 17Oct 1891	Derby	3 - 3	Stoke
DIV 1	Sa 05Sep 1891	Stoke	2 - 1	Derby

1889/1890

DIV 1	Sa 26Oct 1889	Derby	2 - 0	Stoke
DIV 1	Sa 07Sep 1889	Stoke	1 - 1	Derby

1888/1889

DIV 1	Sa 06Apr 1889	Stoke	1 - 1	Derby
DIV 1	Sa 26Jan 1889	Derby	2 - 1	Stoke

DERBY V WALSALL

	DERBY WINS	DRAWS	WALSALL WINS
League	5	3	4
Total	5	3	4

2003/2004

FL DIV 1	Sa 03Apr 2004	Derby	0 - 1	Walsall
FL DIV 1	Sa 13Sep 2003	Walsall	0 - 1	Derby

2002/2003

FL DIV 1	Sa 26Apr 2003	Walsall	3 - 2	Derby
FL DIV 1	Sa 05Oct 2002	Derby	2 - 2	Walsall

1985/1986

DIV 3	Mo 31Mar 1986	Walsall	1 - 1	Derby
DIV 3	We 12Mar 1986	Derby	3 - 1	Walsall

1984/1985

DIV 3	We 06Mar 1985	Derby	2 - 0	Walsall
DIV 3	Tu 23Oct 1984	Walsall	0 - 0	Derby

1962/1963

DIV 2	We 24Apr 1963	Derby	2 - 0	Walsall
DIV 2	Sa 16Mar 1963	Walsall	1 - 3	Derby

1961/1962

DIV 2	Sa 23Dec 1961	Walsall	2 - 0	Derby
DIV 2	Sa 26Aug 1961	Derby	1 - 3	Walsall

DERBY V WEST BROM

	DERBY WINS	DRAWS	WBA WINS
League	39	28	34
FA Cup	6	1	2
League Cup	4	0	1
Total	49	29	37

2009/2010

CHAMP	Sa 27Feb 2010	WBA	3 - 1	Derby
CHAMP	Sa 05Dec 2009	Derby	2 - 2	WBA

2006/2007

CHAMP	Mo 28May 2007	Derby	1 - 0	WBA
CHAMP	Sa 02Dec 2006	WBA	1 - 0	Derby
CHAMP	Sa 04Nov 2006	Derby	2 - 1	WBA

2003/2004

FL DIV 1	Fr 26Dec 2003	WBA	1 - 1	Derby
FL DIV 1	Sa 30Aug 2003	Derby	0 - 1	WBA

2000/2001

FA CUP	Sa 06Jan 2001	Derby	3 - 2	WBA
LC	Tu 26Sep 2000	WBA	2 - 4	Derby
LC	Tu 19Sep 2000	Derby	1 - 2	WBA

1995/1996

FL DIV 1	Su 05May 1996	WBA	3 - 2	Derby
FL DIV 1	Sa 11Nov 1995	Derby	3 - 0	WBA

1994/1995

FL DIV 1	Sa 22Apr 1995	WBA	0 - 0	Derby
FL DIV 1	Mo 02Jan 1995	Derby	1 - 1	WBA

1993/1994

FL DIV 1	Sa 26Mar 1994	WBA	1 - 2	Derby
FL DIV 1	Su 03Oct 1993	Derby	5 - 3	WBA

1989/1990

LC	We 22Nov 1989	Derby	2 - 0	WBA

1986/1987

DIV 2	Sa 21Feb 1987	Derby	1 - 1	WBA
LC	Tu 07Oct 1986	WBA	0 - 1	Derby
DIV 2	Sa 27Sep 1986	WBA	2 - 0	Derby
LC	We 24Sep 1986	Derby	4 - 1	WBA

1979/1980

DIV 1	Sa 03Nov 1979	Derby	2 - 1	WBA
DIV 1	Sa 18Aug 1979	WBA	0 - 0	Derby

1978/1979

DIV 1	Mo 26Mar 1979	WBA	2 - 1	Derby
DIV 1	Sa 16Sep 1978	Derby	3 - 2	WBA

1977/1978

DIV 1	Tu 18Apr 1978	WBA	1 - 0	Derby
FA CUP	Su 01Jan 1978	Derby	2 - 3	WBA
DIV 1	Sa 15Oct 1977	Derby	1 - 1	WBA

1976/1977

DIV 1	Sa 05Mar 1977	WBA	1 - 0	Derby
DIV 1	Sa 25Sep 1976	Derby	2 - 2	WBA

1972/1973				
DIV 1	Sa 27Jan 1973	Derby	2 - 0	WBA
DIV 1	Sa 09Sep 1972	WBA	2 - 1	Derby
1971/1972				
DIV 1	We 05Apr 1972	WBA	0 - 0	Derby
DIV 1	Sa 25Sep 1971	Derby	0 - 0	WBA
1970/1971				
DIV 1	Sa 01May 1971	Derby	2 - 0	WBA
DIV 1	Sa 26Sep 1970	WBA	2 - 1	Derby
1969/1970				
DIV 1	Sa 27Dec 1969	Derby	2 - 0	WBA
DIV 1	Sa 30Aug 1969	WBA	0 - 2	Derby
1952/1953				
DIV 1	Sa 28Mar 1953	WBA	2 - 2	Derby
DIV 1	Sa 08Nov 1952	Derby	1 - 1	WBA
1951/1952				
DIV 1	Sa 12Apr 1952	WBA	1 - 0	Derby
DIV 1	Sa 24Nov 1951	Derby	2 - 1	WBA
1950/1951				
DIV 1	Sa 24Feb 1951	WBA	1 - 2	Derby
FA CUP	We 10Jan 1951	WBA	0 - 1	Derby
FA CUP	Sa 06Jan 1951	Derby	2 - 2	WBA
DIV 1	Sa 07Oct 1950	Derby	1 - 1	WBA
1949/1950				
DIV 1	Mo 10Apr 1950	WBA	1 - 0	Derby
DIV 1	Fr 07Apr 1950	Derby	3 - 1	WBA
1945/1946				
FA CUP	We 30Jan 1946	WBA	1 - 3	Derby
FA CUP	Sa 26Jan 1946	Derby	1 - 0	WBA
1937/1938				
DIV 1	Sa 12Mar 1938	WBA	4 - 2	Derby
DIV 1	Sa 30Oct 1937	Derby	5 - 3	WBA
1936/1937				
DIV 1	Sa 26Dec 1936	Derby	1 - 0	WBA
DIV 1	Sa 29Aug 1936	WBA	1 - 3	Derby
1935/1936				
DIV 1	Sa 07Mar 1936	WBA	0 - 3	Derby
DIV 1	Sa 30Nov 1935	Derby	2 - 0	WBA
1934/1935				
DIV 1	Sa 20Apr 1935	WBA	4 - 3	Derby
DIV 1	Sa 08Dec 1934	Derby	9 - 3	WBA
1933/1934				
DIV 1	Sa 10Feb 1934	Derby	1 - 1	WBA
DIV 1	Sa 30Sep 1933	WBA	5 - 1	Derby
1932/1933				
DIV 1	Sa 21Jan 1933	Derby	2 - 2	WBA
DIV 1	Sa 10Sep 1932	WBA	2 - 0	Derby
1931/1932				
DIV 1	We 17Feb 1932	Derby	3 - 1	WBA
DIV 1	Sa 03Oct 1931	WBA	4 - 0	Derby

1926/1927				
DIV 1	Sa 30Apr 1927	Derby	2 - 1	WBA
DIV 1	Sa 11Dec 1926	WBA	3 - 1	Derby
1920/1921				
DIV 1	Sa 02Oct 1920	WBA	3 - 0	Derby
DIV 1	Sa 25Sep 1920	Derby	1 - 1	WBA
1919/1920				
DIV 1	Sa 27Dec 1919	WBA	3 - 0	Derby
DIV 1	Sa 20Dec 1919	Derby	0 - 4	WBA
1913/1914				
DIV 1	Sa 28Feb 1914	WBA	2 - 1	Derby
DIV 1	Sa 25Oct 1913	Derby	1 - 2	WBA
1912/1913				
DIV 1	Th 26Dec 1912	WBA	0 - 0	Derby
DIV 1	We 25Dec 1912	Derby	1 - 2	WBA
1910/1911				
DIV 2	We 01Mar 1911	Derby	1 - 3	WBA
FA CUP	Sa 04Feb 1911	Derby	2 - 0	WBA
DIV 2	Sa 22Oct 1910	WBA	1 - 1	Derby
1909/1910				
DIV 2	Sa 30Apr 1910	WBA	0 - 0	Derby
DIV 2	Sa 18Dec 1909	Derby	2 - 1	WBA
1908/1909				
DIV 2	Mo 26Apr 1909	Derby	2 - 1	WBA
DIV 2	Sa 21Nov 1908	WBA	2 - 0	Derby
1907/1908				
DIV 2	Sa 11Apr 1908	WBA	1 - 0	Derby
DIV 2	Sa 14Dec 1907	Derby	2 - 0	WBA
1906/1907				
FA CUP	Sa 23Feb 1907	WBA	2 - 0	Derby
1903/1904				
DIV 1	Sa 02Apr 1904	Derby	4 - 2	WBA
DIV 1	Mo 14Dec 1903	WBA	0 - 0	Derby
1902/1903				
DIV 1	Sa 25Apr 1903	WBA	3 - 0	Derby
DIV 1	Sa 27Dec 1902	Derby	1 - 0	WBA
1900/1901				
DIV 1	Sa 01Dec 1900	Derby	4 - 0	WBA
DIV 1	Mo 03Sep 1900	WBA	1 - 1	Derby
1899/1900				
DIV 1	Sa 31Mar 1900	WBA	0 - 0	Derby
DIV 1	Sa 25Nov 1899	Derby	4 - 1	WBA
1898/1899				
DIV 1	Sa 07Jan 1899	Derby	4 - 1	WBA
DIV 1	Sa 10Sep 1898	WBA	1 - 1	Derby
1897/1898				
DIV 1	Sa 20Nov 1897	WBA	3 - 1	Derby
DIV 1	Sa 18Sep 1897	Derby	3 - 2	WBA
1896/1897				
DIV 1	Sa 06Feb 1897	WBA	1 - 4	Derby

DIV 1 Fr 25Dec 1896 Derby 8 - 1 WBA

1895/1896

FA CUP Sa 29Feb 1896 Derby 1 - 0 WBA
DIV 1 Sa 18Jan 1896 WBA 0 - 0 Derby
DIV 1 Sa 14Dec 1895 Derby 4 - 1 WBA

1894/1895

DIV 1 Sa 27Oct 1894 Derby 1 - 1 WBA
DIV 1 Sa 20Oct 1894 WBA 2 - 2 Derby

1893/1894

DIV 1 Sa 24Mar 1894 WBA 0 - 1 Derby
DIV 1 Sa 16Sep 1893 Derby 2 - 3 WBA

1892/1893

DIV 1 Sa 01Apr 1893 WBA 3 - 1 Derby
DIV 1 Sa 24Sep 1892 Derby 1 - 1 WBA

1891/1892

DIV 1 Sa 06Feb 1892 Derby 1 - 1 WBA
DIV 1 Sa 12Dec 1891 WBA 4 - 2 Derby

1890/1891

DIV 1 Sa 29Nov 1890 WBA 3 - 4 Derby
DIV 1 Sa 22Nov 1890 Derby 3 - 1 WBA

1889/1890

DIV 1 Sa 09Nov 1889 WBA 2 - 3 Derby
DIV 1 Sa 14Sep 1889 Derby 3 - 1 WBA

1888/1889

DIV 1 Sa 06Oct 1888 WBA 5 - 0 Derby
DIV 1 Sa 15Sep 1888 Derby 1 - 2 WBA

DERBY V WOLVES

	DERBY WINS	DRAWS	WOLVES WINS
League	55	28	49
FA Cup	6	3	2
Total	61	31	51

2008/2009

CHAMP Mo 13Apr 2009 Derby 2 - 3 Wolves
CHAMP Tu 09Dec 2008 Wolves 3 - 0 Derby

2006/2007

CHAMP Tu 26Dec 2006 Derby 0 - 2 Wolves
CHAMP Tu 12Sep 2006 Wolves 0 - 1 Derby

2005/2006

CHAMP Fr 18Nov 2005 Derby 0 - 3 Wolves
CHAMP Tu 18Oct 2005 Wolves 1 - 1 Derby

2004/2005

CHAMP We 02Mar 2005 Derby 3 - 3 Wolves
CHAMP Tu 19Oct 2004 Wolves 2 - 0 Derby

2002/2003

FL DIV 1 We 01Jan 2003 Wolves 1 - 1 Derby
FL DIV 1 Sa 24Aug 2002 Derby 1 - 4 Wolves

1995/1996

FL DIV 1 Sa 10Feb 1996 Derby 0 - 0 Wolves
FL DIV 1 We 30Aug 1995 Wolves 3 - 0 Derby

1994/1995

FL DIV 1 We 12Apr 1995 Derby 3 - 3 Wolves
FL DIV 1 Su 27Nov 1994 Wolves 0 - 2 Derby

1993/1994

FL DIV 1 Su 05Dec 1993 Wolves 2 - 2 Derby
FL DIV 1 Su 07Nov 1993 Derby 0 - 4 Wolves

1992/1993

FL DIV 1 Sa 08May 1993 Derby 2 - 0 Wolves
FL DIV 1 Sa 31Oct 1992 Wolves 0 - 2 Derby

1991/1992

DIV 2 Sa 21Mar 1992 Derby 1 - 2 Wolves
DIV 2 Sa 09Nov 1991 Wolves 2 - 3 Derby

1985/1986

DIV 3 Sa 28Dec 1985 Wolves 0 - 4 Derby
DIV 3 Mo 26Aug 1985 Derby 4 - 2 Wolves

1982/1983

DIV 2 Sa 12Mar 1983 Derby 1 - 1 Wolves
DIV 2 Sa 30Oct 1982 Wolves 2 - 1 Derby

1979/1980

DIV 1 Tu 09Oct 1979 Wolves 0 - 0 Derby
DIV 1 We 22Aug 1979 Derby 0 - 1 Wolves

1978/1979

DIV 1 Tu 24Apr 1979 Wolves 4 - 0 Derby
DIV 1 Sa 04Nov 1978 Derby 4 - 1 Wolves

1977/1978

DIV 1 Sa 08Apr 1978 Derby 3 - 1 Wolves
DIV 1 Tu 04Oct 1977 Wolves 1 - 2 Derby

1975/1976

DIV 1 Sa 22Nov 1975 Wolves 0 - 0 Derby
DIV 1 Sa 18Oct 1975 Derby 3 - 2 Wolves

1974/1975

DIV 1 We 09Apr 1975 Derby 1 - 0 Wolves
DIV 1 Sa 18Jan 1975 Wolves 0 - 1 Derby

1973/1974

DIV 1 Sa 27Apr 1974 Derby 2 - 0 Wolves
DIV 1 Tu 09Apr 1974 Wolves 4 - 0 Derby

1972/1973

DIV 1 Fr 04May 1973 Derby 3 - 0 Wolves
DIV 1 Sa 02Dec 1972 Wolves 1 - 2 Derby

1971/1972

DIV 1 Sa 04Mar 1972 Derby 2 - 1 Wolves
DIV 1 Sa 13Nov 1971 Wolves 2 - 1 Derby

1970/1971

DIV 1 Sa 09Jan 1971 Derby 1 - 2 Wolves
FA CUP Fr 01Jan 1971 Derby 2 - 1 Wolves
DIV 1 We 19Aug 1970 Wolves 2 - 4 Derby

1969/1970

DIV 1 Sa 04Apr 1970 Derby 2 - 0 Wolves
DIV 1 We 27Aug 1969 Wolves 1 - 1 Derby

1966/1967				
DIV 2	Mo 26Dec 1966	Derby	0 - 3	Wolves
DIV 2	Sa 24Dec 1966	Wolves	5 - 3	Derby
1965/1966				
DIV 2	Sa 26Feb 1966	Derby	2 - 2	Wolves
DIV 2	Sa 11Sep 1965	Wolves	4 - 0	Derby
1952/1953				
DIV 1	Sa 24Jan 1953	Wolves	3 - 1	Derby
DIV 1	Sa 13Sep 1952	Derby	2 - 3	Wolves
1951/1952				
DIV 1	We 29Aug 1951	Derby	1 - 3	Wolves
DIV 1	We 22Aug 1951	Wolves	1 - 2	Derby
1950/1951				
DIV 1	Mo 28Aug 1950	Wolves	2 - 3	Derby
DIV 1	We 23Aug 1950	Derby	1 - 2	Wolves
1949/1950				
DIV 1	Sa 25Feb 1950	Wolves	4 - 1	Derby
DIV 1	Sa 08Oct 1949	Derby	1 - 2	Wolves
1948/1949				
DIV 1	Sa 05Feb 1949	Derby	3 - 2	Wolves
DIV 1	Sa 18Sep 1948	Wolves	2 - 2	Derby
1947/1948				
DIV 1	We 14Apr 1948	Derby	1 - 2	Wolves
DIV 1	Sa 13Sep 1947	Wolves	1 - 0	Derby
1946/1947				
DIV 1	Tu 08Apr 1947	Wolves	7 - 2	Derby
DIV 1	Mo 07Apr 1947	Derby	2 - 1	Wolves
1938/1939				
DIV 1	Sa 24Dec 1938	Wolves	0 - 0	Derby
DIV 1	Sa 27Aug 1938	Derby	2 - 2	Wolves
1937/1938				
DIV 1	Mo 06Sep 1937	Wolves	2 - 2	Derby
DIV 1	We 01Sep 1937	Derby	1 - 2	Wolves
1936/1937				
DIV 1	Sa 01May 1937	Wolves	3 - 1	Derby
DIV 1	We 23Sep 1936	Derby	5 - 1	Wolves
1935/1936				
DIV 1	Sa 08Feb 1936	Wolves	0 - 0	Derby
DIV 1	Sa 05Oct 1935	Derby	3 - 1	Wolves
1934/1935				
DIV 1	We 26Dec 1934	Derby	2 - 0	Wolves
DIV 1	Tu 25Dec 1934	Wolves	5 - 1	Derby
1933/1934				
DIV 1	Sa 14Apr 1934	Wolves	3 - 0	Derby
FA CUP	Sa 27Jan 1934	Derby	3 - 0	Wolves
DIV 1	Sa 02Dec 1933	Derby	3 - 1	Wolves
1932/1933				
DIV 1	Sa 22Apr 1933	Wolves	3 - 1	Derby
FA CUP	Sa 14Jan 1933	Wolves	3 - 6	Derby
DIV 1	Sa 10Dec 1932	Derby	4 - 4	Wolves

1925/1926				
DIV 2	Sa 20Mar 1926	Wolves	2 - 0	Derby
DIV 2	Sa 07Nov 1925	Derby	2 - 0	Wolves
1924/1925				
DIV 2	Sa 24Jan 1925	Derby	0 - 1	Wolves
DIV 2	Sa 20Sep 1924	Wolves	0 - 4	Derby
1922/1923				
DIV 2	Sa 02Sep 1922	Derby	1 - 1	Wolves
DIV 2	Sa 26Aug 1922	Wolves	0 - 1	Derby
1921/1922				
DIV 2	Sa 15Oct 1921	Wolves	0 - 3	Derby
DIV 2	Sa 08Oct 1921	Derby	2 - 3	Wolves
1920/1921				
FA CUP	Th 03Feb 1921	Wolves	1 - 0	Derby
FA CUP	Sa 29Jan 1921	Derby	1 - 1	Wolves
1914/1915				
DIV 2	Sa 16Jan 1915	Wolves	0 - 1	Derby
DIV 2	Sa 12Sep 1914	Derby	3 - 1	Wolves
1911/1912				
DIV 2	Sa 06Apr 1912	Derby	1 - 1	Wolves
DIV 2	Sa 02Dec 1911	Wolves	0 - 1	Derby
1910/1911				
DIV 2	Tu 27Dec 1910	Derby	2 - 0	Wolves
DIV 2	Mo 05Sep 1910	Wolves	1 - 2	Derby
1909/1910				
DIV 2	Sa 29Jan 1910	Wolves	2 - 3	Derby
DIV 2	Sa 18Sep 1909	Derby	5 - 0	Wolves
1908/1909				
DIV 2	Fr 25Dec 1908	Wolves	1 - 1	Derby
DIV 2	We 16Sep 1908	Derby	2 - 1	Wolves
1907/1908				
DIV 2	We 08Apr 1908	Derby	3 - 2	Wolves
DIV 2	Sa 26Oct 1907	Wolves	2 - 2	Derby
1905/1906				
DIV 1	Sa 21Apr 1906	Wolves	7 - 0	Derby
DIV 1	Sa 16Dec 1905	Derby	2 - 0	Wolves
1904/1905				
DIV 1	Sa 28Jan 1905	Derby	2 - 1	Wolves
DIV 1	Sa 01Oct 1904	Wolves	2 - 0	Derby
1903/1904				
FA CUP	Mo 29Feb 1904	Derby	1 - 0	Wolves
FA CUP	We 24Feb 1904	Wolves	2 - 2	Derby
FA CUP	Sa 20Feb 1904	Derby	2 - 2	Wolves
DIV 1	Sa 02Jan 1904	Wolves	2 - 2	Derby
DIV 1	Sa 05Sep 1903	Derby	2 - 1	Wolves
1902/1903				
DIV 1	Sa 08Nov 1902	Derby	3 - 1	Wolves
DIV 1	Mo 01Sep 1902	Wolves	3 - 0	Derby
1901/1902				
DIV 1	We 25Dec 1901	Derby	3 - 1	Wolves

DIV 1	Sa 28Sep 1901	Wolves	0 - 0	Derby
1900/1901				
DIV 1	Sa 19Jan 1901	Wolves	0 - 0	Derby
DIV 1	Sa 22Sep 1900	Derby	4 - 5	Wolves
1899/1900				
DIV 1	Sa 21Apr 1900	Wolves	3 - 0	Derby
DIV 1	Sa 16Dec 1899	Derby	0 - 2	Wolves
1898/1899				
FA CUP	Sa 11Feb 1899	Derby	2 - 1	Wolves
DIV 1	Sa 04Feb 1899	Derby	6 - 2	Wolves
DIV 1	Sa 08Oct 1898	Wolves	2 - 2	Derby
1897/1898				
FA CUP	Sa 12Feb 1898	Wolves	0 - 1	Derby
DIV 1	Sa 08Jan 1898	Derby	3 - 2	Wolves
DIV 1	Sa 04Dec 1897	Wolves	2 - 0	Derby
1896/1897				
DIV 1	Sa 19Sep 1896	Derby	4 - 3	Wolves
DIV 1	Tu 01Sep 1896	Wolves	1 - 0	Derby
1895/1896				
FA CUP	Sa 21Mar 1896	Wolves	2 - 1	Derby
DIV 1	Sa 16Nov 1895	Wolves	2 - 0	Derby
DIV 1	Sa 26Oct 1895	Derby	5 - 2	Wolves
1894/1895				
DIV 1	Sa 26Jan 1895	Derby	1 - 3	Wolves
DIV 1	Sa 08Dec 1894	Wolves	2 - 2	Derby
1893/1894				
DIV 1	Sa 03Feb 1894	Derby	4 - 1	Wolves
DIV 1	Sa 20Jan 1894	Wolves	2 - 4	Derby
1892/1893				
DIV 1	Sa 25Feb 1893	Wolves	2 - 1	Derby
DIV 1	Sa 26Nov 1892	Derby	2 - 2	Wolves
1891/1892				
DIV 1	Sa 31Oct 1891	Derby	2 - 1	Wolves
DIV 1	Sa 26Sep 1891	Wolves	1 - 3	Derby
1890/1891				
DIV 1	Sa 10Jan 1891	Derby	9 - 0	Wolves
DIV 1	Sa 11Oct 1890	Wolves	5 - 1	Derby
1889/1890				
DIV 1	Sa 25Jan 1890	Wolves	2 - 1	Derby
DIV 1	Sa 23Nov 1889	Derby	3 - 3	Wolves
1888/1889				
DIV 1	Sa 12Jan 1889	Derby	3 - 0	Wolves
DIV 1	Sa 03Nov 1888	Wolves	4 - 1	Derby

NOTT'M FOREST V NOTTS CO

	FOREST WINS	DRAWS	COUNTY WINS
League Cup	1	1	0
League	35	23	28
FA Cup	3	1	2
Total	39	25	30

2011/2012

CARLING CUP Tu 09Aug 2011

Nottm Forest 3 - 3 Notts Co

1993/1994		
FL DIV 1	Sa 12Feb 1994	Notts Co 2 - 1 Nottm Forest
FL DIV 1	Sa 30Oct 1993	Nottm Forest 1 - 0 Notts Co
1991/1992		
DIV 1	Sa 11Jan 1992	Nottm Forest 1 - 1 Notts Co
DIV 1	Sa 24Aug 1991	Notts Co 0 - 4 Nottm Forest
1983/1984		
DIV 1	Sa 31Mar 1984	Notts Co 0 - 0 Nottm Forest
DIV 1	Su 16Oct 1983	Nottm Forest 3 - 1 Notts Co
1982/1983		
DIV 1	Sa 23Apr 1983	Nottm Forest 2 - 1 Notts Co
DIV 1	Sa 04Dec 1982	Notts Co 3 - 2 Nottm Forest
1981/1982		
DIV 1	Mo 12Apr 1982	Notts Co 1 - 2 Nottm Forest
DIV 1	Sa 23Jan 1982	Nottm Forest 0 - 2 Notts Co
1977/1978		
LC	Su 01Jan 1978	Nottm Forest 4 - 0 Notts Co
1976/1977		
DIV 2	Sa 09Apr 1977	Notts Co 1 - 1 Nottm Forest
DIV 2	Tu 08Mar 1977	Nottm Forest 1 - 2 Notts Co
1975/1976		
DIV 2	Tu 13Apr 1976	Notts Co 0 - 0 Nottm Forest
DIV 2	Sa 30Aug 1975	Nottm Forest 0 - 1 Notts Co
1974/1975		
DIV 2	Tu 25Mar 1975	Notts Co 2 - 2 Nottm Forest
DIV 2	Sa 28Dec 1974	Nottm Forest 0 - 2 Notts Co
1973/1974		
DIV 2	Su 03Mar 1974	Nottm Forest 0 - 0 Notts Co
DIV 2	We 26Dec 1973	Notts Co 0 - 1 Nottm Forest
1956/1957		
DIV 2	We 01May 1957	Nottm Forest 2 - 4 Notts Co
DIV 2	Sa 20Oct 1956	Notts Co 1 - 2 Nottm Forest
1955/1956		
DIV 2	Sa 11Feb 1956	Notts Co 1 - 3 Nottm Forest
DIV 2	Sa 01Oct 1955	Nottm Forest 0 - 2 Notts Co
1954/1955		
DIV 2	Sa 12Feb 1955	Notts Co 4 - 1 Nottm Forest
DIV 2	Sa 25Sep 1954	Nottm Forest 0 - 1 Notts Co
1953/1954		
DIV 2	Sa 27Feb 1954	Notts Co 1 - 1 Nottm Forest

DIV 2 Sa 10Oct 1953 Nottm Forest 5 - 0 Notts Co

1952/1953

DIV 2 Sa 03Jan 1953 Nottm Forest 1 - 0 Notts Co

DIV 2 Sa 30Aug 1952 Notts Co 3 - 2 Nottm Forest

1951/1952

DIV 2 Sa 19Jan 1952 Nottm Forest 3 - 2 Notts Co

DIV 2 Sa 15Sep 1951 Notts Co 2 - 2 Nottm Forest

1949/1950

DIV 3 (S) Sa 22Apr 1950 Notts Co 2 - 0 Nottm Forest

DIV 3 (S) Sa 03Dec 1949 Nottm Forest 1 - 2 Notts Co

1934/1935

DIV 2 Sa 09Feb 1935 Nottm Forest 2 - 3 Notts Co

DIV 2 Sa 29Sep 1934 Notts Co 3 - 5 Nottm Forest

1933/1934

DIV 2 Sa 17Feb 1934 Notts Co 1 - 0 Nottm Forest

DIV 2 Sa 07Oct 1933 Nottm Forest 2 - 0 Notts Co

1932/1933

DIV 2 Sa 18Feb 1933 Nottm Forest 3 - 0 Notts Co

DIV 2 Sa 08Oct 1932 Notts Co 2 - 4 Nottm Forest

1931/1932

DIV 2 Sa 13Feb 1932 Notts Co 2 - 6 Nottm Forest

DIV 2 Sa 03Oct 1931 Nottm Forest 2 - 1 Notts Co

1929/1930

DIV 2 Sa 04Jan 1930 Notts Co 0 - 0 Nottm Forest

DIV 2 Sa 07Sep 1929 Nottm Forest 1 - 1 Notts Co

1928/1929

DIV 2 Sa 02Mar 1929 Nottm Forest 1 - 2 Notts Co

DIV 2 Sa 20Oct 1928 Notts Co 1 - 1 Nottm Forest

1927/1928

DIV 2 We 22Feb 1928 Notts Co 1 - 2 Nottm Forest

DIV 2 Sa 17Sep 1927 Nottm Forest 2 - 1 Notts Co

1926/1927

DIV 2 Sa 05Feb 1927 Nottm Forest 2 - 0 Notts Co

DIV 2 Sa 18Sep 1926 Notts Co 1 - 2 Nottm Forest

1924/1925

DIV 1 Sa 24Jan 1925 Nottm Forest 0 - 0 Notts Co

DIV 1 Sa 20Sep 1924 Notts Co 0 - 0 Nottm Forest

1923/1924

DIV 1 Sa 29Sep 1923 Nottm Forest 1 - 0 Notts Co

DIV 1 Sa 22Sep 1923 Notts Co 2 - 1 Nottm Forest

1921/1922

DIV 2 Mo 14Nov 1921 Nottm Forest 0 - 0 Notts Co

DIV 2 Sa 05Nov 1921 Notts Co 1 - 1 Nottm Forest

1920/1921

DIV 2 Sa 18Sep 1920 Notts Co 2 - 0 Nottm Forest

DIV 2 Sa 11Sep 1920 Nottm Forest 1 - 0 Notts Co

1913/1914

DIV 2 Fr 26Dec 1913 Nottm Forest 1 - 0 Notts Co

DIV 2 Th 25Dec 1913 Notts Co 2 - 2 Nottm Forest

1910/1911

DIV 1 Sa 31Dec 1910 Nottm Forest 0 - 2 Notts Co

DIV 1 Sa 03Sep 1910 Notts Co 1 - 1 Nottm Forest

1909/1910

DIV 1 Sa 08Jan 1910 Notts Co 4 - 1 Nottm Forest

DIV 1 Sa 04Sep 1909 Nottm Forest 2 - 1 Notts Co

1908/1909

DIV 1 Sa 27Mar 1909 Nottm Forest 1 - 0 Notts Co

DIV 1 Sa 21Nov 1908 Notts Co 3 - 0 Nottm Forest

1907/1908

DIV 1 Sa 04Apr 1908 Notts Co 2 - 0 Nottm Forest

DIV 1 Sa 07Dec 1907 Nottm Forest 2 - 0 Notts Co

1905/1906

DIV 1 Mo 25Dec 1905 Nottm Forest 1 - 2 Notts Co

DIV 1 Sa 04Nov 1905 Notts Co 1 - 1 Nottm Forest

1904/1905

DIV 1 Sa 25Mar 1905 Notts Co 1 - 2 Nottm Forest

DIV 1 Sa 26Nov 1904 Nottm Forest 2 - 1 Notts Co

1903/1904

DIV 1 Fr 25Dec 1903 Nottm Forest 0 - 1 Notts Co

DIV 1 Sa 28Nov 1903 Notts Co 1 - 3 Nottm Forest

1902/1903

DIV 1 Fr 26Dec 1902 Notts Co 1 - 1 Nottm Forest

DIV 1 Sa 15Nov 1902 Nottm Forest 0 - 0 Notts Co

1901/1902

DIV 1 Th 26Dec 1901 Nottm Forest 1 - 0 Notts Co

DIV 1 Sa 16Nov 1901 Notts Co 3 - 0 Nottm Forest

1900/1901

DIV 1 We 26Dec 1900 Notts Co 1 - 0 Nottm Forest

DIV 1 Sa 24Nov 1900 Nottm Forest 5 - 0 Notts Co

1899/1900

DIV 1 Sa 17Mar 1900 Nottm Forest 0 - 3 Notts Co

DIV 1 Sa 11Nov 1899 Notts Co 1 - 2 Nottm Forest

1898/1899

DIV 1 Sa 04Feb 1899 Nottm Forest 0 - 0 Notts Co

DIV 1 Sa 08Oct 1898 Notts Co 2 - 2 Nottm Forest

1897/1898

DIV 1 Sa 09Oct 1897 Notts Co 1 - 3 Nottm Forest

DIV 1 Sa 04Sep 1897 Nottm Forest 1 - 1 Notts Co

1893/1894

FA CUP Sa 03Mar 1894 Notts Co 4 - 1 Nottm Forest

FA CUP Sa 24Feb 1894 Nottm Forest 1 - 1 Notts Co

1892/1893

DIV 1 Sa 25Feb 1893 Nottm Forest 3 - 1 Notts Co

DIV 1 Sa 08Oct 1892 Notts Co 3 - 0 Nottm Forest

1887/1888

FA CUP Sa 26Nov 1887 Nottm Forest 2 - 1 Notts Co

1883/1884

FA CUP Sa 01Dec 1883 Notts Co 3 - 0 Nottm Forest

1879/1880

FA CUP Sa 08Nov 1879 Nottm Forest 4 - 0 Notts Co
1878/1879
FA CUP Sa 16Nov 1878 Notts Co 1 - 3 Nottm Forest

LEICESTER V NOTTM FOREST

	LEICESTER WINS	DRAWS	NOTTM FOREST WINS
League	37	21	35
League Cup	1	1	1
FA Cup	0	0	1
Total	38	22	37

2011/2012
CHAMP Sa 20Aug 2011 Forest 2 - 2 Leicester
2010/2011
CHAMP Fr 22Apr 2011 Forest 3 - 2 Leicester
CHAMP Mo 29Nov 2010 Leicester 1 - 0 Forest
2009/2010
CHAMP Sa 27Feb 2010 Leicester 3 - 0 Forest
CHAMP Sa 05Dec 2009 Forest 5 - 1 Leicester
2007/2008
LC Tu 18Sep 2007 Forest 2 - 3 Leicester
2004/2005
CHAMP Sa 05Mar 2005 Leicester 0 - 1 Forest
CHAMP Fr 17Dec 2004 Forest 1 - 1 Leicester
2002/2003
FL DIV 1 Tu 08Apr 2003 Leicester 1 - 0 Forest
FL DIV 1 Sa 26Oct 2002 Forest 2 - 2 Leicester
1998/1999
FAPL Su 16May 1999 Forest 1 - 0 Leicester
FAPL Sa 12Dec 1998 Leicester 3 - 1 Forest
1996/1997
FAPL Sa 28Dec 1996 Leicester 2 - 2 Forest
FAPL Sa 07Sep 1996 Forest 0 - 0 Leicester
1994/1995
FAPL Sa 11Mar 1995 Leicester 2 - 4 Forest
FAPL Sa 27Aug 1994 Forest 1 - 0 Leicester
1993/1994
FL DIV 1 Su 06Feb 1994 Forest 4 - 0 Leicester
FL DIV 1 Su 24Oct 1993 Leicester 1 - 0 Forest
1988/1989
LC We 14Dec 1988 Forest 2 - 1 Leicester
LC We 30Nov 1988 Leicester 0 - 0 Forest
1986/1987
DIV 1 Su 22Mar 1987 Forest 2 - 1 Leicester
DIV 1 Sa 11Oct 1986 Leicester 3 - 1 Forest
1985/1986
DIV 1 Sa 22Mar 1986 Forest 4 - 3 Leicester
DIV 1 Su 08Sep 1985 Leicester 0 - 3 Forest
1984/1985
DIV 1 Sa 27Apr 1985 Leicester 1 - 0 Forest
DIV 1 Su 25Nov 1984 Forest 2 - 1 Leicester
1983/1984
DIV 1 Sa 05May 1984 Leicester 2 - 1 Forest
DIV 1 Su 04Dec 1983 Forest 3 - 2 Leicester
1980/1981
DIV 1 Sa 28Feb 1981 Leicester 1 - 1 Forest
DIV 1 Sa 20Sep 1980 Forest 5 - 0 Leicester
1977/1978
DIV 1 Tu 14Mar 1978 Forest 1 - 0 Leicester
DIV 1 Sa 24Sep 1977 Leicester 0 - 3 Forest
1971/1972
DIV 1 Sa 22Jan 1972 Forest 1 - 2 Leicester
DIV 1 We 18Aug 1971 Leicester 2 - 1 Forest
1968/1969
DIV 1 Sa 18Jan 1969 Forest 0 - 0 Leicester
DIV 1 Sa 09Nov 1968 Leicester 2 - 2 Forest
1967/1968
DIV 1 Sa 04May 1968 Leicester 4 - 2 Forest
DIV 1 Tu 19Mar 1968 Forest 2 - 1 Leicester
1966/1967
DIV 1 Sa 25Feb 1967 Forest 1 - 0 Leicester
DIV 1 Sa 08Oct 1966 Leicester 3 - 0 Forest
1965/1966
DIV 1 Sa 30Apr 1966 Leicester 2 - 1 Forest
DIV 1 Sa 04Dec 1965 Forest 2 - 0 Leicester
1964/1965
DIV 1 Sa 27Feb 1965 Forest 2 - 1 Leicester
DIV 1 Sa 17Oct 1964 Leicester 3 - 2 Forest
1963/1964
DIV 1 Sa 29Feb 1964 Leicester 1 - 1 Forest
DIV 1 Tu 08Oct 1963 Forest 2 - 0 Leicester
1962/1963
DIV 1 Tu 19Feb 1963 Forest 0 - 2 Leicester
DIV 1 Sa 25Aug 1962 Leicester 2 - 1 Forest
1961/1962
DIV 1 Sa 28Apr 1962 Leicester 2 - 1 Forest
DIV 1 Sa 09Dec 1961 Forest 0 - 0 Leicester
1960/1961
DIV 1 Sa 22Apr 1961 Forest 2 - 2 Leicester
DIV 1 Sa 03Dec 1960 Leicester 1 - 1 Forest
1959/1960
DIV 1 Sa 02Apr 1960 Leicester 0 - 1 Forest
DIV 1 Sa 14Nov 1959 Forest 1 - 0 Leicester
1958/1959
DIV 1 Sa 18Apr 1959 Forest 1 - 4 Leicester
DIV 1 Sa 29Nov 1958 Leicester 0 - 3 Forest
1957/1958
DIV 1 Sa 01Mar 1958 Forest 3 - 1 Leicester

DIV 1 Sa 19Oct 1957 Leicester 3 - 1 Forest
1956/1957
DIV 2 Sa 30Mar 1957 Forest 1 - 2 Leicester
DIV 2 Sa 17Nov 1956 Leicester 0 - 0 Forest
1955/1956
DIV 2 We 31Aug 1955 Forest 2 - 0 Leicester
DIV 2 Mo 22Aug 1955 Leicester 5 - 2 Forest
1953/1954
DIV 2 Sa 23Jan 1954 Forest 3 - 1 Leicester
DIV 2 Sa 12Sep 1953 Leicester 1 - 0 Forest
1952/1953
DIV 2 Sa 28Feb 1953 Leicester 1 - 1 Forest
DIV 2 Sa 11Oct 1952 Forest 1 - 3 Leicester
1951/1952
DIV 2 Sa 05Jan 1952 Leicester 3 - 1 Forest
DIV 2 Sa 08Sep 1951 Forest 2 - 2 Leicester
1948/1949
DIV 2 Sa 09Apr 1949 Forest 2 - 1 Leicester
DIV 2 Sa 13Nov 1948 Leicester 4 - 2 Forest
1947/1948
DIV 2 Sa 28Feb 1948 Forest 1 - 0 Leicester
DIV 2 Sa 11Oct 1947 Leicester 3 - 1 Forest
1946/1947
DIV 2 Sa 01Mar 1947 Leicester 1 - 1 Forest
DIV 2 Sa 26Oct 1946 Forest 2 - 0 Leicester
1936/1937
DIV 2 Sa 24Apr 1937 Leicester 2 - 1 Forest
DIV 2 Sa 19Dec 1936 Forest 0 - 3 Leicester
1935/1936
DIV 2 Th 30Jan 1936 Forest 0 - 1 Leicester
DIV 2 Sa 21Sep 1935 Leicester 2 - 1 Forest
1921/1922
DIV 2 Sa 15Oct 1921 Forest 0 - 0 Leicester
DIV 2 Sa 08Oct 1921 Leicester 2 - 2 Forest
1920/1921
DIV 2 Sa 19Feb 1921 Leicester 2 - 0 Forest
DIV 2 Sa 12Feb 1921 Forest 1 - 2 Leicester
1919/1920
DIV 2 Sa 13Mar 1920 Leicester 0 - 0 Forest
DIV 2 Sa 06Mar 1920 Forest 0 - 0 Leicester
1914/1915
DIV 2 Sa 20Feb 1915 Forest 1 - 3 Leicester
DIV 2 Sa 17Oct 1914 Leicester 3 - 1 Forest
1913/1914
DIV 2 Th 11Sep 1913 Leicester 5 - 1 Forest
DIV 2 We 03Sep 1913 Forest 1 - 3 Leicester
1912/1913
DIV 2 Sa 28Dec 1912 Forest 4 - 2 Leicester
DIV 2 Sa 07Sep 1912 Leicester 3 - 1 Forest
1911/1912
DIV 2 Th 29Feb 1912 Leicester 1 - 1 Forest
DIV 2 Sa 16Sep 1911 Forest 4 - 1 Leicester
1908/1909
DIV 1 We 21Apr 1909 Forest 12 - 0 Leicester
DIV 1 Sa 07Nov 1908 Leicester 0 - 3 Forest
1906/1907
DIV 2 Sa 20Apr 1907 Leicester 1 - 2 Forest
DIV 2 Sa 15Dec 1906 Forest 2 - 1 Leicester
1900/1901
FA CUP Sa 09Feb 1901 Forest 5 - 1 Leicester

LEICESTER V STOKE

	LEICESTER WINS	DRAWS	STOKE WINS
League	26	25	27
Cup	1	1	0
League Cup	1	1	0
FA Cup	3	4	2
Total	31	31	29

2007/2008
CHAMP Su 04May 2008 Stoke 0 - 0 Leicester
CHAMP Sa 29Sep 2007 Leicester 1 - 1 Stoke
2006/2007
CHAMP Sa 31Mar 2007 Stoke 4 - 2 Leicester
CHAMP Tu 31Oct 2006 Leicester 2 - 1 Stoke
2005/2006
CHAMP Fr 09Dec 2005 Stoke 3 - 2 Leicester
CHAMP Tu 09Aug 2005 Leicester 4 - 2 Stoke
2004/2005
CHAMP Tu 22Feb 2005 Stoke 3 - 2 Leicester
CHAMP Sa 23Oct 2004 Leicester 1 - 1 Stoke
2002/2003
FL DIV 1 Sa 11Jan 2003 Leicester 0 - 0 Stoke
FL DIV 1 We 14Aug 2002 Stoke 0 - 1 Leicester
1995/1996
PLAY-OFF We 15May 1996 Stoke 0 - 1 Leicester
PLAY-OFF Su 12May 1996 Leicester 0 - 0 Stoke
FL DIV 1 Sa 13Jan 1996 Stoke 1 - 0 Leicester
FL DIV 1 Sa 19Aug 1995 Leicester 2 - 3 Stoke
1993/1994
FL DIV 1 Sa 30Apr 1994 Leicester 1 - 1 Stoke
FL DIV 1 Su 14Nov 1993 Stoke 1 - 0 Leicester
1989/1990
DIV 2 Sa 24Feb 1990 Leicester 2 - 1 Stoke
DIV 2 Sa 25Nov 1989 Stoke 0 - 1 Leicester
1988/1989
DIV 2 Sa 25Feb 1989 Stoke 2 - 2 Leicester
DIV 2 Sa 15Oct 1988 Leicester 2 - 0 Stoke
1987/1988
DIV 2 We 16Mar 1988 Leicester 1 - 1 Stoke
DIV 2 Mo 31Aug 1987 Stoke 2 - 1 Leicester

1984/1985

DIV 1	Sa 12Jan 1985	Leicester	0 - 0	Stoke
DIV 1	Sa 15Sep 1984	Stoke	2 - 2	Leicester

1983/1984

DIV 1	Mo 02Jan 1984	Stoke	0 - 1	Leicester
DIV 1	Sa 24Sep 1983	Leicester	2 - 2	Stoke

1980/1981

DIV 1	Sa 20Dec 1980	Stoke	1 - 0	Leicester
DIV 1	We 08Oct 1980	Leicester	1 - 1	Stoke

1978/1979

DIV 2	Sa 07Apr 1979	Leicester	1 - 1	Stoke
DIV 2	Sa 02Dec 1978	Stoke	0 - 0	Leicester

1976/1977

DIV 1	Sa 19Mar 1977	Stoke	0 - 1	Leicester
DIV 1	We 29Sep 1976	Leicester	1 - 0	Stoke

1975/1976

DIV 1	Sa 07Feb 1976	Stoke	1 - 2	Leicester
DIV 1	We 27Aug 1975	Leicester	1 - 1	Stoke

1974/1975

DIV 1	Sa 18Jan 1975	Leicester	1 - 1	Stoke
DIV 1	Sa 30Nov 1974	Stoke	1 - 0	Leicester

1973/1974

DIV 1	Tu 16Apr 1974	Leicester	1 - 1	Stoke
DIV 1	Mo 15Apr 1974	Stoke	1 - 0	Leicester

1972/1973

DIV 1	Sa 24Mar 1973	Leicester	2 - 0	Stoke
DIV 1	Sa 28Oct 1972	Stoke	1 - 0	Leicester

1971/1972

DIV 1	Sa 29Jan 1972	Leicester	2 - 1	Stoke
DIV 1	We 25Aug 1971	Stoke	3 - 1	Leicester

1968/1969

DIV 1	Sa 15Mar 1969	Leicester	0 - 0	Stoke
DIV 1	Sa 24Aug 1968	Stoke	1 - 0	Leicester

1967/1968

DIV 1	Sa 11May 1968	Leicester	0 - 0	Stoke
DIV 1	We 06Sep 1967	Stoke	3 - 2	Leicester

1966/1967

DIV 1	Sa 29Apr 1967	Stoke	3 - 1	Leicester
DIV 1	Sa 03Dec 1966	Leicester	4 - 2	Stoke

1965/1966

DIV 1	Sa 01Jan 1966	Leicester	1 - 0	Stoke
DIV 1	Sa 09Oct 1965	Stoke	1 - 0	Leicester

1964/1965

DIV 1	Mo 26Apr 1965	Leicester	0 - 1	Stoke
DIV 1	Sa 24Oct 1964	Stoke	3 - 3	Leicester

1963/1964

LC	We 22Apr 1964	Leicester	3 - 2	Stoke
LC	We 15Apr 1964	Stoke	1 - 1	Leicester
DIV 1	Sa 11Jan 1964	Leicester	2 - 1	Stoke
DIV 1	Sa 07Sep 1963	Stoke	3 - 3	Leicester

1961/1962

FA CUP	Mo 15Jan 1962	Stoke	5 - 2	Leicester
FA CUP	We 10Jan 1962	Leicester	1 - 1	Stoke

1956/1957

DIV 2	Sa 22Dec 1956	Leicester	3 - 2	Stoke
DIV 2	Sa 25Aug 1956	Stoke	3 - 1	Leicester

1955/1956

DIV 2	Sa 11Feb 1956	Stoke	2 - 0	Leicester
FA CUP	Mo 30Jan 1956	Stoke	2 - 1	Leicester
FA CUP	Sa 28Jan 1956	Leicester	3 - 3	Stoke
DIV 2	Sa 01Oct 1955	Leicester	3 - 1	Stoke

1953/1954

FA CUP	Tu 02Feb 1954	Leicester	3 - 1	Stoke
FA CUP	Sa 30Jan 1954	Stoke	0 - 0	Leicester
DIV 2	Mo 14Sep 1953	Stoke	2 - 2	Leicester
DIV 2	Mo 07Sep 1953	Leicester	4 - 0	Stoke

1938/1939

FA CUP	We 11Jan 1939	Leicester	2 - 1	Stoke
FA CUP	Sa 07Jan 1939	Stoke	1 - 1	Leicester
DIV 1	Sa 24Dec 1938	Stoke	1 - 0	Leicester
DIV 1	Sa 27Aug 1938	Leicester	2 - 2	Stoke

1937/1938

DIV 1	Sa 23Apr 1938	Stoke	1 - 2	Leicester
DIV 1	Sa 11Dec 1937	Leicester	2 - 0	Stoke

1934/1935

DIV 1	Sa 23Mar 1935	Stoke	3 - 0	Leicester
DIV 1	Sa 10Nov 1934	Leicester	0 - 3	Stoke

1933/1934

DIV 1	Tu 26Dec 1933	Leicester	3 - 1	Stoke
DIV 1	Mo 25Dec 1933	Stoke	2 - 1	Leicester

1924/1925

DIV 2	Sa 17Jan 1925	Stoke	1 - 1	Leicester
FA CUP	Sa 10Jan 1925	Leicester	3 - 0	Stoke
DIV 2	Sa 13Sep 1924	Leicester	0 - 1	Stoke

1923/1924

DIV 2	Mo 03Sep 1923	Stoke	1 - 0	Leicester
DIV 2	Mo 27Aug 1923	Leicester	5 - 0	Stoke

1921/1922

DIV 2	Sa 11Feb 1922	Leicester	3 - 4	Stoke
DIV 2	Sa 04Feb 1922	Stoke	1 - 1	Leicester

1920/1921

DIV 2	Mo 27Dec 1920	Stoke	1 - 1	Leicester
DIV 2	Sa 25Dec 1920	Leicester	3 - 1	Stoke

1919/1920

DIV 2	Sa 27Dec 1919	Stoke	3 - 0	Leicester
DIV 2	Sa 20Dec 1919	Leicester	3 - 1	Stoke

1907/1908

DIV 2	Mo 27Apr 1908	Stoke	0 - 1	Leicester
DIV 2	Sa 26Oct 1907	Leicester	1 - 0	Stoke

LEICESTER V WALSALL

	LEICESTER WINS	DRAWS	WALSALL WINS
League	12	4	2
FA Cup	0	0	1
Total	12	4	3

2008/2009

FL DIV 1 Tu 03Feb 2009 Walsall 1 - 4 Leicester
FL DIV 1 Tu 21Oct 2008 Leicester 2 - 2 WalsalL

2002/2003

FL DIV 1 Sa 08Feb 2003 Walsall 1 - 4 Leicester
FL DIV 1 Sa 09Nov 2002 Leicester 2 - 0 Walsall

1988/1989

DIV 2 Sa 04Mar 1989 Leicester 1 - 0 Walsall
DIV 2 Sa 12Nov 1988 Walsall 0 - 1 Leicester

1977/1978

FA CUP Su 01Jan 1978 Walsall 1 - 0 Leicester

1900/1901

DIV 2 Sa 30Mar 1901 Leicester 5 - 0 Walsall
DIV 2 Sa 24Nov 1900 Walsall 2 - 0 Leicester

1899/1900

DIV 2 We 27Dec 1899 Leicester 2 - 1 Walsall
DIV 2 Mo 25Sep 1899 Walsall 1 - 2 Leicester

1898/1899

DIV 2 Sa 25Feb 1899 Leicester 2 - 2 Walsal
IDIV 2 Mo 26Sep 1898 Walsall 1 - 1 Leicester

1897/1898

DIV 2 Sa 26Feb 1898 Walsall 2 - 1 Leicester
DIV 2 Sa 16Oct 1897 Leicester 3 - 1 Walsall

1896/1897

DIV 2 Sa 20Mar 1897 Walsall 1 - 1 Leicester
DIV 2 Sa 28Nov 1896 Leicester 4 - 2 Walsall

1894/1895

DIV 2 Sa 05Jan 1895 Leicester 9 - 1 Walsall
DIV 2 Sa 08Dec 1894 Walsall 1 - 3 Leicester

LEICESTER V WEST BROM

	LEICESTER WINS	DRAWS	WEST BROM WINS
League Cup	0	1	4
League	30	20	44
FA Cup	2	0	1
Total	32	21	49

2010/2011

LC Tu 26Oct 2010 Leicester 1 - 4 West Brom

2009/2010

CHAMP Fr 02Apr 2010 West Brom 3 - 0 Leicester
CHAMP Sa 07Nov 2009 Leicester 1 - 2 West Brom

2007/2008

CHAMP Sa 15Mar 2008 West Brom 1 - 4 Leicester
CHAMP Sa 08Dec 2007 Leicester 1 - 2 West Brom

2006/2007

CHAMP Sa 24Feb 2007 Leicester 1 - 1 West Brom
CHAMP Sa 09Sep 2006 West Brom 2 - 0 Leicester

2001/2002

FA CUP Sa 26Jan 2002 West Brom 1 - 0 Leicester

1995/1996

FL DIV 1 Tu 09Apr 1996 Leicester 1 - 2 West Brom
FL DIV 1 Su 05Nov 1995 West Brom 2 - 3 Leicester

1993/1994

FL DIV 1 Sa 19Feb 1994 West Brom 1 - 2 Leicester
FL DIV 1 We 12Jan 1994 Leicester 4 - 2 West Brom

1990/1991

DIV 2 Sa 13Apr 1991 West Brom 2 - 1 Leicester
DIV 2 Tu 01Jan 1991 Leicester 2 - 1 West Brom

1989/1990

DIV 2 We 21Feb 1990 West Brom 0 - 1 Leicester
DIV 2 Sa 09Sep 1989 Leicester 1 - 3 West Brom

1988/1989

DIV 2 Sa 21Jan 1989 West Brom 1 - 1 Leicester
DIV 2 Sa 27Aug 1988 Leicester 1 - 1 West Brom

1987/1988

DIV 2 Sa 09Apr 1988 West Brom 1 - 1 Leicester
DIV 2 We 21Oct 1987 Leicester 3 - 0 West Brom

1985/1986

DIV 1 Sa 15Mar 1986 West Brom 2 - 2 Leicester
DIV 1 Sa 12Oct 1985 Leicester 2 - 2 West Brom

1984/1985

DIV 1 Sa 30Mar 1985 West Brom 2 - 0 Leicester
DIV 1 Sa 22Sep 1984 Leicester 2 - 1 West Brom

1983/1984

DIV 1 Sa 31Dec 1983 Leicester 1 - 1 West Brom
DIV 1 Sa 03Sep 1983 West Brom 1 - 0 Leicester

1980/1981

DIV 1 Sa 10Jan 1981 Leicester 0 - 2 West Brom
LC Th 01Jan 1981 West Brom 1 - 0 Leicester
LC Th 01Jan 1981 Leicester 0 - 1 West Brom
DIV 1 Sa 22Nov 1980 West Brom 3 - 1 Leicester

1977/1978

DIV 1 Sa 01Apr 1978 Leicester 0 - 1 West Brom
DIV 1 Sa 05Nov 1977 West Brom 2 - 0 Leicester

1976/1977

DIV 1 Sa 07May 1977 Leicester 0 - 5 West Brom
DIV 1 Sa 11Dec 1976 West Brom 2 - 2 Leicester

1972/1973

DIV 1 Sa 07Apr 1973 West Brom 1 - 0 Leicester
DIV 1 Sa 02Dec 1972 Leicester 3 - 1 West Brom

1971/1972

DIV 1 Sa 12Feb 1972 Leicester 0 - 1 West Brom
DIV 1 Sa 23Oct 1971 West Brom 0 - 1 Leicester

1969/1970

LC Th 01Jan 1970 Leicester 0 - 0 West Brom

LC	Th 01Jan 1970	West Brom	2 - 1	Leicester
1968/1969				
FA CUP	Sa 29Mar 1969	Leicester	1 - 0	West Brom
DIV 1	Sa 14Dec 1968	West Brom	1 - 1	Leicester
DIV 1	Sa 12Oct 1968	Leicester	0 - 2	West Brom
1967/1968				
DIV 1	Sa 23Mar 1968	Leicester	2 - 3	West Brom
DIV 1	Sa 28Oct 1967	West Brom	0 - 0	Leicester
1966/1967				
DIV 1	Sa 15Apr 1967	West Brom	1 - 0	Leicester
DIV 1	Sa 19Nov 1966	Leicester	2 - 1	West Brom
1965/1966				
DIV 1	Fr 22Apr 1966	West Brom	5 - 1	Leicester
DIV 1	Sa 27Nov 1965	Leicester	2 - 1	West Brom
1964/1965				
DIV 1	Sa 13Mar 1965	West Brom	6 - 0	Leicester
DIV 1	We 30Sep 1964	Leicester	4 - 2	West Brom
1963/1964				
DIV 1	Sa 14Dec 1963	Leicester	0 - 2	West Brom
DIV 1	Sa 24Aug 1963	West Brom	1 - 1	Leicester
1962/1963				
DIV 1	Sa 04May 1963	West Brom	2 - 1	Leicester
DIV 1	Sa 15Sep 1962	Leicester	1 - 0	West Brom
1961/1962				
DIV 1	Sa 23Dec 1961	West Brom	2 - 0	Leicester
DIV 1	Sa 26Aug 1961	Leicester	1 - 0	West Brom
1960/1961				
DIV 1	Sa 11Mar 1961	West Brom	1 - 0	Leicester
DIV 1	Sa 22Oct 1960	Leicester	2 - 2	West Brom
1959/1960				
FA CUP	Sa 20Feb 1960	Leicester	2 - 1	West Brom
DIV 1	Sa 16Jan 1960	Leicester	0 - 1	West Brom
DIV 1	Sa 05Sep 1959	West Brom	5 - 0	Leicester
1958/1959				
DIV 1	Sa 07Feb 1959	West Brom	2 - 2	Leicester
DIV 1	Sa 20Sep 1958	Leicester	2 - 2	West Brom
1957/1958				
DIV 1	Sa 12Apr 1958	West Brom	6 - 2	Leicester
DIV 1	Sa 30Nov 1957	Leicester	3 - 3	West Brom
1954/1955				
DIV 1	Sa 12Feb 1955	Leicester	6 - 3	West Brom
DIV 1	Sa 25Sep 1954	West Brom	6 - 4	Leicester
1948/1949				
DIV 2	Th 05May 1949	Leicester	0 - 3	West Brom
DIV 2	Sa 25Sep 1948	West Brom	2 - 1	Leicester
1947/1948				
DIV 2	Sa 14Feb 1948	West Brom	1 - 3	Leicester
DIV 2	Sa 27Sep 1947	Leicester	1 - 1	West Brom
1946/1947				
DIV 2	Sa 26Apr 1947	Leicester	1 - 1	West Brom
DIV 2	Sa 21Dec 1946	West Brom	4 - 2	Leicester
1937/1938				
DIV 1	Sa 26Feb 1938	West Brom	1 - 3	Leicester
DIV 1	Sa 16Oct 1937	Leicester	4 - 1	West Brom
1934/1935				
DIV 1	Sa 13Apr 1935	Leicester	0 - 0	West Brom
DIV 1	Sa 01Dec 1934	West Brom	4 - 1	Leicester
1933/1934				
DIV 1	Sa 21Apr 1934	West Brom	2 - 0	Leicester
DIV 1	Sa 09Dec 1933	Leicester	0 - 1	West Brom
1932/1933				
DIV 1	Sa 06May 1933	Leicester	6 - 2	West Brom
DIV 1	Sa 24Dec 1932	West Brom	4 - 3	Leicester
1931/1932				
DIV 1	Sa 16Apr 1932	West Brom	1 - 2	Leicester
DIV 1	Sa 05Dec 1931	Leicester	2 - 3	West Brom
1926/1927				
DIV 1	Mo 27Dec 1926	West Brom	0 - 1	Leicester
DIV 1	Sa 25Dec 1926	Leicester	5 - 0	West Brom
1925/1926				
DIV 1	Sa 27Feb 1926	West Brom	3 - 1	Leicester
DIV 1	Sa 17Oct 1925	Leicester	3 - 0	West Brom
1910/1911				
DIV 2	Sa 11Mar 1911	Leicester	2 - 3	West Brom
DIV 2	Sa 05Nov 1910	West Brom	5 - 1	Leicester
1909/1910				
DIV 2	Sa 26Mar 1910	Leicester	2 - 1	West Brom
DIV 2	Sa 13Nov 1909	West Brom	1 - 2	Leicester
1907/1908				
DIV 2	Sa 29Feb 1908	Leicester	3 - 0	West Brom
DIV 2	Sa 02Nov 1907	West Brom	1 - 1	Leicester
1906/1907				
DIV 2	Sa 06Apr 1907	West Brom	0 - 1	Leicester
DIV 2	Sa 01Dec 1906	Leicester	3 - 0	West Brom
1905/1906				
DIV 2	Sa 31Mar 1906	West Brom	3 - 0	Leicester
DIV 2	Sa 25Nov 1905	Leicester	0 - 0	West Brom
1904/1905				
DIV 2	Sa 08Apr 1905	West Brom	2 - 0	Leicester
DIV 2	Th 15Dec 1904	Leicester	3 - 1	West Brom
1901/1902				
DIV 2	Mo 06Jan 1902	West Brom	1 - 0	Leicester
DIV 2	Sa 28Dec 1901	Leicester	0 - 3	West Brom

LEICESTER V WOLVES

	LEICESTER WINS	DRAWS	WOLVES WINS
League	34	31	35
FA Cup	1	1	5
Total	35	32	40

2007/2008				
CHAMP	Sa 22Dec 2007	Wolves	1 - 1	Leicester
CHAMP	Tu 02Oct 2007	Leicester	0 - 0	Wolves
2006/2007				
CHAMP	Su 06May 2007	Leicester	1 - 4	Wolves
CHAMP	Sa 09Dec 2006	Wolves	1 - 2	Leicester
2005/2006				
CHAMP	Sa 04Feb 2006	Leicester	1 - 0	Wolves
CHAMP	Sa 17Sep 2005	Wolves	0 - 0	Leicester
2004/2005				
CHAMP	Tu 05Apr 2005	Leicester	1 - 1	Wolves
CHAMP	Sa 28Aug 2004	Wolves	1 - 1	Leicester
2003/2004				
FAPL	Sa 28Feb 2004	Leicester	0 - 0	Wolves
FAPL	Sa 25Oct 2003	Wolves	4 - 3	Leicester
2002/2003				
FL DIV 1	Su 04May 2003	Wolves	1 - 1	Leicester
FA CUP	Sa 25Jan 2003	Wolves	4 - 1	Leicester
FL DIV 1	Sa 28Sep 2002	Leicester	1 - 0	Wolves
1995/1996				
FL DIV 1	We 21Feb 1996	Wolves	2 - 3	Leicester
FL DIV 1	Sa 02Sep 1995	Leicester	1 - 0	Wolves
1994/1995				
FA CUP	Sa 18Feb 1995	Wolves	1 - 0	Leicester
1993/1994				
FL DIV 1	Su 08May 1994	Wolves	1 - 1	Leicester
FL DIV 1	Sa 27Nov 1993	Leicester	2 - 2	Wolves
1992/1993				
FL DIV 1	Su 13Sep 1992	Leicester	0 - 0	Wolves
FL DIV 1	Tu 18Aug 1992	Wolves	3 - 0	Leicester
1991/1992				
DIV 2	Sa 01Feb 1992	Wolves	1 - 0	Leicester
DIV 2	Sa 19Oct 1991	Leicester	3 - 0	Wolves
1990/1991				
DIV 2	Tu 05Mar 1991	Wolves	2 - 1	Leicester
DIV 2	Sa 17Nov 1990	Leicester	1 - 0	Wolves
1989/1990				
DIV 2	Tu 10Apr 1990	Wolves	5 - 0	Leicester
DIV 2	We 01Nov 1989	Leicester	0 - 0	Wolves
1983/1984				
DIV 1	Mo 07May 1984	Wolves	1 - 0	Leicester
DIV 1	Sa 10Dec 1983	Leicester	5 - 1	Wolves
1982/1983				
DIV 2	Sa 26Feb 1983	Leicester	5 - 0	Wolves
DIV 2	Sa 16Oct 1982	Wolves	0 - 3	Leicester
1980/1981				
DIV 1	Sa 28Mar 1981	Wolves	0 - 1	Leicester
DIV 1	Sa 25Oct 1980	Leicester	2 - 0	Wolves
1977/1978				
DIV 1	Sa 25Feb 1978	Leicester	1 - 0	Wolves
DIV 1	Sa 01Oct 1977	Wolves	3 - 0	Leicester
1975/1976				
DIV 1	Sa 27Mar 1976	Wolves	2 - 2	Leicester
DIV 1	Sa 06Dec 1975	Leicester	2 - 0	Wolves
1974/1975				
DIV 1	Sa 22Mar 1975	Leicester	3 - 2	Wolves
DIV 1	Sa 07Sep 1974	Wolves	1 - 1	Leicester
1973/1974				
DIV 1	Tu 23Apr 1974	Wolves	1 - 0	Leicester
DIV 1	We 26Dec 1973	Leicester	2 - 2	Wolves
1972/1973				
DIV 1	Tu 26Dec 1972	Wolves	2 - 0	Leicester
DIV 1	Sa 23Sep 1972	Leicester	1 - 1	Wolves
1971/1972				
DIV 1	Sa 01Apr 1972	Wolves	0 - 1	Leicester
FA CUP	Sa 01Jan 1972	Wolves	1 - 1	Leicester
FA CUP	Sa 01Jan 1972	Leicester	2 - 0	Wolves
DIV 1	Mo 27Dec 1971	Leicester	1 - 2	Wolves
1968/1969				
DIV 1	We 09Oct 1968	Leicester	2 - 0	Wolves
DIV 1	We 28Aug 1968	Wolves	1 - 0	Leicester
1967/1968				
DIV 1	Sa 13Jan 1968	Leicester	3 - 1	Wolves
DIV 1	Sa 09Sep 1967	Wolves	1 - 3	Leicester
1964/1965				
DIV 1	We 02Sep 1964	Wolves	1 - 1	Leicester
DIV 1	We 26Aug 1964	Leicester	3 - 2	Wolves
1963/1964				
DIV 1	Sa 22Feb 1964	Wolves	1 - 2	Leicester
DIV 1	Mo 14Oct 1963	Leicester	0 - 1	Wolves
1962/1963				
DIV 1	Sa 20Apr 1963	Leicester	1 - 1	Wolves
DIV 1	Sa 01Dec 1962	Wolves	1 - 3	Leicester
1961/1962				
DIV 1	Sa 24Mar 1962	Wolves	1 - 1	Leicester
DIV 1	Sa 04Nov 1961	Leicester	3 - 0	Wolves
1960/1961				
DIV 1	We 14Sep 1960	Leicester	2 - 0	Wolves
DIV 1	We 07Sep 1960	Wolves	3 - 2	Leicester
1959/1960				
DIV 1	Sa 19Mar 1960	Leicester	2 - 1	Wolves
FA CUP	Sa 12Mar 1960	Leicester	1 - 2	Wolves
DIV 1	Sa 12Dec 1959	Wolves	0 - 3	Leicester
1958/1959				
DIV 1	We 22Apr 1959	Wolves	3 - 0	Leicester

DIV 1 Sa 13Dec 1958 Leicester 1 - 0 Wolves
1957/1958
DIV 1 Sa 01Feb 1958 Wolves 5 - 1 Leicester
DIV 1 Sa 21Sep 1957 Leicester 2 - 3 Wolves
1954/1955
DIV 1 Sa 05Mar 1955 Wolves 5 - 0 Leicester
DIV 1 Sa 11Dec 1954 Leicester 1 - 2 Wolves
1948/1949
FA CUP Sa 30Apr 1949 Wolves 3 - 1 Leicester
1938/1939
DIV 1 Th 04May 1939 Leicester 0 - 2 Wolves
FA CUP Sa 21Jan 1939 Wolves 5 - 1 Leicester
DIV 1 Mo 29Aug 1938 Wolves 0 - 0 Leicester
1937/1938
DIV 1 Mo 18Apr 1938 Leicester 1 - 1 Wolves
DIV 1 Fr 15Apr 1938 Wolves 10 - 1 Leicester
1934/1935
DIV 1 Sa 29Dec 1934 Wolves 3 - 1 Leicester
DIV 1 Sa 25Aug 1934 Leicester 1 - 1 Wolves
1933/1934
DIV 1 Tu 03Apr 1934 Leicester 1 - 1 Wolves
DIV 1 Mo 02Apr 1934 Wolves 1 - 1 Leicester
1932/1933
DIV 1 Sa 07Jan 1933 Leicester 2 - 2 Wolves
DIV 1 Sa 03Sep 1932 Wolves 1 - 1 Leicester
1924/1925
DIV 2 Mo 30Mar 1925 Wolves 0 - 1 Leicester
DIV 2 Sa 01Nov 1924 Leicester 2 - 0 Wolves
1922/1923
DIV 2 Sa 10Mar 1923 Leicester 7 - 0 Wolves
DIV 2 Sa 03Mar 1923 Wolves 1 - 2 Leicester
1921/1922
DIV 2 Sa 29Oct 1921 Wolves 1 - 1 Leicester
DIV 2 Sa 22Oct 1921 Leicester 0 - 1 Wolves
1920/1921
DIV 2 Sa 30Apr 1921 Wolves 3 - 0 Leicester
DIV 2 Th 28Apr 1921 Leicester 0 - 0 Wolves
1919/1920
DIV 2 Sa 06Sep 1919 Wolves 1 - 1 Leicester
DIV 2 Sa 30Aug 1919 Leicester 1 - 2 Wolves
1914/1915
DIV 2 Sa 20Mar 1915 Leicester 0 - 3 Wolves
DIV 2 Sa 14Nov 1914 Wolves 7 - 0 Leicester
1913/1914
DIV 2 Sa 28Mar 1914 Leicester 2 - 3 Wolves
DIV 2 Sa 22Nov 1913 Wolves 2 - 1 Leicester
1912/1913
DIV 2 Sa 22Mar 1913 Wolves 1 - 1 Leicester
DIV 2 Sa 16Nov 1912 Leicester 0 - 1 Wolves
1911/1912
DIV 2 Tu 26Dec 1911 Wolves 1 - 0 Leicester
DIV 2 Mo 25Dec 1911 Leicester 1 - 1 Wolves
1910/1911
DIV 2 Sa 07Jan 1911 Leicester 2 - 3 Wolves
DIV 2 Sa 10Sep 1910 Wolves 1 - 0 Leicester
1909/1910
DIV 2 Tu 28Dec 1909 Wolves 4 - 1 Leicester
DIV 2 We 01Sep 1909 Leicester 2 - 1 Wolves
1907/1908
DIV 2 Sa 14Sep 1907 Wolves 0 - 0 Leicester
DIV 2 Mo 09Sep 1907 Leicester 1 - 0 Wolves
1906/1907
DIV 2 Sa 09Feb 1907 Wolves 1 - 0 Leicester
DIV 2 Sa 06Oct 1906 Leicester 2 - 0 Wolves

NOTTM FOREST V STOKE

	FOREST WINS	DRAWS	STOKE WINS
League	41	28	29
FA Cup	2	2	1
Total	43	30	30

2004/2005
CHAMP Sa 01Jan 2005 Forest 1 - 0 Stoke
CHAMP Sa 18Sep 2004 Stoke 0 - 0 Forest
2003/2004
FL DIV 1 Sa 10Apr 2004 Forest 0 - 0 Stoke
FL DIV 1 Sa 04Oct 2003 Stoke 2 - 1 Forest
2002/2003
FL DIV 1 Sa 22Feb 2003 Forest 6 - 0 Stoke
FL DIV 1 We 25Sep 2002 Stoke 2 - 2 Forest
1997/1998
FL DIV 1 Sa 21Feb 1998 Stoke 1 - 1 Forest
FL DIV 1 Sa 27Sep 1997 Forest 1 - 0 Stoke
1995/1996
FA CUP We 17Jan 1996 Forest 2 - 0 Stoke
FA CUP Sa 06Jan 1996 Stoke 1 - 1 Forest
1993/1994
FL DIV 1 Sa 12Mar 1994 Stoke 0 - 1 Forest
FL DIV 1 Su 19Sep 1993 Forest 2 - 3 Stoke
1984/1985
DIV 1 Sa 23Mar 1985 Stoke 1 - 4 Forest
DIV 1 Sa 06Oct 1984 Forest 1 - 1 Stoke
1983/1984
DIV 1 Sa 28Apr 1984 Forest 0 - 0 Stoke
DIV 1 Sa 26Nov 1983 Stoke 1 - 1 Forest
1982/1983
DIV 1 We 16Mar 1983 Stoke 1 - 0 Forest
DIV 1 Sa 02Oct 1982 Forest 1 - 0 Stoke
1981/1982
DIV 1 Sa 30Jan 1982 Forest 0 - 0 Stoke

DIV 1 Sa 19Sep 1981 Stoke 1 - 2 Forest

1980/1981

DIV 1 We 18Feb 1981 Stoke 1 - 2 Forest

DIV 1 Sa 30Aug 1980 Forest 5 - 0 Stoke

1979/1980

DIV 1 We 10Oct 1979 Stoke 1 - 1 Forest

DIV 1 We 22Aug 1979 Forest 1 - 0 Stoke

1971/1972

DIV 1 Mo 10Apr 1972 Stoke 0 - 2 Forest

DIV 1 Tu 31Aug 1971 Forest 0 - 0 Stoke

1970/1971

DIV 1 Tu 27Apr 1971 Forest 0 - 0 Stoke

DIV 1 We 02Sep 1970 Stoke 0 - 0 Forest

1969/1970

DIV 1 We 20Aug 1969 Stoke 1 - 1 Forest

DIV 1 Tu 12Aug 1969 Forest 0 - 0 Stoke

1968/1969

DIV 1 Th 26Dec 1968 Stoke 3 - 1 Forest

DIV 1 Sa 05Oct 1968 Forest 3 - 3 Stoke

1967/1968

DIV 1 Sa 30Dec 1967 Stoke 1 - 3 Forest

DIV 1 Tu 26Dec 1967 Forest 3 - 0 Stoke

1966/1967

DIV 1 Sa 17Dec 1966 Stoke 1 - 2 Forest

DIV 1 Sa 20Aug 1966 Forest 1 - 2 Stoke

1965/1966

DIV 1 Sa 19Mar 1966 Forest 4 - 3 Stoke

DIV 1 Sa 25Sep 1965 Stoke 1 - 0 Forest

1964/1965

DIV 1 Sa 13Feb 1965 Forest 3 - 1 Stoke

DIV 1 Sa 03Oct 1964 Stoke 1 - 1 Forest

1963/1964

DIV 1 Sa 18Jan 1964 Forest 0 - 0 Stoke

DIV 1 Sa 14Sep 1963 Stoke 0 - 1 Forest

1956/1957

DIV 2 Sa 16Mar 1957 Forest 4 - 0 Stoke

DIV 2 Sa 03Nov 1956 Stoke 2 - 1 Forest

1955/1956

DIV 2 Sa 31Dec 1955 Stoke 1 - 1 Forest

DIV 2 Sa 03Sep 1955 Forest 2 - 3 Stoke

1954/1955

DIV 2 Mo 30Aug 1954 Stoke 2 - 0 Forest

DIV 2 We 25Aug 1954 Forest 0 - 3 Stoke

1953/1954

DIV 2 Sa 06Feb 1954 Stoke 1 - 1 Forest

DIV 2 Sa 19Sep 1953 Forest 5 - 4 Stoke

1932/1933

DIV 2 Tu 27Dec 1932 Forest 1 - 0 Stoke

DIV 2 Mo 26Dec 1932 Stoke 0 - 1 Forest

1931/1932

DIV 2 Sa 26Dec 1931 Forest 1 - 1 Stoke

DIV 2 Fr 25Dec 1931 Stoke 2 - 1 Forest

1930/1931

DIV 2 Sa 17Jan 1931 Stoke 1 - 0 Forest

DIV 2 Sa 13Sep 1930 Forest 3 - 0 Stoke

1929/1930

DIV 2 Sa 15Mar 1930 Stoke 6 - 0 Forest

DIV 2 Sa 09Nov 1929 Forest 2 - 1 Stoke

1928/1929

DIV 2 Sa 29Dec 1928 Stoke 1 - 1 Forest

DIV 2 Sa 25Aug 1928 Forest 1 - 5 Stoke

1927/1928

DIV 2 Sa 28Apr 1928 Forest 0 - 2 Stoke

DIV 2 Sa 17Dec 1927 Stoke 1 - 3 Forest

1925/1926

DIV 2 Sa 24Apr 1926 Forest 1 - 2 Stoke

DIV 2 Sa 12Dec 1925 Stoke 1 - 1 Forest

1922/1923

DIV 1 Sa 07Apr 1923 Forest 0 - 1 Stoke

DIV 1 Sa 31Mar 1923 Stoke 0 - 1 Forest

1921/1922

DIV 2 Sa 22Apr 1922 Forest 3 - 1 Stoke

DIV 2 Sa 15Apr 1922 Stoke 1 - 1 Forest

1920/1921

DIV 2 Sa 04Sep 1920 Stoke 4 - 0 Forest

DIV 2 Sa 28Aug 1920 Forest 2 - 2 Stoke

1919/1920

DIV 2 We 28Jan 1920 Forest 0 - 2 Stoke

DIV 2 Sa 24Jan 1920 Stoke 0 - 2 Forest

1905/1906

DIV 1 Sa 17Mar 1906 Stoke 4 - 0 Forest

DIV 1 Sa 11Nov 1905 Forest 3 - 1 Stoke

1904/1905

DIV 1 Sa 28Jan 1905 Stoke 0 - 0 Forest

DIV 1 Sa 01Oct 1904 Forest 0 - 1 Stoke

1903/1904

DIV 1 Sa 05Mar 1904 Stoke 2 - 3 Forest

DIV 1 We 25Nov 1903 Forest 4 - 2 Stoke

1902/1903

FA CUP Th 26Feb 1903 Stoke 2 - 0 Forest

FA CUP Sa 21Feb 1903 Forest 0 - 0 Stoke

DIV 1 Sa 14Feb 1903 Stoke 3 - 2 Forest

DIV 1 Sa 18Oct 1902 Forest 1 - 3 Stoke

1901/1902

FA CUP Sa 22Feb 1902 Forest 2 - 0 Stoke

DIV 1 Sa 01Feb 1902 Forest 2 - 0 Stoke

DIV 1 Sa 05Oct 1901 Stoke 1 - 1 Forest

1900/1901

DIV 1 Sa 16Feb 1901 Stoke 0 - 3 Forest

DIV 1 Sa 13Oct 1900 Forest 1 - 1 Stoke

1899/1900

DIV 1 Sa 20Jan 1900 Stoke 0 - 0 Forest

DIV 1 Sa 23Sep 1899 Forest 1 - 0 Stoke

1898/1899

DIV 1 Mo 26Dec 1898 Stoke 2 - 1 Forest

DIV 1 Sa 15Oct 1898 Forest 2 - 1 Stoke

1897/1898

DIV 1 Sa 19Feb 1898 Forest 3 - 1 Stoke

DIV 1 Sa 20Nov 1897 Stoke 1 - 2 Forest

1896/1897

DIV 1 Sa 17Oct 1896 Stoke 3 - 0 Forest

DIV 1 Sa 12Sep 1896 Forest 4 - 0 Stoke

1895/1896

DIV 1 Sa 21Mar 1896 Stoke 1 - 0 Forest

DIV 1 Th 28Nov 1895 Forest 4 - 0 Stoke

1894/1895

DIV 1 Sa 23Feb 1895 Forest 3 - 1 Stoke

DIV 1 Sa 13Oct 1894 Stoke 0 - 3 Forest

1893/1894

DIV 1 Sa 21Oct 1893 Forest 2 - 0 Stoke

DIV 1 Sa 09Sep 1893 Stoke 2 - 1 Forest

1892/1893

DIV 1 Sa 22Oct 1892 Stoke 3 - 0 Forest

DIV 1 Sa 10Sep 1892 Forest 3 - 4 Stoke

NOTTM FOREST V WALSALL

	FOREST WINS	DRAWS	WALSALL WINS
League	6	4	6
League Cup	1	1	2
Total	7	5	8

2007/2008

FL 1 Sa 15Mar 2008 Forest 1 - 1 Walsall

FL 1 Tu 04Dec 2007 Walsall 1 - 0 Forest

2005/2006

FL 1 Sa 10Dec 2005 Forest 1 - 1 Walsall

FL 1 Tu 09Aug 2005 Walsall 3 - 2 Forest

2003/2004

FL DIV 1 Sa 14Feb 2004 Forest 3 - 3 Walsall

FL DIV 1 Tu 04Nov 2003 Walsall 4 - 1 Forest

2002/2003

FL DIV 1 We 01Jan 2003 Forest 1 - 1 Walsall

LC We 02Oct 2002 Forest 1 - 2 Walsall

FL DIV 1 Sa 24Aug 2002 Walsall 2 - 1 Forest

2001/2002

FL DIV 1 Mo 01Apr 2002 Forest 2 - 3 Walsall

FL DIV 1 Su 11Nov 2001 Walsall 2 - 0 Forest

1999/2000

FL DIV 1 Sa 12Feb 2000 Walsall 0 - 2 Forest

FL DIV 1 Sa 04Sep 1999 Forest 4 - 1 Walsall

1997/1998

LC We 24Sep 1997 Walsall 2 - 2 Forest

LC We 17Sep 1997 Forest 0 - 1 Walsall

1976/1977

LC Sa 01Jan 1977 Walsall 2 - 4 Forest

1950/1951

DIV 3 (S) Sa 10Mar 1951 Walsall 0 - 2 Forest

DIV 3 (S) Sa 21Oct 1950 Forest 4 - 0 Walsall

1949/1950

DIV 3 (S) Sa 24Dec 1949 Walsall 1 - 3 Forest

DIV 3 (S) Sa 27Aug 1949 Forest 1 - 0 Walsall

NOTT'M FOREST V WEST BROM

	FOREST WINS	DRAWS	WEST BROM WINS
League	40	23	51
FA Cup	4	7	4
League Cup	1	0	2
Total	45	30	57

2009/2010

CHAMP Fr 08Jan 2010 West Brom 1 - 3 Forest

CHAMP Sa 15Aug 2009 Forest 0 - 1 West Brom

2003/2004

FL DIV 1 Su 09May 2004 West Brom 0 - 2 Forest

FA CUP Sa 03Jan 2004 Forest 1 - 0 West Brom

FL DIV 1 Sa 29Nov 2003 Forest 0 - 3 West Brom

2001/2002

FL DIV 1 Fr 22Mar 2002 Forest 0 - 1 West Brom

FL DIV 1 Su 04Nov 2001 West Brom 1 - 0 Forest

2000/2001

FL DIV 1 Sa 23Dec 2000 West Brom 3 - 0 Forest

FL DIV 1 Sa 12Aug 2000 Forest 1 - 0 West Brom

1999/2000

FL DIV 1 Sa 22Jan 2000 Forest 0 - 0 West Brom

FL DIV 1 Fr 20Aug 1999 West Brom 1 - 1 Forest

1997/1998

FL DIV 1 Su 03May 1998 West Brom 1 - 1 Forest

FL DIV 1 Tu 21Oct 1997 Forest 1 - 0 West Brom

1993/1994

FL DIV 1 Su 24Apr 1994 Forest 2 - 0 West Brom

FL DIV 1 Su 21Nov 1993 West Brom 0 - 2 Forest

1985/1986

DIV 1 Sa 05Apr 1986 West Brom 1 - 1 Forest

DIV 1 Su 03Nov 1985 Forest 2 - 1 West Brom

1984/1985

DIV 1 Sa 16Mar 1985 Forest 1 - 2 West Brom

DIV 1 Sa 13Oct 1984 West Brom 4 - 1 Forest

1983/1984

DIV 1 Sa 07Apr 1984 Forest 3 - 1 West Brom

Comp	Date	Home	Score	Away
DIV 1	We 08Feb 1984	West Brom	0 - 5	Forest
1982/1983				
DIV 1	Sa 19Feb 1983	Forest	0 - 0	West Brom
LC	Sa 01Jan 1983	Forest	6 - 1	West Brom
LC	Sa 01Jan 1983	West Brom	3 - 1	Forest
DIV 1	Sa 09Oct 1982	West Brom	2 - 1	Forest
1981/1982				
DIV 1	Sa 06Feb 1982	West Brom	2 - 1	Forest
DIV 1	Sa 12Sep 1981	Forest	0 - 0	West Brom
1980/1981				
DIV 1	Sa 21Mar 1981	West Brom	2 - 1	Forest
DIV 1	Sa 18Oct 1980	Forest	2 - 1	West Brom
1979/1980				
DIV 1	Sa 12Jan 1980	Forest	3 - 1	West Brom
DIV 1	Sa 01Sep 1979	West Brom	1 - 5	Forest
1978/1979				
DIV 1	Fr 18May 1979	West Brom	0 - 1	Forest
DIV 1	Sa 02Sep 1978	Forest	0 - 0	West Brom
1977/1978				
DIV 1	Tu 02May 1978	West Brom	2 - 2	Forest
FA CUP	Su 01Jan 1978	West Brom	2 - 0	Forest
DIV 1	Sa 26Nov 1977	Forest	0 - 0	West Brom
1975/1976				
DIV 2	Sa 17Apr 1976	West Brom	2 - 0	Forest
DIV 2	Fr 26Dec 1975	Forest	0 - 2	West Brom
1974/1975				
DIV 2	Sa 26Apr 1975	Forest	2 - 1	West Brom
DIV 2	Sa 19Oct 1974	West Brom	0 - 1	Forest
1973/1974				
DIV 2	Sa 12Jan 1974	Forest	1 - 4	West Brom
DIV 2	Sa 15Sep 1973	West Brom	3 - 3	Forest
1972/1973				
FA CUP	Mo 29Jan 1973	West Brom	3 - 1	Forest
FA CUP	Mo 01Jan 1973	Forest	0 - 0	West Brom
FA CUP	Mo 01Jan 1973	West Brom	1 - 1	Forest
1971/1972				
DIV 1	Sa 04Mar 1972	West Brom	1 - 0	Forest
DIV 1	Sa 13Nov 1971	Forest	4 - 1	West Brom
1970/1971				
DIV 1	Sa 09Jan 1971	West Brom	0 - 1	Forest
DIV 1	Tu 18Aug 1970	Forest	3 - 3	West Brom
1969/1970				
DIV 1	Sa 04Apr 1970	West Brom	4 - 0	Forest
DIV 1	Tu 26Aug 1969	Forest	1 - 0	West Brom
1968/1969				
DIV 1	Sa 22Mar 1969	Forest	3 - 0	West Brom
LC	We 01Jan 1969	Forest	2 - 3	West Brom
DIV 1	Sa 07Sep 1968	West Brom	2 - 5	Forest
1967/1968				
DIV 1	Sa 20Jan 1968	Forest	3 - 2	West Brom
DIV 1	Sa 16Sep 1967	West Brom	2 - 1	Forest
1966/1967				
DIV 1	Sa 07Jan 1967	West Brom	1 - 2	Forest
DIV 1	Sa 03Sep 1966	Forest	2 - 1	West Brom
1965/1966				
DIV 1	Sa 05Feb 1966	West Brom	5 - 3	Forest
DIV 1	Sa 28Aug 1965	Forest	3 - 2	West Brom
1964/1965				
DIV 1	Sa 02Jan 1965	West Brom	2 - 2	Forest
DIV 1	Sa 05Sep 1964	Forest	0 - 0	West Brom
1963/1964				
DIV 1	Sa 11Apr 1964	West Brom	2 - 3	Forest
DIV 1	Sa 30Nov 1963	Forest	0 - 3	West Brom
1962/1963				
DIV 1	Tu 14May 1963	Forest	2 - 2	West Brom
FA CUP	Mo 11Mar 1963	Forest	2 - 1	West Brom
FA CUP	We 06Mar 1963	West Brom	0 - 0	Forest
DIV 1	Sa 24Nov 1962	West Brom	1 - 4	Forest
1961/1962				
DIV 1	Sa 17Mar 1962	West Brom	2 - 2	Forest
DIV 1	Sa 28Oct 1961	Forest	4 - 4	West Brom
1960/1961				
DIV 1	Sa 04Feb 1961	West Brom	1 - 2	Forest
DIV 1	Sa 17Sep 1960	Forest	1 - 2	West Brom
1959/1960				
DIV 1	Mo 28Dec 1959	Forest	1 - 2	West Brom
DIV 1	Sa 26Dec 1959	West Brom	2 - 3	Forest
1958/1959				
DIV 1	Sa 25Apr 1959	West Brom	2 - 0	Forest
DIV 1	Sa 06Dec 1958	Forest	1 - 1	West Brom
1957/1958				
DIV 1	Sa 08Feb 1958	West Brom	3 - 2	Forest
FA CUP	Tu 28Jan 1958	Forest	1 - 5	West Brom
FA CUP	Sa 25Jan 1958	West Brom	3 - 3	Forest
DIV 1	Sa 28Sep 1957	Forest	0 - 2	West Brom
1948/1949				
DIV 2	Sa 18Dec 1948	West Brom	2 - 1	Forest
DIV 2	Sa 21Aug 1948	Forest	0 - 1	West Brom
1947/1948				
DIV 2	Sa 10Apr 1948	Forest	3 - 1	West Brom
DIV 2	Sa 22Nov 1947	West Brom	3 - 2	Forest
1946/1947				
DIV 2	Sa 17May 1947	West Brom	5 - 1	Forest
DIV 2	Sa 12Oct 1946	Forest	1 - 1	West Brom
1938/1939				
DIV 2	Mo 10Apr 1939	West Brom	0 - 0	Forest
DIV 2	Fr 07Apr 1939	Forest	2 - 0	West Brom
1930/1931				
DIV 2	Sa 04Apr 1931	West Brom	2 - 1	Forest
DIV 2	Sa 29Nov 1930	Forest	1 - 6	West Brom

1929/1930

DIV 2	We 19Mar 1930	West Brom	1 - 3	Forest
DIV 2	Sa 12Oct 1929	Forest	0 - 2	West Brom

1928/1929

DIV 2	Mo 01Apr 1929	West Brom	3 - 0	Forest
DIV 2	Fr 29Mar 1929	Forest	1 - 2	West Brom

1927/1928

DIV 2	Sa 14Apr 1928	Forest	0 - 2	West Brom
DIV 2	Sa 03Dec 1927	West Brom	2 - 3	Forest

1924/1925

DIV 1	Sa 18Apr 1925	Forest	0 - 1	West Brom
DIV 1	Sa 13Dec 1924	West Brom	5 - 1	Forest

1923/1924

DIV 1	Mo 03Sep 1923	West Brom	3 - 2	Forest
DIV 1	Mo 27Aug 1923	Forest	1 - 1	West Brom

1922/1923

DIV 1	Sa 10Mar 1923	West Brom	0 - 0	Forest
DIV 1	Sa 03Mar 1923	Forest	0 - 4	West Brom

1906/1907

DIV 2	Sa 13Apr 1907	Forest	3 - 1	West Brom
DIV 2	Sa 08Dec 1906	West Brom	3 - 1	Forest

1903/1904

DIV 1	We 30Mar 1904	Forest	2 - 0	West Brom
FA CUP	Sa 13Feb 1904	Forest	3 - 1	West Brom
FA CUP	We 10Feb 1904	West Brom	1 - 1	Forest
DIV 1	Sa 17Oct 1903	West Brom	1 - 1	Forest

1902/1903

DIV 1	Sa 07Mar 1903	Forest	3 - 1	West Brom
DIV 1	Sa 08Nov 1902	West Brom	2 - 0	Forest

1900/1901

DIV 1	We 13Mar 1901	Forest	2 - 3	West Brom
DIV 1	Sa 20Oct 1900	West Brom	1 - 6	Forest

1899/1900

DIV 1	Mo 16Apr 1900	West Brom	8 - 0	Forest
DIV 1	Sa 07Oct 1899	Forest	6 - 1	West Brom

1898/1899

DIV 1	Sa 22Apr 1899	Forest	3 - 0	West Brom
DIV 1	Sa 24Dec 1898	West Brom	2 - 0	Forest

1897/1898

FA CUP	Sa 26Feb 1898	West Brom	2 - 3	Forest
DIV 1	Sa 11Dec 1897	Forest	0 - 1	West Brom
DIV 1	Sa 11Sep 1897	West Brom	2 - 0	Forest

1896/1897

DIV 1	Sa 23Jan 1897	West Brom	4 - 0	Forest
DIV 1	Sa 02Jan 1897	Forest	0 - 1	West Brom

1895/1896

DIV 1	Sa 16Nov 1895	Forest	2 - 0	West Brom
DIV 1	Sa 28Sep 1895	West Brom	3 - 1	Forest

1894/1895

DIV 1	Mo 15Apr 1895	West Brom	1 - 0	Forest
DIV 1	Sa 08Dec 1894	Forest	5 - 3	West Brom

1893/1894

DIV 1	Mo 26Mar 1894	West Brom	3 - 0	Forest
DIV 1	Sa 30Sep 1893	Forest	2 - 3	West Brom

1892/1893

DIV 1	Mo 03Apr 1893	West Brom	2 - 2	Forest
DIV 1	Th 02Mar 1893	Forest	3 - 4	West Brom

1891/1892

FA CUP	We 09Mar 1892	West Brom	6 - 2	Forest
FA CUP	Sa 05Mar 1892	West Brom	1 - 1	Forest
FA CUP	Sa 27Feb 1892	West Brom	1 - 1	Forest

NOTTM FOREST V WOLVES

	NOTTM FOREST WINS	DRAWS	WOLVES WINS
League	37	24	53
FA Cup	2	0	2
League Cup	1	0	1
Cup	0	0	1
Total	40	24	57

2008/2009

CHAMP	Sa 21Mar 2009	Forest	0 - 1	Wolves
CHAMP	Sa 30Aug 2008	Wolves	5 - 1	Forest

2004/2005

CHAMP	Sa 06Nov 2004	Wolves	2 - 1	Forest
CHAMP	Fr 15Oct 2004	Forest	1 - 0	Wolves

2002/2003

FL DIV 1	Fr 11Apr 2003	Forest	2 - 2	Wolves
FL DIV 1	Sa 23Nov 2002	Wolves	2 - 1	Forest

2001/2002

FL DIV 1	We 06Mar 2002	Forest	2 - 2	Wolves
FL DIV 1	Tu 25Sep 2001	Wolves	1 - 0	Forest

2000/2001

FL DIV 1	Sa 03Mar 2001	Wolves	2 - 0	Forest
FA CUP	Su 07Jan 2001	Forest	0 - 1	Wolves
FL DIV 1	Sa 30Sep 2000	Forest	0 - 0	Wolves

1999/2000

FL DIV 1	Sa 26Feb 2000	Wolves	3 - 0	Forest
FL DIV 1	Su 19Sep 1999	Forest	1 - 1	Wolves

1997/1998

FL DIV 1	Mo 13Apr 1998	Forest	3 - 0	Wolves
FL DIV 1	Su 14Dec 1997	Wolves	2 - 1	Forest

1994/1995

LC	We 26Oct 1994	Wolves	2 - 3	Forest

1993/1994

FL DIV 1	Su 23Jan 1994	Forest	0 - 0	Wolves
FL DIV 1	We 10Nov 1993	Wolves	1 - 1	Forest

1991/1992

FA CUP	Sa 04Jan 1992	Forest	1 - 0	Wolves

1983/1984

DIV 1	Sa 03Mar 1984	Wolves	1 - 0	Forest

DIV 1 Sa 05Nov 1983 Forest 5 - 0 Wolves
1981/1982
DIV 1 Sa 10Apr 1982 Forest 0 - 1 Wolves
DIV 1 Tu 16Feb 1982 Wolves 0 - 0 Forest
1980/1981
DIV 1 Mo 20Apr 1981 Forest 1 - 0 Wolves
DIV 1 Fr 26Dec 1980 Wolves 1 - 4 Forest
1979/1980
DIV 1 Mo 12May 1980 Wolves 3 - 1 Forest
LC Sa 15Mar 1980 Wolves 1 - 0 Forest
DIV 1 Sa 06Oct 1979 Forest 3 - 2 Wolves
1978/1979
DIV 1 Mo 30Apr 1979 Wolves 1 - 0 Forest
DIV 1 Sa 07Oct 1978 Forest 3 - 1 Wolves
1977/1978
DIV 1 Sa 04Feb 1978 Forest 2 - 0 Wolves
DIV 1 Sa 10Sep 1977 Wolves 2 - 3 Forest
1976/1977
DIV 2 Sa 05Feb 1977 Wolves 2 - 1 Forest
DIV 2 Sa 28Aug 1976 Forest 1 - 3 Wolves
1971/1972
DIV 1 Tu 25Apr 1972 Forest 1 - 3 Wolves
DIV 1 Sa 25Sep 1971 Wolves 4 - 2 Forest
1970/1971
DIV 1 Sa 03Apr 1971 Wolves 4 - 0 Forest
DIV 1 Sa 29Aug 1970 Forest 4 - 1 Wolves
1969/1970
DIV 1 Sa 20Dec 1969 Forest 4 - 2 Wolves
DIV 1 Sa 06Sep 1969 Wolves 3 - 3 Forest
1968/1969
DIV 1 Sa 11Jan 1969 Wolves 1 - 0 Forest
DIV 1 Sa 02Nov 1968 Forest 0 - 0 Wolves
1967/1968
DIV 1 Sa 06Apr 1968 Wolves 6 - 1 Forest
DIV 1 Sa 11Nov 1967 Forest 3 - 1 Wolves
1964/1965
DIV 1 Sa 24Apr 1965 Forest 0 - 2 Wolves
DIV 1 Sa 31Oct 1964 Wolves 1 - 2 Forest
1963/1964
DIV 1 Sa 11Jan 1964 Wolves 2 - 3 Forest
DIV 1 Sa 07Sep 1963 Forest 3 - 0 Wolves
1962/1963
DIV 1 Tu 30Apr 1963 Forest 2 - 0 Wolves
FA CUP Tu 29Jan 1963 Forest 4 - 3 Wolves
DIV 1 Sa 15Sep 1962 Wolves 1 - 1 Forest
1961/1962
DIV 1 We 27Sep 1961 Wolves 2 - 1 Forest
DIV 1 Tu 19Sep 1961 Forest 3 - 1 Wolves
1960/1961
DIV 1 Sa 25Mar 1961 Forest 1 - 1 Wolves
DIV 1 Sa 05Nov 1960 Wolves 5 - 3 Forest
1959/1960
DIV 1 Tu 19Apr 1960 Forest 0 - 0 Wolves
DIV 1 Mo 18Apr 1960 Wolves 3 - 1 Forest
CHARITY SHIELD Tu 18Aug 1959 Wolves 3 - 1 Forest
1958/1959
DIV 1 Sa 20Dec 1958 Forest 1 - 3 Wolves
DIV 1 Sa 23Aug 1958 Wolves 5 - 1 Forest
1957/1958
DIV 1 Sa 15Mar 1958 Forest 1 - 4 Wolves
DIV 1 Sa 02Nov 1957 Wolves 2 - 0 Forest
1931/1932
DIV 2 Sa 16Jan 1932 Wolves 0 - 0 Forest
DIV 2 Sa 05Sep 1931 Forest 2 - 0 Wolves
1930/1931
DIV 2 Sa 27Dec 1930 Wolves 4 - 2 Forest
DIV 2 Sa 30Aug 1930 Forest 3 - 4 Wolves
1929/1930
DIV 2 Sa 22Mar 1930 Forest 5 - 2 Wolves
DIV 2 Sa 16Nov 1929 Wolves 2 - 1 Forest
1928/1929
DIV 2 We 26Dec 1928 Forest 2 - 1 Wolves
DIV 2 Tu 25Dec 1928 Wolves 2 - 3 Forest
1927/1928
DIV 2 Tu 27Dec 1927 Wolves 1 - 0 Forest
DIV 2 Mo 26Dec 1927 Forest 3 - 2 Wolves
1926/1927
DIV 2 Sa 19Mar 1927 Wolves 2 - 0 Forest
FA CUP Sa 29Jan 1927 Wolves 2 - 0 Forest
DIV 2 Sa 30Oct 1926 Forest 1 - 1 Wolves
1925/1926
DIV 2 Mo 08Feb 1926 Wolves 4 - 0 Forest
DIV 2 Sa 19Sep 1925 Forest 1 - 4 Wolves
1921/1922
DIV 2 Tu 27Dec 1921 Wolves 2 - 0 Forest
DIV 2 Mo 26Dec 1921 Forest 0 - 0 Wolves
1920/1921
DIV 2 Mo 14Feb 1921 Wolves 2 - 1 Forest
DIV 2 Sa 05Feb 1921 Forest 1 - 1 Wolves
1919/1920
DIV 2 Sa 01Nov 1919 Wolves 4 - 0 Forest
DIV 2 Sa 25Oct 1919 Forest 1 - 0 Wolves
1914/1915
DIV 2 Sa 13Mar 1915 Wolves 5 - 1 Forest
DIV 2 Sa 07Nov 1914 Forest 3 - 1 Wolves
1913/1914
DIV 2 Sa 27Dec 1913 Wolves 4 - 1 Forest
DIV 2 Sa 06Sep 1913 Forest 1 - 3 Wolves

1912/1913

DIV 2	We 25Dec 1912	Forest	2 - 0	Wolves
DIV 2	Mo 16Sep 1912	Wolves	2 - 3	Forest

1911/1912

DIV 2	Sa 06Jan 1912	Forest	0 - 0	Wolves
DIV 2	Sa 09Sep 1911	Wolves	1 - 0	Forest

1906/1907

DIV 2	Sa 16Feb 1907	Forest	1 - 0	Wolves
DIV 2	Sa 13Oct 1906	Wolves	2 - 0	Forest

1905/1906

DIV 1	Sa 30Dec 1905	Wolves	2 - 1	Forest
DIV 1	Sa 02Sep 1905	Forest	3 - 1	Wolves

1904/1905

DIV 1	Sa 31Dec 1904	Forest	2 - 2	Wolves
DIV 1	Sa 03Sep 1904	Wolves	3 - 2	Forest

1903/1904

DIV 1	Sa 23Jan 1904	Forest	5 - 0	Wolves
DIV 1	Sa 26Sep 1903	Wolves	3 - 2	Forest

1902/1903

DIV 1	Sa 11Apr 1903	Wolves	2 - 1	Forest
DIV 1	Sa 13Dec 1902	Forest	2 - 0	Wolves

1901/1902

DIV 1	Sa 07Dec 1901	Forest	2 - 0	Wolves
DIV 1	Mo 02Sep 1901	Wolves	2 - 0	Forest

1900/1901

DIV 1	Sa 13Apr 1901	Wolves	1 - 0	Forest
DIV 1	Sa 08Dec 1900	Forest	2 - 1	Wolves

1899/1900

DIV 1	Sa 06Jan 1900	Forest	0 - 0	Wolves
DIV 1	Sa 09Sep 1899	Wolves	2 - 2	Forest

1898/1899

DIV 1	Sa 21Jan 1899	Forest	3 - 0	Wolves
DIV 1	Sa 24Sep 1898	Wolves	0 - 2	Forest

1897/1898

DIV 1	Fr 08Apr 1898	Forest	1 - 1	Wolves
DIV 1	Sa 25Sep 1897	Wolves	0 - 0	Forest

1896/1897

DIV 1	Sa 10Apr 1897	Forest	1 - 2	Wolves
DIV 1	Sa 05Dec 1896	Wolves	4 - 1	Forest

1895/1896

DIV 1	Sa 04Apr 1896	Forest	3 - 2	Wolves
DIV 1	Sa 28Mar 1896	Wolves	6 - 1	Forest

1894/1895

DIV 1	Sa 13Apr 1895	Forest	0 - 2	Wolves
DIV 1	Sa 10Nov 1894	Wolves	1 - 1	Forest

1893/1894

DIV 1	Sa 14Oct 1893	Wolves	3 - 1	Forest
DIV 1	Sa 02Sep 1893	Forest	7 - 1	Wolves

1892/1893

DIV 1	Sa 24Dec 1892	Forest	3 - 1	Wolves
DIV 1	Sa 05Nov 1892	Wolves	2 - 2	Forest

STOKE V WALSALL

	STOKE WINS	DRAWS	WALSALL WINS
FA Cup	1	0	1
League	8	4	6
Cup	1	0	0
League Cup	1	0	1
Total	11	4	8

2005/2006

FA CUP	Sa 28Jan 2006	Stoke	2 - 1	Walsall

2003/2004

FL DIV 1	Sa 31Jan 2004	Stoke	3 - 2	Walsall
FL DIV 1	Sa 23Aug 2003	Walsall	1 - 1	Stoke

2002/2003

FL DIV 1	We 26Feb 2003	Stoke	1 - 0	Walsall
FL DIV 1	Sa 02Nov 2002	Walsall	4 - 2	Stoke

2000/2001

FL DIV 2	We 16May 2001	Walsall	4 - 2	Stoke
FL DIV 2	Su 13May 2001	Stoke	0 - 0	Walsall
FL DIV 2	Sa 14Apr 2001	Stoke	0 - 0	Walsall
FL TROPHY	We 07Feb 2001	Stoke	4 - 0	Walsall
FL DIV 2	Tu 24Oct 2000	Walsall	3 - 0	Stoke

1998/1999

FL DIV 2	Sa 08May 1999	Stoke	2 - 0	Walsall
FL DIV 2	Sa 19Dec 1998	Walsall	1 - 0	Stoke

1988/1989

DIV 2	Sa 22Apr 1989	Stoke	0 - 3	Walsall
DIV 2	Sa 24Sep 1988	Walsall	1 - 2	Stoke

1966/1967

LC	Su 01Jan 1967	Walsall	2 - 1	Stoke

1965/1966

FA CUP	Sa 22Jan 1966	Stoke	0 - 2	Walsall

1962/1963

DIV 2	Sa 02Mar 1963	Stoke	3 - 0	Walsall
DIV 2	Sa 13Oct 1962	Walsall	0 - 0	Stoke
LC	Tu 25Sep 1962	Walsall	1 - 2	Stoke

1961/1962

DIV 2	Fr 30Mar 1962	Walsall	3 - 1	Stoke
DIV 2	Sa 11Nov 1961	Stoke	2 - 1	Walsall

1926/1927

DIV 3	Sa 22Jan 1927	Stoke	4 - 1	Walsall
DIV 3	Sa 04Sep 1926	Walsall	0 - 1	Stoke

STOKE V WBA

	WBA WINS	DRAWS	STOKE WINS
League	38	31	55
FA Cup	3	2	0
Total	41	33	55

2010/2011
FAPL Mo 28Feb 2011 Stoke 1 - 1 West Brom
FAPL Sa 20Nov 2010 West Brom 0 - 3 Stoke
2008/2009
FAPL Sa 04Apr 2009 West Brom 0 - 2 Stoke
FAPL Sa 22Nov 2008 Stoke 1 - 0 West Brom
2007/2008
CHAMP Sa 22Dec 2007 Stoke 3 - 1 West Brom
CHAMP We 03Oct 2007 West Brom 1 - 1 Stoke
2006/2007
CHAMP Sa 07Apr 2007 West Brom 1 - 3 Stoke
CHAMP Sa 25Nov 2006 Stoke 1 - 0 West Brom
2003/2004
FL DIV 1 Tu 04May 2004 Stoke 4 - 1 West Brom
FL DIV 1 Sa 27Sep 2003 West Brom 1 - 0 Stoke
1997/1998
FA CUP Tu 13Jan 1998 West Brom 3 - 1 Stoke
FL DIV 1 Su 28Dec 1997 West Brom 1 - 1 Stoke
FL DIV 1 We 03Sep 1997 Stoke 0 - 0 West Brom
1996/1997
FL DIV 1 Su 04May 1997 Stoke 2 - 1 West Brom
FL DIV 1 We 16Oct 1996 West Brom 0 - 2 Stoke
1995/1996
FL DIV 1 Sa 09Dec 1995 West Brom 0 - 1 Stoke
FL DIV 1 Su 24Sep 1995 Stoke 2 - 1 West Brom
1994/1995
FL DIV 1 Sa 25Feb 1995 West Brom 1 - 3 Stoke
FL DIV 1 Su 02Oct 1994 Stoke 4 - 1 West Brom
1993/1994
FL DIV 1 Sa 05Mar 1994 West Brom 0 - 0 Stoke
FL DIV 1 Sa 28Aug 1993 Stoke 1 - 0 West Brom
1992/1993
FL DIV 2 Sa 23Jan 1993 West Brom 1 - 2 Stoke
FL DIV 2 Sa 19Sep 1992 Stoke 4 - 3 West Brom
1991/1992
DIV 3 We 12Feb 1992 Stoke 1 - 0 West Brom
DIV 3 Sa 30Nov 1991 West Brom 2 - 2 Stoke
1989/1990
DIV 2 Sa 24Mar 1990 West Brom 1 - 1 Stoke
DIV 2 Tu 17Oct 1989 Stoke 2 - 1 West Brom
1988/1989
DIV 2 Tu 04Apr 1989 Stoke 0 - 0 West Brom
DIV 2 Su 18Dec 1988 West Brom 6 - 0 Stoke
1987/1988
DIV 2 Sa 02Apr 1988 West Brom 2 - 0 Stoke
DIV 2 Sa 07Nov 1987 Stoke 3 - 0 West Brom
1986/1987
DIV 2 Sa 14Feb 1987 West Brom 4 - 1 Stoke
DIV 2 Tu 02Sep 1986 Stoke 1 - 1 West Brom
1984/1985
DIV 1 Tu 12Mar 1985 Stoke 0 - 0 West Brom
DIV 1 Sa 10Nov 1984 West Brom 2 - 0 Stoke
1983/1984
DIV 1 Sa 24Mar 1984 West Brom 3 - 0 Stoke
DIV 1 Mo 29Aug 1983 Stoke 3 - 1 West Brom
1982/1983
DIV 1 Sa 05Feb 1983 West Brom 1 - 1 Stoke
DIV 1 We 08Sep 1982 Stoke 0 - 3 West Brom
1981/1982
DIV 1 Th 20May 1982 Stoke 3 - 0 West Brom
DIV 1 Sa 14Nov 1981 West Brom 1 - 2 Stoke
1980/1981
DIV 1 Tu 25Nov 1980 West Brom 0 - 0 Stoke
DIV 1 We 20Aug 1980 Stoke 0 - 0 West Brom
1979/1980
DIV 1 Sa 03May 1980 West Brom 0 - 1 Stoke
DIV 1 Sa 08Dec 1979 Stoke 3 - 2 West Brom
1976/1977
DIV 1 Sa 14May 1977 West Brom 3 - 1 Stoke
DIV 1 Sa 18Dec 1976 Stoke 0 - 2 West Brom
1972/1973
DIV 1 Sa 31Mar 1973 Stoke 2 - 0 West Brom
DIV 1 Sa 25Nov 1972 West Brom 2 - 1 Stoke
1971/1972
DIV 1 Fr 05May 1972 Stoke 1 - 1 West Brom
DIV 1 Sa 06Nov 1971 West Brom 0 - 1 Stoke
1970/1971
DIV 1 Sa 16Jan 1971 Stoke 2 - 0 West Brom
DIV 1 We 26Aug 1970 West Brom 5 - 2 Stoke
1969/1970
DIV 1 We 15Apr 1970 Stoke 3 - 2 West Brom
DIV 1 We 17Sep 1969 West Brom 1 - 3 Stoke
1968/1969
DIV 1 Sa 01Feb 1969 Stoke 1 - 1 West Brom
DIV 1 Sa 16Nov 1968 West Brom 2 - 1 Stoke
1967/1968
DIV 1 We 13Mar 1968 West Brom 3 - 0 Stoke
DIV 1 Sa 09Sep 1967 Stoke 0 - 0 West Brom
1966/1967
DIV 1 Sa 04Feb 1967 Stoke 1 - 1 West Brom
DIV 1 Sa 24Sep 1966 West Brom 0 - 1 Stoke
1965/1966
DIV 1 Sa 12Mar 1966 Stoke 1 - 1 West Brom
DIV 1 Sa 18Sep 1965 West Brom 6 - 2 Stoke

1964/1965
DIV 1 Sa 16Jan 1965 Stoke 2 - 0 West Brom
DIV 1 Sa 12Sep 1964 West Brom 5 - 3 Stoke
1963/1964
DIV 1 Sa 07Mar 1964 Stoke 1 - 1 West Brom
DIV 1 Sa 26Oct 1963 West Brom 2 - 3 Stoke
1952/1953
DIV 1 Sa 24Jan 1953 Stoke 5 - 1 West Brom
DIV 1 Sa 13Sep 1952 West Brom 3 - 2 Stoke
1951/1952
DIV 1 We 29Aug 1951 West Brom 1 - 0 Stoke
DIV 1 Mo 20Aug 1951 Stoke 1 - 1 West Brom
1950/1951
DIV 1 Sa 23Dec 1950 Stoke 1 - 1 West Brom
DIV 1 Sa 26Aug 1950 West Brom 1 - 1 Stoke
1949/1950
DIV 1 Sa 14Jan 1950 West Brom 0 - 0 Stoke
DIV 1 Sa 10Sep 1949 Stoke 1 - 3 West Brom
1937/1938
DIV 1 Mo 06Sep 1937 Stoke 4 - 0 West Brom
DIV 1 Mo 30Aug 1937 West Brom 0 - 1 Stoke
1936/1937
DIV 1 Th 04Feb 1937 Stoke 10 - 3 West Brom
DIV 1 Sa 26Sep 1936 West Brom 2 - 2 Stoke
1935/1936
DIV 1 Sa 04Jan 1936 Stoke 3 - 2 West Brom
DIV 1 Sa 07Sep 1935 West Brom 2 - 0 Stoke
1934/1935
DIV 1 We 26Dec 1934 Stoke 3 - 0 West Brom
DIV 1 Tu 25Dec 1934 West Brom 3 - 0 Stoke
1933/1934
DIV 1 Th 08Mar 1934 Stoke 4 - 1 West Brom
DIV 1 Sa 21Oct 1933 West Brom 5 - 1 Stoke
1930/1931
DIV 2 Th 30Apr 1931 Stoke 0 - 1 West Brom
DIV 2 Sa 20Dec 1930 West Brom 4 - 0 Stoke
1929/1930
DIV 2 Sa 26Apr 1930 Stoke 0 - 3 West Brom
DIV 2 Sa 21Dec 1929 West Brom 2 - 3 Stoke
1928/1929
DIV 2 Sa 05Jan 1929 West Brom 2 - 3 Stoke
DIV 2 Sa 01Sep 1928 Stoke 4 - 1 West Brom
1927/1928
DIV 2 Mo 05Sep 1927 Stoke 1 - 1 West Brom
DIV 2 We 31Aug 1927 West Brom 2 - 4 Stoke
1922/1923
DIV 1 Sa 30Sep 1922 West Brom 0 - 1 Stoke
DIV 1 Sa 23Sep 1922 Stoke 0 - 2 West Brom
1907/1908
DIV 2 We 04Mar 1908 Stoke 1 - 1 West Brom
DIV 2 Sa 16Nov 1907 West Brom 1 - 0 Stoke
1906/1907
FA CUP Mo 21Jan 1907 West Brom 2 - 1 Stoke
FA CUP Th 17Jan 1907 Stoke 2 - 2 West Brom
FA CUP Sa 12Jan 1907 West Brom 1 - 1 Stoke
1903/1904
DIV 1 Sa 26Mar 1904 West Brom 3 - 0 Stoke
DIV 1 Sa 28Nov 1903 Stoke 5 - 0 West Brom
1902/1903
DIV 1 Sa 04Apr 1903 Stoke 3 - 0 West Brom
DIV 1 Sa 06Dec 1902 West Brom 2 - 1 Stoke
1900/1901
DIV 1 Sa 09Mar 1901 Stoke 2 - 0 West Brom
DIV 1 Sa 03Nov 1900 West Brom 2 - 2 Stoke
1899/1900
DIV 1 Mo 19Mar 1900 West Brom 4 - 0 Stoke
DIV 1 Sa 21Oct 1899 Stoke 1 - 0 West Brom
1898/1899
DIV 1 Sa 04Mar 1899 West Brom 0 - 1 Stoke
DIV 1 Sa 05Nov 1898 Stoke 2 - 1 West Brom
1897/1898
DIV 1 Sa 30Oct 1897 Stoke 0 - 0 West Brom
DIV 1 Sa 25Sep 1897 West Brom 2 - 0 Stoke
1896/1897
DIV 1 Sa 12Dec 1896 West Brom 1 - 2 Stoke
DIV 1 Sa 21Nov 1896 Stoke 2 - 2 West Brom
1895/1896
DIV 1 Sa 09Nov 1895 West Brom 1 - 0 Stoke
DIV 1 Sa 21Sep 1895 Stoke 3 - 1 West Brom
1894/1895
DIV 1 Mo 25Mar 1895 Stoke 1 - 1 West Brom
DIV 1 Sa 15Dec 1894 West Brom 3 - 2 Stoke
1893/1894
DIV 1 Sa 20Jan 1894 Stoke 3 - 1 West Brom
DIV 1 Sa 04Nov 1893 West Brom 4 - 2 Stoke
1892/1893
DIV 1 Sa 11Feb 1893 Stoke 1 - 2 West Brom
DIV 1 Sa 26Nov 1892 West Brom 1 - 2 Stoke
1891/1892
DIV 1 Sa 23Apr 1892 Stoke 1 - 0 West Brom
DIV 1 Mo 11Apr 1892 West Brom 2 - 2 Stoke
1889/1890
DIV 1 Sa 15Mar 1890 West Brom 2 - 1 Stoke
DIV 1 Sa 16Nov 1889 Stoke 1 - 3 West Brom
1888/1889
DIV 1 Sa 29Dec 1888 West Brom 2 - 0 Stoke
DIV 1 Sa 08Sep 1888 Stoke 0 - 2 West Brom
1887/1888
FA CUP Sa 07Jan 1888 West Brom 4 - 1 Stoke

STOKE V WOLVES

	STOKE WINS	DRAWS	WOLVES WINS
League	47	33	58
FA Cup	1	1	6
Total	48	34	64

2010/2011

FAPL Tu 26Apr 2011 Stoke 3 - 0 Wolves
FA CUP Su 30Jan 2011 Wolves 0 - 1 Stoke
FAPL Sa 14Aug 2010 Wolves 2 - 1 Stoke

2009/2010

FAPL Su 11Apr 2010 Wolves 0 - 0 Stoke
FAPL Sa 31Oct 2009 Stoke 2 - 2 Wolves

2007/2008

CHAMP Sa 09Feb 2008 Wolves 2 - 4 Stoke
CHAMP Sa 01Sep 2007 Stoke 0 - 0 Wolves

2006/2007

CHAMP Sa 13Jan 2007 Stoke 1 - 1 Wolves
CHAMP Sa 23Sep 2006 Wolves 2 - 0 Stoke

2005/2006

CHAMP Tu 07Mar 2006 Wolves 0 - 0 Stoke
CHAMP Sa 24Sep 2005 Stoke 1 - 3 Wolves

2004/2005

CHAMP Sa 19Mar 2005 Wolves 1 - 1 Stoke
CHAMP Su 08Aug 2004 Stoke 2 - 1 Wolves

2002/2003

FL DIV 1 Tu 18Mar 2003 Wolves 0 - 0 Stoke
FL DIV 1 Sa 19Oct 2002 Stoke 0 - 2 Wolves

1997/1998

FL DIV 1 We 04Mar 1998 Wolves 1 - 1 Stoke
FL DIV 1 Sa 08Nov 1997 Stoke 3 - 0 Wolves

1996/1997

FL DIV 1 Tu 18Mar 1997 Stoke 1 - 0 Wolves
FL DIV 1 Sa 01Feb 1997 Wolves 2 - 0 Stoke

1995/1996

FL DIV 1 We 03Apr 1996 Stoke 2 - 0 Wolves
FL DIV 1 Sa 14Oct 1995 Wolves 1 - 4 Stoke

1994/1995

FL DIV 1 Sa 14Jan 1995 Wolves 2 - 0 Stoke
FL DIV 1 Su 30Oct 1994 Stoke 1 - 1 Wolves

1993/1994

FL DIV 1 Sa 05Feb 1994 Stoke 1 - 1 Wolves
FL DIV 1 Sa 23Oct 1993 Wolves 1 - 1 Stoke

1989/1990

DIV 2 Sa 17Feb 1990 Stoke 2 - 0 Wolves
DIV 2 Sa 09Sep 1989 Wolves 0 - 0 Stoke

1983/1984

DIV 1 Sa 12May 1984 Stoke 4 - 0 Wolves
DIV 1 Sa 17Dec 1983 Wolves 0 - 0 Stoke

1981/1982

DIV 1 Sa 24Apr 1982 Stoke 2 - 1 Wolves
DIV 1 Sa 28Nov 1981 Wolves 2 - 0 Stoke

1980/1981

DIV 1 Sa 02May 1981 Stoke 3 - 2 Wolves
FA CUP Th 01Jan 1981 Wolves 2 - 1 Stoke
FA CUP Th 01Jan 1981 Stoke 2 - 2 Wolves
DIV 1 Sa 29Nov 1980 Wolves 1 - 0 Stoke

1979/1980

DIV 1 Sa 22Mar 1980 Wolves 3 - 0 Stoke
DIV 1 Sa 10Nov 1979 Stoke 0 - 1 Wolves

1975/1976

DIV 1 Sa 31Jan 1976 Wolves 2 - 1 Stoke
DIV 1 We 20Aug 1975 Stoke 2 - 2 Wolves

1974/1975

DIV 1 Sa 15Feb 1975 Stoke 2 - 2 Wolves
DIV 1 Sa 23Nov 1974 Wolves 2 - 2 Stoke

1973/1974

DIV 1 Sa 02Feb 1974 Wolves 1 - 1 Stoke
DIV 1 Sa 15Dec 1973 Stoke 2 - 3 Wolves

1972/1973

DIV 1 Tu 24Apr 1973 Stoke 2 - 0 Wolves
DIV 1 Sa 30Sep 1972 Wolves 5 - 3 Stoke

1971/1972

DIV 1 Sa 18Dec 1971 Wolves 2 - 0 Stoke
DIV 1 Sa 04Sep 1971 Stoke 0 - 1 Wolves

1970/1971

DIV 1 We 07Apr 1971 Stoke 1 - 0 Wolves
DIV 1 Sa 05Sep 1970 Wolves 1 - 1 Stoke

1969/1970

DIV 1 Sa 14Feb 1970 Stoke 1 - 1 Wolves
DIV 1 Sa 09Aug 1969 Wolves 3 - 1 Stoke

1968/1969

DIV 1 Sa 22Mar 1969 Stoke 4 - 1 Wolves
DIV 1 Sa 31Aug 1968 Wolves 1 - 1 Stoke

1967/1968

DIV 1 Sa 13Apr 1968 Stoke 0 - 2 Wolves
DIV 1 Sa 18Nov 1967 Wolves 3 - 4 Stoke

1964/1965

DIV 1 Sa 20Mar 1965 Wolves 3 - 1 Stoke
DIV 1 Sa 07Nov 1964 Stoke 0 - 2 Wolves

1963/1964

DIV 1 Sa 21Dec 1963 Stoke 0 - 2 Wolves
DIV 1 Sa 31Aug 1963 Wolves 2 - 1 Stoke

1952/1953

DIV 1 Sa 04Apr 1953 Wolves 3 - 0 Stoke
DIV 1 Sa 15Nov 1952 Stoke 1 - 2 Wolves

1951/1952

DIV 1 Sa 08Mar 1952 Wolves 3 - 0 Stoke
DIV 1 Sa 20Oct 1951 Stoke 1 - 0 Wolves

1950/1951

DIV 1 Sa 14Apr 1951 Wolves 2 - 3 Stoke

DIV 1 Sa 25Nov 1950 Stoke 0 - 1 Wolves
1949/1950
DIV 1 Sa 25Mar 1950 Wolves 2 - 1 Stoke
DIV 1 Sa 05Nov 1949 Stoke 2 - 1 Wolves
1948/1949
DIV 1 Sa 09Apr 1949 Wolves 3 - 1 Stoke
DIV 1 Sa 13Nov 1948 Stoke 2 - 1 Wolves
1947/1948
DIV 1 Sa 17Apr 1948 Stoke 2 - 3 Wolves
DIV 1 Sa 29Nov 1947 Wolves 1 - 2 Stoke
1946/1947
DIV 1 Sa 01Mar 1947 Wolves 3 - 0 Stoke
DIV 1 Sa 26Oct 1946 Stoke 0 - 3 Wolves
1938/1939
DIV 1 We 29Mar 1939 Stoke 5 - 3 Wolves
DIV 1 Sa 19Nov 1938 Wolves 3 - 0 Stoke
1937/1938
DIV 1 Sa 19Mar 1938 Wolves 2 - 2 Stoke
DIV 1 Sa 06Nov 1937 Stoke 1 - 1 Wolves
1936/1937
DIV 1 Sa 20Mar 1937 Wolves 2 - 1 Stoke
DIV 1 Sa 14Nov 1936 Stoke 2 - 1 Wolves
1935/1936
DIV 1 Sa 11Apr 1936 Wolves 1 - 1 Stoke
DIV 1 Sa 07Dec 1935 Stoke 4 - 1 Wolves
1934/1935
DIV 1 Sa 27Apr 1935 Wolves 2 - 1 Stoke
DIV 1 Sa 15Dec 1934 Stoke 1 - 2 Wolves
1933/1934
DIV 1 Sa 10Feb 1934 Wolves 0 - 2 Stoke
DIV 1 Sa 30Sep 1933 Stoke 1 - 1 Wolves
1931/1932
DIV 2 Sa 20Feb 1932 Stoke 2 - 1 Wolves
DIV 2 Sa 10Oct 1931 Wolves 0 - 1 Stoke
1930/1931
DIV 2 Mo 15Sep 1930 Stoke 1 - 2 Wolves
DIV 2 Mo 08Sep 1930 Wolves 5 - 1 Stoke
1929/1930
DIV 2 Mo 21Apr 1930 Wolves 2 - 1 Stoke
DIV 2 Mo 30Sep 1929 Stoke 3 - 0 Wolves
1928/1929
DIV 2 Sa 20Apr 1929 Wolves 4 - 0 Stoke
DIV 2 Sa 08Dec 1928 Stoke 4 - 3 Wolves
1927/1928
DIV 2 Sa 10Mar 1928 Stoke 2 - 2 Wolves
DIV 2 Sa 29Oct 1927 Wolves 1 - 2 Stoke
1925/1926
DIV 2 Sa 20Feb 1926 Wolves 5 - 1 Stoke
DIV 2 Sa 10Oct 1925 Stoke 0 - 0 Wolves
1924/1925
DIV 2 Sa 14Mar 1925 Stoke 0 - 3 Wolves
DIV 2 Sa 08Nov 1924 Wolves 1 - 0 Stoke
1921/1922
DIV 2 Sa 08Apr 1922 Stoke 3 - 0 Wolves
DIV 2 Sa 01Apr 1922 Wolves 1 - 1 Stoke
1920/1921
DIV 2 Th 10Mar 1921 Stoke 1 - 0 Wolves
DIV 2 Sa 26Feb 1921 Wolves 3 - 3 Stoke
FA CUP Sa 08Jan 1921 Wolves 3 - 2 Stoke
1919/1920
DIV 2 Sa 01May 1920 Stoke 3 - 0 Wolves
DIV 2 Mo 26Apr 1920 Wolves 4 - 0 Stoke
1907/1908
FA CUP Sa 07Mar 1908 Stoke 0 - 1 Wolves
DIV 2 Sa 25Jan 1908 Stoke 0 - 0 Wolves
DIV 2 Sa 28Sep 1907 Wolves 2 - 0 Stoke
1905/1906
DIV 1 Sa 06Jan 1906 Stoke 4 - 0 Wolves
DIV 1 Sa 09Sep 1905 Wolves 1 - 2 Stoke
1904/1905
DIV 1 Sa 01Apr 1905 Wolves 1 - 3 Stoke
DIV 1 Sa 03Dec 1904 Stoke 2 - 1 Wolves
1903/1904
DIV 1 Mo 04Apr 1904 Wolves 0 - 0 Stoke
DIV 1 Sa 19Dec 1903 Stoke 5 - 1 Wolves
1902/1903
DIV 1 Sa 10Jan 1903 Wolves 1 - 0 Stoke
DIV 1 Sa 13Sep 1902 Stoke 3 - 0 Wolves
1901/1902
DIV 1 Sa 28Dec 1901 Wolves 4 - 1 Stoke
DIV 1 Mo 11Nov 1901 Stoke 3 - 0 Wolves
1900/1901
DIV 1 Tu 09Apr 1901 Wolves 0 - 2 Stoke
DIV 1 Sa 22Dec 1900 Stoke 3 - 0 Wolves
1899/1900
DIV 1 Sa 07Oct 1899 Wolves 0 - 2 Stoke
DIV 1 Mo 18Sep 1899 Stoke 1 - 3 Wolves
1898/1899
DIV 1 Sa 01Apr 1899 Wolves 3 - 2 Stoke
DIV 1 Sa 03Dec 1898 Stoke 2 - 4 Wolves
1897/1898
DIV 1 Sa 05Feb 1898 Wolves 4 - 2 Stoke
DIV 1 Sa 16Oct 1897 Stoke 0 - 2 Wolves
1896/1897
DIV 1 Sa 10Oct 1896 Wolves 1 - 2 Stoke
DIV 1 Sa 05Sep 1896 Stoke 2 - 1 Wolves
1895/1896
FA CUP Sa 29Feb 1896 Wolves 3 - 0 Stoke
DIV 1 Sa 23Nov 1895 Stoke 4 - 1 Wolves

DIV 1 Sa 05Oct 1895 Wolves 1 - 0 Stoke

1894/1895

FA CUP Sa 16Feb 1895 Wolves 2 - 0 Stoke

DIV 1 Mo 04Feb 1895 Stoke 0 - 0 Wolves

DIV 1 Sa 24Nov 1894 Wolves 0 - 0 Stoke

1893/1894

DIV 1 Sa 30Dec 1893 Stoke 0 - 3 Wolves

DIV 1 Sa 25Nov 1893 Wolves 4 - 2 Stoke

1892/1893

DIV 1 Sa 03Dec 1892 Wolves 1 - 0 Stoke

DIV 1 Sa 29Oct 1892 Stoke 2 - 1 Wolves

1891/1892

DIV 1 Sa 02Jan 1892 Wolves 4 - 1 Stoke

DIV 1 Sa 12Sep 1891 Stoke 1 - 3 Wolves

1889/1890

FA CUP Sa 22Feb 1890 Wolves 8 - 0 Stoke

DIV 1 Sa 12Oct 1889 Wolves 2 - 2 Stoke

DIV 1 Sa 28Sep 1889 Stoke 2 - 1 Wolves

1888/1889

DIV 1 Sa 22Dec 1888 Wolves 4 - 1 Stoke

DIV 1 Sa 17Nov 1888 Stoke 0 - 1 Wolves

WALSALL V WBA

	WBA WINS	DRAWS	WALSALL WINS
League	2	2	4
League Cup	1	1	1
FA Cup	1	1	0
Total	4	4	5

2003/2004

FL DIV 1 Fr 09Jan 2004 West Brom 2 - 0 Walsall

FL DIV 1 Sa 09Aug 2003 Walsall 4 - 1 West Brom

2001/2002

FL DIV 1 Su 20Jan 2002 West Brom 1 - 0 Walsall

FL DIV 1 Sa 11Aug 2001 Walsall 2 - 1 West Brom

1999/2000

FL DIV 1 Sa 22Apr 2000 Walsall 2 - 1 West Brom

FL DIV 1 Sa 16Oct 1999 West Brom 0 - 1 Walsall

1988/1989

DIV 2 Sa 01Apr 1989 Walsall 0 - 0 West Brom

DIV 2 Sa 17Sep 1988 West Brom 0 - 0 Walsall

1987/1988

LC Tu 25Aug 1987 Walsall 0 - 0 West Brom

LC We 19Aug 1987 West Brom 2 - 3 Walsall

1965/1966

LC We 22Sep 1965 West Brom 3 - 1 Walsall

1899/1900

FA CUP Th 01Feb 1900 West Brom 6 - 1 Walsall

FA CUP Sa 27Jan 1900 Walsall 1 - 1 West Brom

WALSALL V WOLVES

	WOLVES WINS	DRAWS	WALSALL WINS
League	4	4	2
League Cup	0	1	1
FA Cup	1	0	0
Total	5	5	3

2002/2003

FL DIV 1 Sa 11Jan 2003 Walsall 0 - 1 Wolves

FL DIV 1 We 14Aug 2002 Wolves 3 - 1 Walsall

2001/2002

FL DIV 1 Tu 26Feb 2002 Wolves 3 - 0 Walsall

FL DIV 1 Fr 21Sep 2001 Walsall 0 - 3 Wolves

1999/2000

FL DIV 1 Sa 29Jan 2000 Walsall 1 - 1 Wolves

FL DIV 1 Sa 28Aug 1999 Wolves 1 - 2 Walsall

1985/1986

DIV 3 Su 09Feb 1986 Walsall 1 - 1 Wolves

DIV 3 Sa 19Oct 1985 Wolves 0 - 0 Walsall

LC Tu 03Sep 1985 Wolves 0 - 1 Walsall

LC Tu 20Aug 1985 Walsall 1 - 1 Wolves

1923/1924

DIV 3 (NORTH) Mo 07Apr 1924 Walsall 2 - 1 Wolves

DIV 3 (NORTH) Sa 22Dec 1923 Wolves 0 - 0 Walsall

1888/1889

FA CUP Sa 16Feb 1889 Wolves 6 - 1 Walsall

WEST BROM VS. WOLVES

	WBA WINS	DRAWS	WOLVES WINS
League	54	40	52
FA Cup	8	2	1
Cup	0	1	0
Total	62	43	53

2010/2011

FAPL Su 08May 2011 Wolves 3 - 1 West Brom

FAPL Su 20Feb 2011 West Brom 1 - 1 Wolves

2007/2008

CHAMP Tu 15Apr 2008 Wolves 0 - 1 West Brom

CHAMP Su 25Nov 2007 West Brom 0 - 0 Wolves

2006/2007

CHAMP We 16May 2007 West Brom 1 - 0 Wolves

CHAMP Su 13May 2007 Wolves 2 - 3 West Brom

CHAMP Su 11Mar 2007 Wolves 1 - 0 West Brom

FA CUP Su 28Jan 2007 Wolves 0 - 3 West Brom

CHAMP Su 22Oct 2006 West Brom 3 - 0 Wolves

2001/2002

FL DIV 1 Su 02Dec 2001 Wolves 0 - 1 West Brom

FL DIV 1 Th 25Oct 2001 West Brom 1 - 1 Wolves

2000/2001
FL DIV 1 Su 18Mar 2001 Wolves 3 - 1 West Brom
FL DIV 1 Tu 17Oct 2000 West Brom 1 - 0 Wolves
1999/2000
FL DIV 1 Su 31Oct 1999 West Brom 1 - 1 Wolves
FL DIV 1 Su 03Oct 1999 Wolves 1 - 1 West Brom
1998/1999
FL DIV 1 Su 25Apr 1999 Wolves 1 - 1 West Brom
FL DIV 1 Su 29Nov 1998 West Brom 2 - 0 Wolves
1997/1998
FL DIV 1 Sa 31Jan 1998 Wolves 0 - 1 West Brom
FL DIV 1 Su 24Aug 1997 West Brom 1 - 0 Wolves
1996/1997
FL DIV 1 Su 12Jan 1997 Wolves 2 - 0 West Brom
FL DIV 1 Su 15Sep 1996 West Brom 2 - 4 Wolves
1995/1996
FL DIV 1 Sa 13Jan 1996 West Brom 0 - 0 Wolves
FL DIV 1 Su 20Aug 1995 Wolves 1 - 1 West Brom
1994/1995
FL DIV 1 We 15Mar 1995 West Brom 2 - 0 Wolves
FL DIV 1 Su 28Aug 1994 Wolves 2 - 0 West Brom
1993/1994
FL DIV 1 Sa 26Feb 1994 Wolves 1 - 2 West Brom
FL DIV 1 Su 05Sep 1993 West Brom 3 - 2 Wolves
1990/1991
DIV 2 Sa 06Apr 1991 Wolves 2 - 2 West Brom
DIV 2 Sa 29Dec 1990 West Brom 1 - 1 Wolves
1989/1990
DIV 2 Tu 20Mar 1990 Wolves 2 - 1 West Brom
DIV 2 Su 15Oct 1989 West Brom 1 - 2 Wolves
1983/1984
DIV 1 Sa 28Apr 1984 Wolves 0 - 0 West Brom
DIV 1 Sa 26Nov 1983 West Brom 1 - 3 Wolves
1981/1982
DIV 1 Sa 01May 1982 Wolves 1 - 2 West Brom
DIV 1 Sa 05Dec 1981 West Brom 3 - 0 Wolves
1980/1981
DIV 1 Sa 31Jan 1981 Wolves 2 - 0 West Brom
DIV 1 Sa 23Aug 1980 West Brom 1 - 1 Wolves
1979/1980
DIV 1 Sa 19Apr 1980 West Brom 0 - 0 Wolves
DIV 1 Sa 24Nov 1979 Wolves 0 - 0 West Brom
1978/1979
DIV 1 Sa 21Apr 1979 West Brom 1 - 1 Wolves
DIV 1 Sa 16Dec 1978 Wolves 0 - 3 West Brom
1977/1978
DIV 1 Tu 14Mar 1978 Wolves 1 - 1 West Brom
DIV 1 Sa 17Sep 1977 West Brom 2 - 2 Wolves
1972/1973
DIV 1 Tu 20Mar 1973 Wolves 2 - 0 West Brom
DIV 1 Sa 21Oct 1972 West Brom 1 - 0 Wolves
1971/1972
DIV 1 Sa 15Apr 1972 Wolves 0 - 1 West Brom
DIV 1 Sa 27Nov 1971 West Brom 2 - 3 Wolves
1970/1971
DIV 1 Sa 20Mar 1971 West Brom 2 - 4 Wolves
DIV 1 Sa 07Nov 1970 Wolves 2 - 1 West Brom
1969/1970
DIV 1 Sa 28Feb 1970 West Brom 3 - 3 Wolves
DIV 1 Sa 01Nov 1969 Wolves 1 - 0 West Brom
1968/1969
DIV 1 Sa 12Apr 1969 Wolves 0 - 1 West Brom
DIV 1 Sa 21Sep 1968 West Brom 0 - 0 Wolves
1967/1968
DIV 1 We 30Aug 1967 West Brom 4 - 1 Wolves
DIV 1 We 23Aug 1967 Wolves 3 - 3 West Brom
1964/1965
DIV 1 Mo 15Mar 1965 Wolves 3 - 2 West Brom
DIV 1 Sa 10Oct 1964 West Brom 5 - 1 Wolves
1963/1964
DIV 1 Sa 29Feb 1964 West Brom 3 - 1 Wolves
DIV 1 We 02Oct 1963 Wolves 0 - 0 West Brom
1962/1963
DIV 1 We 03Apr 1963 West Brom 2 - 2 Wolves
DIV 1 Sa 16Mar 1963 Wolves 7 - 0 West Brom
1961/1962
DIV 1 We 28Mar 1962 Wolves 1 - 5 West Brom
FA CUP Sa 27Jan 1962 Wolves 1 - 2 West Brom
DIV 1 Tu 26Dec 1961 West Brom 1 - 1 Wolves
1960/1961
DIV 1 Mo 03Apr 1961 West Brom 2 - 1 Wolves
DIV 1 Sa 28Jan 1961 Wolves 4 - 2 West Brom
1959/1960
DIV 1 Sa 27Feb 1960 Wolves 3 - 1 West Brom
DIV 1 Sa 05Dec 1959 West Brom 0 - 1 Wolves
1958/1959
DIV 1 Sa 21Mar 1959 Wolves 5 - 2 West Brom
DIV 1 Sa 01Nov 1958 West Brom 2 - 1 Wolves
1957/1958
DIV 1 Sa 29Mar 1958 West Brom 0 - 3 Wolves
DIV 1 Sa 16Nov 1957 Wolves 1 - 1 West Brom
1956/1957
DIV 1 Mo 15Apr 1957 Wolves 5 - 2 West Brom
DIV 1 Sa 06Oct 1956 West Brom 1 - 1 Wolves
1955/1956
FA CUP Sa 07Jan 1956 Wolves 1 - 2 West Brom
DIV 1 Sa 17Dec 1955 Wolves 3 - 2 West Brom
DIV 1 Sa 20Aug 1955 West Brom 1 - 1 Wolves
1954/1955
DIV 1 We 16Mar 1955 West Brom 1 - 0 Wolves

DIV 1 Sa 23Oct 1954 Wolves 4 - 0 West Brom
CHARITY SHIELD We 29Sep 1954
Wolves 4 - 4 West Brom
1953/1954
DIV 1 Sa 03Apr 1954 West Brom 0 - 1 Wolves
DIV 1 Sa 14Nov 1953 Wolves 1 - 0 West Brom
1952/1953
DIV 1 Sa 07Mar 1953 Wolves 2 - 0 West Brom
DIV 1 Sa 18Oct 1952 West Brom 1 - 1 Wolves
1951/1952
DIV 1 Tu 15Apr 1952 Wolves 1 - 4 West Brom
DIV 1 Mo 14Apr 1952 West Brom 2 - 1 Wolves
1950/1951
DIV 1 Sa 21Apr 1951 West Brom 3 - 2 Wolves
DIV 1 Sa 02Dec 1950 Wolves 3 - 1 West Brom
1949/1950
DIV 1 Sa 04Mar 1950 West Brom 1 - 1 Wolves
DIV 1 Sa 15Oct 1949 Wolves 1 - 1 West Brom
1948/1949
FA CUP Sa 26Feb 1949 Wolves 1 - 0 West Brom
1937/1938
DIV 1 Mo 02May 1938 Wolves 2 - 1 West Brom
DIV 1 Mo 27Dec 1937 West Brom 2 - 2 Wolves
1936/1937
DIV 1 We 14Apr 1937 Wolves 5 - 2 West Brom
DIV 1 Sa 17Oct 1936 West Brom 2 - 1 Wolves
1935/1936
DIV 1 Sa 14Mar 1936 Wolves 2 - 0 West Brom
DIV 1 Sa 26Oct 1935 West Brom 2 - 1 Wolves
1934/1935
DIV 1 Sa 23Feb 1935 West Brom 5 - 2 Wolves
DIV 1 Sa 13Oct 1934 Wolves 3 - 2 West Brom
1933/1934
DIV 1 Sa 17Feb 1934 West Brom 2 - 0 Wolves
DIV 1 Sa 07Oct 1933 Wolves 0 - 0 West Brom
1932/1933
DIV 1 Sa 18Feb 1933 Wolves 3 - 3 West Brom
DIV 1 Sa 08Oct 1932 West Brom 4 - 1 Wolves
1930/1931
FA CUP We 04Mar 1931 Wolves 1 - 2 West Brom
FA CUP Sa 28Feb 1931 West Brom 1 - 1 Wolves
DIV 2 We 18Feb 1931 Wolves 1 - 4 West Brom
DIV 2 Sa 11Oct 1930 West Brom 2 - 1 Wolves
1929/1930
DIV 2 Sa 28Dec 1929 West Brom 7 - 3 Wolves
DIV 2 Sa 31Aug 1929 Wolves 2 - 4 West Brom
1928/1929
DIV 2 Sa 23Mar 1929 Wolves 0 - 1 West Brom
DIV 2 Sa 10Nov 1928 West Brom 0 - 2 Wolves
1927/1928
DIV 2 Sa 18Feb 1928 West Brom 4 - 0 Wolves
DIV 2 Sa 08Oct 1927 Wolves 4 - 1 West Brom
1923/1924
FA CUP We 27Feb 1924 Wolves 0 - 2 West Brom
FA CUP Sa 23Feb 1924 West Brom 1 - 1 Wolves
1910/1911
DIV 2 Sa 18Mar 1911 West Brom 2 - 1 Wolves
DIV 2 Sa 12Nov 1910 Wolves 2 - 3 West Brom
1909/1910
DIV 2 Sa 25Dec 1909 West Brom 0 - 1 Wolves
DIV 2 Sa 16Oct 1909 Wolves 3 - 1 West Brom
1908/1909
DIV 2 Sa 03Oct 1908 Wolves 0 - 1 West Brom
DIV 2 Mo 07Sep 1908 West Brom 0 - 2 Wolves
1907/1908
DIV 2 Sa 05Oct 1907 West Brom 1 - 0 Wolves
DIV 2 Mo 02Sep 1907 Wolves 1 - 2 West Brom
1906/1907
DIV 2 Mo 01Apr 1907 West Brom 1 - 1 Wolves
DIV 2 Sa 29Sep 1906 Wolves 0 - 3 West Brom
1903/1904
DIV 1 Sa 05Mar 1904 West Brom 1 - 2 Wolves
DIV 1 Sa 07Nov 1903 Wolves 1 - 0 West Brom
1902/1903
DIV 1 Sa 31Jan 1903 West Brom 2 - 2 Wolves
DIV 1 Sa 04Oct 1902 Wolves 1 - 2 West Brom
1900/1901
DIV 1 Sa 29Dec 1900 West Brom 1 - 2 Wolves
DIV 1 Sa 01Sep 1900 Wolves 0 - 0 West Brom
1899/1900
DIV 1 Sa 10Mar 1900 West Brom 3 - 2 Wolves
DIV 1 Sa 04Nov 1899 Wolves 2 - 0 West Brom
1898/1899
DIV 1 Tu 27Dec 1898 Wolves 5 - 1 West Brom
DIV 1 Sa 15Oct 1898 West Brom 1 - 2 Wolves
1897/1898
DIV 1 Tu 28Dec 1897 Wolves 1 - 1 West Brom
DIV 1 Sa 23Oct 1897 West Brom 2 - 2 Wolves
1896/1897
DIV 1 Mo 28Dec 1896 Wolves 6 - 1 West Brom
DIV 1 Sa 17Oct 1896 West Brom 1 - 0 Wolves
1895/1896
DIV 1 Sa 07Mar 1896 Wolves 1 - 2 West Brom
DIV 1 Sa 30Nov 1895 West Brom 2 - 1 Wolves
1894/1895
FA CUP Sa 02Mar 1895 West Brom 1 - 0 Wolves
DIV 1 Th 27Dec 1894 Wolves 3 - 1 West Brom
DIV 1 Sa 08Sep 1894 West Brom 5 - 1 Wolves
1893/1894

DIV 1 We 27Dec 1893 Wolves 0 - 8 West Brom
DIV 1 Sa 07Oct 1893 West Brom 0 - 0 Wolves
1892/1893
DIV 1 Tu 27Dec 1892 Wolves 1 - 1 West Brom
DIV 1 Sa 17Sep 1892 West Brom 2 - 1 Wolves
1891/1892
DIV 1 Mo 28Dec 1891 Wolves 2 - 1 West Brom
DIV 1 Sa 19Sep 1891 West Brom 4 - 3 Wolves
1890/1891
DIV 1 Sa 03Jan 1891 Wolves 4 - 0 West Brom
DIV 1 Sa 13Dec 1890 West Brom 0 - 1 Wolves
1889/1890
DIV 1 Sa 28Dec 1889 Wolves 1 - 1 West Brom
DIV 1 Sa 19Oct 1889 West Brom 1 - 4 Wolves
1888/1889
DIV 1 Sa 05Jan 1889 West Brom 1 - 3 Wolves
DIV 1 Sa 15Dec 1888 Wolves 2 - 1 West Brom
1887/1888
FA CUP Sa 26Nov 1887 West Brom 2 - 0 Wolves
1885/1886
FA CUP Sa 02Jan 1886 West Brom 3 - 1 Wolves

MIDLANDS FOOTY FANS MEMORIES

1) BURTON ALBION 5- 6 CHELTENHAM TOWN SATURDAY, 13 MARCH 2010

For Cheltenham Town's trip to mid-table Burton Albion for a League 2 game, the atmosphere in the Cheltenham camp was on an all time low, after being relegated; Town had not expected a relegation battle. Never the less Cheltenham went in to this match knowing a win was vital to their survival, little did Burton or Cheltenham know they were about to make history.

From start Burton were straight on the attack, winning a free kick thanks to David Hutton's hand ball outside the Cheltenham box. From the kick Shaun Harrad lost his marker and fired a volley pass Scott Brown into the bottom-left hand corner of the net to put Albion in the lead, Cheltenham did not look happy but Burton didn't mind. For the next 30 minutes neither team was able to get that all important second or equalising goal, that was until Shaun Harrad got in to the Cheltenham box and drew a challenge from Michael Townsend. Harrad udsted himself down and scored the penalty to put the home side 2-0 up and that's the way it stayed until half-time.

Burton must have thought the 3 points were theirs at the interval but Mark Yates must have had words with the Cheltenham player as 8 minutes after the restart they were back in the game with a goal from Justin Richards, the Town striker scoring from 6 years out after Hutton won the ball on the right wing allowing him to pick Richards out and set him up for a tap-in he couldn't miss. With no time to catch your breath Town went on the attack again with Pook crossing the ball and Elito smashing it into the top right corner of the net to equalise! But just as Cheltenham breathed a sigh of relief Burton regained the advantage - a cross by Burton deflecting off Michael Townsend into the Cheltenham net. It was not a good day for Townsend after he had given away the penalty in the first half and now the own goal.

Cheltenham responded by testing the Burton defence but with little success. Then on 72 minutes Burton's defending paid off when Steven Kubba struck the ball from 12 yards out to make it 4-2 after a poor defensive clearance from Lescott. Cheltenham looked down and out with Burton only 18 minutes away from 3 points. To the visitor's credit they kept attacking and nearly score a 3rd but a save from the Burton keeper maintained their 2 goal lead, Hutton also came close with an amazing over head kick that just went over the bar.

But still Cheltenham were pressing and they got a goal back on the 84th minute thanks to Pook's drilled free kick into the bottom corner of the net - 4-3 and all of a sudden it was game on! Almost from Burton's kick off, Kubba got on the end of a low cross to side foot it in the net - 5-3 Burton, the game has to be over now surely. Almost immediately, Cheltenham went up the other end and Michael Pook fired in a 20 yard drive which deflected off Boco and looped in over Krysiak. Unbelievable! Burton 5-4 Cheltenham and three minutes remained!

Searching an equaliser, Scott Brown took a free kick from inside his half and launched it into the danger area. It was flicked on by Julian Alsop into the path of Richards. Richards calmly slipped the ball past Krysiak to draw Cheltenham level in injury time.

Then, to complete the comeback Cheltenham win it in the 4th minute of added time as Pook completes his a hat trick with a superb drive into the back of the net from 25 yards. As the referee blew for full time Cheltenham somehow went home with 3 points and took a step closer to League 2 survival.

By Lewis Morgan, 15, Weston-Super-Mare
Cheltenham Town supporter!

2) My favourite memory was watching Burton Albion play Oldham Athletic in the FA Cup first round back in 2002. We were a Conference side and they were top of League One. Loads of us made the trip up to Boundary Park and it's was a really cold day. The Albion had our centre half sent off early in the game but still held their own. I can remember Craig Dudley scoring a great solo goal and a few Albion fans ran on the pitch. The police tried to get them back over the hoardings and even tried to cart Aaron Webster off! He had to point out that he was a player and even showed the policeman the football boots he was wearing. All game the Albion fans were singing "ten men...we've only got ten men". Even old men with flat caps were singing their heads off. Just a great feeling!!! It got to the last couple of minutes and it was 2-1 to the Albion. It was a proper nail biting finish I couldn't watch. Then Oldham scored to make it 2-2. A real heartbreaker. We lost the replay down at Eton Park on penalties after extra time. That was another great night at our tiny little ground and the place was rocking. This is my favourite memory and I hope you like it.

Wayne Bennett
Burton Albion Supporter

3) After a twenty-six year wait, Aston Villa finally beat Manchester United at Old Trafford through a goal from Birmingham born Gabriel Agbonlahor.

Agbonlahor scored in the twenty-first minute at the Theatre of Dreams past a helpless Thomas Kuszczak following a perfectly weighted cross from Ashley Young.

1999 was the last time Villa had beaten Sir Alex Ferguson's Red Devils, however this was in a league cup match, and the last victory at Old Trafford stretched back to 1983.

Villa secured their hundredth Barclays Premier League win away from Villa Park in style with pace and power, and a resolute backline of newcomers Stephen Warnock and Richard Dunne but with the regulars of Carlos Cuellar and Luke Young.

Right from the first whistle blown by Atkinson, Martin O'Neill's men looked determined to end their dismal record against United. With talk of Manchester City and Tottenham Hotspur breaking into the top four, Villa looked to prove a point and they certainly looked like they were going to do just that. With the two lightning bolts in the likes of Ashley Young and Gabby Agbonlahor up front for Villa, they looked like a force to be reckoned with.

Both were involved in the winning goal and it seemed Villa would be challenging for top four for the majority of the season. It certainly seemed like it as Villa showed their character and composure against the big clubs, as they established themselves as one and kept one at bay.

No wonder they call Old Trafford the Theatre of Dreams because it definitely was the day where claret and blue dreams came true.

Molly Jennens, 13 years old
Old Hill, Cradley Heath
Aston Villa Supporter

4) One of my favourite memories was the second leg against Bolton in the Carling Cup semi final. We were 5-2 down from the first leg and no one gave us a hope. We had McCann sent off, yet we played them off the pitch for 90 mins. Villa Park was full and the crowd didnt stop singing from start to finish - Hitzlsperger scored, then Samuel on 83 minutes. We needed one more goal and we were denied a blatant penalty for a hand ball by campo. We didnt go through but I felt so proud walking out with fellow villans still singing - what a night!

Danny Finnegan
Aston Villa Supporter

5) As a West Bromwich Albion fan, I have lots of memories of my club. The greatest has to be the great escape in 2005, at the time I was a 12 year old boy supporting my local team. My favourite manager was Bryan Robson for me he did the club proud as a player and a manager. The players that will always stick in my mind for West Bromwich Albion are Jason Koumas, Lee Hughes and Kevin Phillips. Jason Koumas because the effort he put in to the club and decided to leave, then returned. Lee Hughes might not have a good reputation but for me he never lost faith in West Brom, the game against Wolves when he lifted his top with the words "boing boing" showed that he still had passion for the club. Kevin Phillips was also a tremendous player for West Bromwich Albion; the effort, the charisma the atmosphere at The Hawthorns when he scored with twenty thousand fans chanting "super Kev" was just immense.

Jason Ashfield. 18
Princes End
Tipton
West Bromwich Albion Supporter

6) It was a Tuesday night at the Ricoh, the date was 1st September 2007... Our attendances are not great and i think there was 22k there which is very impressive for Coventry considering the game on telly. There was lots of noise before the game with talk of us going top of the table with a win. Only three points would do. We started off well controling the match and playing good football, it looked good. Then a freak goal against the run of play from Preston North End gave them the lead which silenced the very loud crowd.

Fustration grew amongst the fans as the second half didnt start off well either and we all feared the worst. In the 80th minuite or so dele adebola got a goal following a twist and shot that took everybody by suprise. Then a 90th minuite winner by Michael Doyle who scored a screamer from about 30 yards out. The roof came of the Ricoh for the first time! We were top of the league! After the game we decided to walk back towards the pub called the Cherry Tree and it went past the Preston fans coaches where they were being stopped from leaving by a massive amount of Coventry fans blocking the way singing chants. while some people jumped on cars which made the moment as crazy as ever. Finally the police moved everyone away from there and people began to leave the ground, thinking that this year might be a sky blue one.

Asher Hastie
Coventry City Supporter

7) 96,527 people packed into Wembley to see Wolves beat the favorites Nottingham Forest in the 1980 League Cup final. Forest created many chances throughout the game but Paul Bradshaw was too good in the Wolves goal. On 67 minutes Andy Gray struck a shot past shilton in the Nottingham goal following a long lob upfield by Peter Daniel to secure the only goal and the League Cup. The trophy was then handed to Wolves captain Emlyn Hughes who had now won every major domestic honours. What a proud moment that will go down in the

history of football and a great moment for my team Wolverhampton Wanderers

NOTTINGHAM FOREST:

1 Peter Shilton, 2 Viv Anderson , 3 Frank Gray , 4 John McGovern (c), 5 David Needham, 6 Kenny Burns , 7 Martin O'Neill, 8 Ian Bowyer, 9 Garry Birtles, 10 Trevor Francis, 11 John Robertson

Substitute: 12 John O'Hare

Manager: Brian Clough

WOLVERHAMPTON WANDERERS:

1 Paul Bradshaw, 2 Geoff Palmer, 3 Derek Parkin, 4 Peter Daniel, 5 Emlyn Hughes (c), 6 George Berry, 7 Kenny Hibbitt, 8 Willie Carr, 9 Andy Gray, 10 John Richards, 11 Mel Eves

Substitute: 12 Colin Brazier

Manager: John Barnwell

Nathaniel Prendergast, 16

Hednesford

Wolves Supporter

8) My favourite memories are when Graham had successful seasons in the 70's and when we gave Gillingham a 7-0 thrashing in the 08/09 season, and you cant go without mentioning Grant Holt, what a star player he was, every bit of credit to him. Not forgetting to mention Joe Hart who was League Two's player of the season and now plays top football with Manchester City and England. I remember watching Gillingham v Shrewsbury in the play-off finals in the 08/09 season - what a smashing day out, even if we lost 1-0 that day :(and Im from Birmingham.

Charlie Brittain

19 years old,

Birmingham

Shrewsbury Town Supporter

9) Being a bluenose I'm used to alot of low points following the blues. This season will go down in histroy; winning the Carling Cup. I was at the semi final second leg vs West Ham and it is the greatest game I have ever been to! Everyone in the stands was singing their hearts out and the atmsphere was tense when they scored, electric when we scored and extremely tense at the end of 90 mins. But when the final whistle went the crowed erputed with keep right on. I sang my heart out and all week my throate was killing me. KRO

Lewis Carey, 19
Swadlincote.
Birmingham City Supporter

10) Having been a fan of Derby county for over forty years, I am one of the lucky ones who has many happy memories. From league titles to big European games, I could probably write my own book on the many matches that I have witnessed.

One might figure that watching The Rams beat opponents such as Real Madrid and Benfica would be at the top of the list of memories, however there is nothing quite like beating your local rivals for the bragging rightts in the East Midlands Derby.

Nottingham Forest and not Leicester City are seen as the real East midlands rivals to any Derby County supporter. Over the years the pendulum has swung one way and the other many times.

Whilst we were under the reign of Clough and Taylor, I remember us winning at the City Ground and it wasn't until his son Nigel had taken over the managerial reigns that we managed another win in Nottingham.

Clough and Taylor, when in charge of our rivals, did put one over us during their Championship winning season. An easy 3-0 victory for the red side of the A52, which was difficult for any Rams fan to take.

It was however whilst they were between winning European cups and we were on our way to relegation from the top flight that we scored one of our better victories. A 4-1 victory saw The Rams give the Reds a real footballing lesson. Cloughie couldn't believe his eyes as Shilton dropped one for John Duncan to smash into the net.

A few years later we had Clough (Forest, riding high in the first Division) v Taylor (In charge of a struggling Second Division Derby) in an FA Cup tie. It was the latter who emerged victorious. A superb

Archie Gemmil free-kick and another goal by Andy Hill saw David beat Goliath.

During the George Burley era as manager we had the infamous 'Kenco Cup' game. Derby won the game 4-2. The Forest goalkeeper blamed a misskick that led to Paul Peschisolido scoring for us on a vending machine coffee cup getting caught up with his boot!

The following season saw a 3-0 stroll at Pride Park. Tommy Smith scoring early in the first half and Grzegorz Rasiak adding a brace in the second. That defeat was a final nail in the coffin of Joe Kinnear as Forest manager.

In 2008-09, the clubs met four times. Two draws at Pride Park, and two wins for The Rams at the City Ground. The early league game at Pride Park was when Paul Jewell was nearing the end of his tenure as manager of Derby. Likewise Colin Calderwood was asked to leave as The Reds manager a few weeks later.

After a dull first half the game livened after half time. A Forest attack saw Bywater make a save, but the ball rebounded of Emanuel Villa and into the Derby net to put the 'Red Dogs' one up. Villa made up for his error a few minutes later when he mat a Kris Commons cross to level the scores. However, it was two incidents in this game and two contreversial decisions by referee Stuart Atwell that will keep people talking about the game for years.

Miles Addison leapt to meet a cross and seemingly put Derby ahead. Atwell ruled no goal, but gave a penalty to us instead. What for ? Who knows? The spot kick was then saved by Lee Camp, a former Rams keeper. Can lightning strike twice? Well it did in Mr Atwell's case. As the game was edging towards full time, Addison again jumped and scored what looked like a well headed goal. Unbelievably Atwell ruled foul and no goal. The game ended 1-1. No one who witnessed the game could believe what theyhad seen. Former Rams and Reds legend Archie Gemmill agreed that Derby had been robbed.

It wasn't long after the appointment of Nigel Clough as manager that we were drawn at home to our rivals in the FA Cup. Nigel was a legend inhis own right in Nottingham where he scored bucket loads of goals for them during his playing days.

Rob Hulse opened the scoring for us in the first half only for ex-Ram Robert Earnshaw to level things in the second half. We pounded the Forest goal, but Paul Smith played a blinder in their goal, stopping everything we threw at him.

It was on to the City ground for the replay and many pundits were tipping a home win. We hadn't won there since the Clough and Taylor years. The game was barely a few minutes old when Chris Cohen cut in from the right and fired theminto the lead. Minutes later Stephen Bywater brought down Nathan Tyson and they were awarded a penalty that Tyson duly converted. by this time many Derby fans were fearing the worst. The Trent end were in full voice as they sensed what surely would be a victory.

After twenty minutes or so, Derby began to feel their way into the game. Rob Hulse met a cross to pull one back by half time there was a feeling that just maybe we could get backinto the game. That belief was well founded when Paul Green equalised early in the second half. It was game on and by now the Derby fans in the Bridgford End were making plenty of noise. When Kris Commons hit the woodwork I was convinced we were going to win. Moments later he hit one that hit the bottom right of the Forest net. What a feeling that was! I can't remember the last few minutes of the game, but I certainly can remember the celebrations. At the end Robbie Savage celebrated by waving a Black and White scarf at the Derby fans.

It was barely two weeks later when we returned for the league game. They promised that they would make us pay. Revenge is what their players promised. The game however was far from that. Nyatanga scored early on in the first, Hulse added a second after the break and a Steve Davies penalty wrapped up what was a very easy win. Earnshaw scored a consolation for them, but the final score was Nottingham Forest 1 Derby County 3. that was the easiest win over them I have ever seen.

I've no doubt that our Red Rivals will be able to recall their own victories and disagree with certain points made, but I'm sure that they'll agree that for passion and pride The East Midlands Derby is second to none. What it does need is a bigger stage. Both of these sides should be gracing the Premier League.

Andy Buckley-Taylor (Derby fan since 1969)

11) My favourite memory was The Play-Off Final against. Norwich. The atmosphere at the game was amazing! There's no one like Geoff Horsfield to make us go mental! I remember watching the penalties and watching Carter take the kick that sent us into the Premier League after 16 years out of the top flight.

Dec James Davis

12) My best memories were from Notts County vs League 1 champions Brighton, as we were on the brink of relegation we were in a slightly awkward position, so to push the boys on - a huge crowd of Notts and Brighton fans arrived at meadow lane. The kop stand was deafening and the game ended in a 1-1 draw which consiquently helped us to survive. Our fans spilled onto the pitch to celebrate with the Brighton fans, both teams singing in unison. Brighton were chanting "you are staying up!" and Notts fans were chanting back "you are going up!" it was a brilliant moment for both teams and it made me feel proud to be part of it, the best game of my life!

Jack Wilden

13) My favourite memory of the blues has got to be the semi-final of the Carling Cup! Being 1-0 down and the fans still singing their hearts out, and then for the lads to come out fighting and win 3-1 was brilliant! I remember the feeling when I saw Gardner's goal go in, it sent shivers down my spine! The atmosphere on that night was unreal, especially at the end of the match. It meant so much to every single fan and player on that pitch. To then go and beat Arsenal at Wembley and see Stephen Carr lifting the cup, really was something special! Niamh McLaughlin, 13

Tamworth

14) My best memory was this season - 2010/11. It was my birthday and we were playing West Ham at home in November and it was a surprise for me and it was the best day ever. On that day me, my dad, my brother and my grandad went as well and I loved that day and when I was there I loved the game and I was by one of the goal end on the old stand and when West Ham scored I cried but then we scored two goals I stood up and cheered with the rest of the blues fans. and also the sprinklers came

on and that was funny as the game had not long started.

Eleanor Neale, 14
West Midlands

15) My favourite memory was from last season - Wolves winning at Anfield. We were all bigging up Stephen Ward during the game for his effort, then he scores to shut up Reina. I was sitting next to the scouse fans and having banter all game, well giving it. Then Skrtl scored and all the Liverpool fans were near enough in my face, only for me to be pointing to the linesman with his flag up for offside and seeing the scousers sit back down. I had a big smile on my face! Once a wolf, Forever a wolf!

Steffan Freeman

16) My best memory in recent years as a villain in the Holte is without a doubt Darren's goal against Manchester City. They bought our two best players for two seasons running, causing a hatred from myself, and indeed the majority of Villa supporters and - with our season in shambles and relegation becoming a more possibility, the only beacon of hope the could lift Villa Park was the arrival of Darren Bent.

So imagine my joy when Bent picked up the scraps from Young's saved shot and poked in the winner to send the scum of Manchester home depressed, as James Milner looked on in his tracksuit from the bench, drowning in a pool of his own wasted talent - and with Barry watching from the centre circle, barely able to stand under the weight of his seemingly imminent morbid obesity.

Tom Careless

17) My First Game - WBA v WYCOMBE - Tuesday 21st September 1998. Football League Cup 2nd Round Second Leg.

I'll never forget the first time I set foot in the Hawthorns. I'd been looking for a team to follow for a while,I was a 15 year old football fanatic without a team to follow, I'd been to St Andrews and didn't like it,I'd been to the Molineux and didn't like it. My best mate at the time was a mad Albion fan and told me he had a spare ticket if I wanted to go

It was a cup game Wycombe Wanderers from what my mate had told me the first leg had ended 1 -1 so it was all to play for. Him and his dad come to pick me up and we stated off on our journey,We lived in Harborne at the time so it wasn't too far. We parked up on a side street about a 5 minute walk from the ground on the way our small group began to swell and by the time we had got to the ground there was about 40 or 50 so people hanging around the entrance to the Smethwick End. We got through the turnstiles and walked through the concourse and I will never ever forget the next feeling I got. I began to walk up the steps to the entrance to the actual ground and seated area,as I got closer I felt all the hairs stand up on the back of my neck as I walked up the steps and began to see the pitch,; the Brummy End ,the floodlights and hearing the songs and general hubbub of a football match,I never got this feeling at any other ground I went to and I was excited that I may have found my team.

We took our seats in the Smethwick End and I flicked through my mate's program and waited for the teams to come out. When Albion came out the cheers started and before we knew it the ref had got the game underway. Wycombe had a really good chance of progressing to the 3rd Round for the first time ever but found themselves tested after their goalkeeper Martin Taylor and defender Paul McCarthy were declared unfit.

I remember Wycombe got off to a flying start when an early Sean Devine shot in the area following a corner from the left to give Wycombe the lead. Unlike any of the other games I'd been to I felt really angry we had gone one down and told some bloke next to me we had defended like idiots and he nodded in agreement by this point my love affair with the Albion had started and I didn't even know it.

Wycombe's defense was finally tested and after pilling the pressure on West Brom and finally the equalizer came in the 16th minute following a header by Paul Raven from Richard Sneekes' corner,I practically jumped on my mates back and celebrated like a mad woman!. It was 1-1 at half-time.

Wycombe came out and stated the second half like little rockets! After 90 Minutes it was 2-2 and 3-3 on aggregate so the game went into extra-time

We went on to score twice and go through winning on the night 4-3 and 4-5 aggregate. I left the ground knowing I had found my football team and spent most the night awake in bed re-living the Albion goals in my head and wondering how the hell I was going to fund my new

found obsession and Season Ticket for the following season!
Leanne Williams

18) Sunderland away, FA Cup 3rd round. High tension and nerves on the drive up there. We got into the ground and were greated by a few thousand Notts fans, everyone was talking about how badly we'd get beat, it was a great laugh before the game, everyone was drinking, chanting and dancing around. And as kick-off came upon us we begun to fill up their away end, non-stop singing from the Notts fans and Westcar's goal got us jumping. Then Mr Lee Hughes knocked in a 2nd and we went mental, people ran to the bottom of the stand to celebrate with hughsey, we went on to win 2-1. An amazing day and great atmosphere! YOU PIES!
Jack WIlden

19) 2010/11 beating Fleetwood 2-1 to keep alive our chances of the play-offs. It was the best atmosphere seen at Aggy in ages. Northwich Victoria away back in 08/09 season, we lost 3-2 but won on aggregate to be the first team at the New Wembley. Stevenage at home - we beat them 4-2 in our promotion push. Brilliant day because we were 2-0 down, came back against the odds and sang 2-0 and you f★★★★d it up (what Stevenage sang to us when we lost against them in the FA trophy final at Wembley)
Jack Goldstraw

20) My favourite memory for Derby County was when we went to the City ground for an FA cup replay. We were 2-0 down and pulled it back to win 3-2. It was my first trip to the City Ground and it was only 3-4 years back. I can remember when Commons (ex-Forest) smashed the winner in from 25 yards and the whole away end went mad. Me and my dad were almost in tears, that's how much we hate Nottingham Forest. I'll always look back to that day and think 'Born a ram, live a ram, die a ram!'
Jack Orton, 15
Derby County

21) When asked to write a few memories of Port Vale for this book my mind was swamped with options, sadly most are from our bygone glory years of the late 80's through to 2001 however a couple have sneaked in from recent times so here goes in no particular order!

PORT VALE V STOKE CITY FA CUP 1ST ROUND REPLAY 24TH NOVEMBER 1992

After a fairly drab first game which ended 0-0 (despite a stroke of luck in a good Stoke goal being ruled out for offside) this game took place at fortress Vale Park, a place where at the time we rarely lost, however the pitch was known to hold water, so the deluge on the day of the game left most wondering if it would be called off. Of course it was live on sky (possibly the saving grace for keeping the game on) a full house and around 20 minutes in Lee Sandford puts Stoke 1-0 up infront of the home fans in the Bycars End. Vale hit back through Martin Foyle almost immediately, and just before half time Andy Porter sent the Vale in 2-1 up with a tremendous strike.

The second half produced one of the funniest moments in the Vale/ Stoke rivalry (At the time it was pure hatred to rival the most famous derbies you could name), the deluge of rain that continued all through the game had swamped the stands, and the pitch. I was drenched at the front of the Bycars End, with my bottoms slowly sliding to my ankles such was the weight of water and the pitch resembled a quagmire (see the youtube videos). The ball ran loose and Paul Musslewhite haired out of goal to clear, miskicked and left Stoke substitute Dave Regis to roll the ball into an empty net....or so he thought, he reeled away to celebrate infront of the Stokies only to see the ball stop in the mud in the Vale goal, just short of crossing the line to which a laughing out loud Peter Swan gratfully cleared the ball and the game remained 2-1 until the last minutes when Martin Foyle again broke free and slid the ball past Ronnie Sinclair to make it 3-1 and all the glory and bragging rights to the Vale.

BRENTFORD V PORT VALE. MILLENIUM STADIUM, CARDIFF - 22ND APRIL 2001

This game was special to me for more than it being a chance to see the Vale in a Cup Final. I attended with my late grandfather who rarely got to see the Vale due to work, however we treated him to this game and what a day it was....again it poured down all day (A familiar feature whenever the Vale play it seems) and we went into the game as heavy favourites following the start of a good unbeaten run, we had the mecurial Alex Smith down the left, Dave Brammer in the middle pulling the strings, the beef of Steve Brooker and the tricky, nippy Tony Naylor up front supplied by the majestic Marc Bridge-Wilkinson, and those attack minded players were supported by the outstanding Mark Goodlad in goal.

We conceeded an early goal from a set piece to Brentford, to go a goal behind, but that was to prove one of only 2/3 attacks they had on our goal as Vale proceeded to dominate the game, passing on a zippy surface as the rain teemed down on the 20,000+ in attendance. Half time came and went and as the game approached the last 25 minutes it felt like we wouldnt get back into the game, but in the 76th Minute Tony Naylor was tripped and Bridge-Wilkinson smashed home the penalty, and seven minutes later Steve Brooker finished an excellent move to put the Vale 2-1 up and it seemed there would be no way back.

Brentford then piled on the pressure and had numerous late chances; the first falling to Mark McCammon whose first touch of the game was a poor header that could have found the net if it he had got it on target, it was a very bad miss. The last kick of the game could have taken it to extra time, however Owusu headed wide from the keeper's overhead kick – the Brentford goalkeeper doing more than making up the numbers in the Vale box during the last seconds of injury time.

Not only will I remember this game fondly for the success but also for the sheer joy of seeing my grandfather jumping for joy and punching the air with a big grin on his face like a teenage kid relieving his earlier years supporting the club. I attended numerous games with my grandfather, sadly few reached the successful heights of this day, but none the less were enjoyable due to his company and friendship.

PORT VALE V STOKE CITY, 1996

This time it was snow and ice that threatend the game, however somehow the pitch was deemed fit and we piled into Vale Park, for our league game against fierce rivals Stoke, Ian Bogie managed to carve out a habit of scoring against Stoke, he scored in the reverse fixture in this season, but this goal was special, but quite a few Vale fans missed it as they were late getting into the ground.

Vale kicked off, and the ball was played to right back Andy Hill, who played a ball into Ian Bogie, who in turn ghosted past the Stoke defence and rocketed the ball into Ronnie Sinclair's top right hand corner to put the Vale 1-0 up after just 12 seconds. However if you watch the videos on Youtube you will see that from kick off to the ball entering the net it can be timed at just 5 seconds.

Stoke went on the have large amounts of possession and we had more than our fair share of nervy moments, however we stood firm and held on to win 1-0 and once again laugh at our neighbours who by now were struggling to remember the last time they actually beat us!!

PORT VALE V STOKE CITY OCTOBER 13TH 1996

I've chosen this game for one simple reason, having gone 1-0 up Stoke, who in fairness had dominated the game, were celebrating in the Hamil End what should have been a Stoke victory however earlier in the game we brought on substitute Lee Mills, a tall battering ram of a player, and deep into injury time Vale had a free kick, which was pumped into the Stoke box in front of the home fans in the Bycars End, the Stoke keeper came out to punch the ball claer, but was out jumped by Mills whose header flew into the net to the unadulterated delight of the Vale fans who danced in the aisles and celebrated as if they had just gained promotion, to see the looks on the faces of the Stoke fans who thought they had won was brilliant!

I consider myself lucky to have lived through Vale's best period, going to Wembley twice in a week was an amazing experience, we won the Autoglass Trophy and had an open top parade through the town of Burslem, and then on the Sunday went back in the playoff final against West Brom. Things didn't go our way that day but the experience was one that not many teams even in the top flight can boast about.

One of the best days out was last season at Stockport County, we were under Mickey Adams' management and Stockport were struggling, we took a fantastic away following for a midweek game and ran riot winning 5-0, it was great to see so much confidence in the team and everything we did that night came off, short passes, long defence splitting passes, hard tackles and the goals were a delight.

All supporters should have good memories of their team, these are just some that constantly stick in my mind and with my belief that football goes in cycles, it wont be long before i have a few more to put into the memory bank... i hope!

Carl Ziemann, Port Vale Supporter

22) Here's some of my long sticking Burton Albion memories. 1. My first season as a whole supporting Burton Albion, which was 10 seasons ago was when Burton Albion played in the Unibond Premier in 2001/2002 (then the league below the Conference National). And I was extremely spoilt that season, as we totally stormed the league, with a 3 figure points and 3 figure goals total, where every player scored including goalkeeper Matt Duke from a penalty. We also got to the FA Trophy semi final that season. Winning the league away at Vauxhall Motors 4-2 was amazing.

2. In the 2005/2006 season where we'd had a terrible start to the season in our brand new Pirelli Stadium we'd just moved to, bottom of the league for a while and fans calling for Nigel Clough's head. A memorable FA Cup run seemingly saved his bacon and was a big turning point in our history after a few relegation battles. We drew 0-0 away at then League 2 Peterborough United, and beat them 1-0 in a replay. The 2nd round was a home game against Burscough who were two leagues below Burton Albion. The match got postponed on the original day due to a waterlogged pitch. And when the FA Cup 3rd round draw was done, Burton Albion/Burscough got drawn at home to Manchester United. That made the 2nd round match between two non league teams a massive occasion which was played on the Tuesday after that FA Cup draw, and the euphoria when Burton Albion won 4-1 was massive. FA Cup fever had hit Burton on Trent. The whole town was talking about the big game and Burton Albion had never had a game as high profile as this, the local team in the Conference National taking on the mighty Manchester United. Even the most die hard fan didn't seriously expect Burton Albion to get a result from this game, but low and behold, they pulled it off with a 0-0 draw. The FA Cup fever in Burton was fever pitch after that. And Burton Albion, who got average crowds of 1500 in those days, took 12,000 fans to Old Trafford for a televised midweek game. Manchester United won the replay 5-0, but the memories were priceless. And Burton earned an estimated £1 million out of the FA Cup run. Burton went on to get their highest ever league finish that season too with

a comfortable top half finish. And the prize money had set Burton Albion up nicely for the future.

3. The 08/09 season for Burton Albion, who were still part time, won the Conference National was extremely special. Despite a bad run of results in the new year trimming a 19 point gap to 2 points at the end of the season. It was a season of ups and downs, with Burton Albion breaking a then league record by getting 13 consecutive wins. Then legendary manager Nigel Clough left Albion in his 10th season to take the Derby County job, leaving us with Roy McFarland as the caretaker manager until the end of the season. Despite the fans having no fingernails left to bite when we left it till the final day of the season to win the league, and despite us losing that match and relying on nearest rival Cambridge United's result, the joy of Burton Albion finally making it into the football league was amazing. And it was a brilliant moment for the town.

4. The football league first season was special for the fans who never seriously believed Burton Albion would ever reach this level of football. And Burton Albion stayed up comfortably, with Paul Peschisolido, who is still our manager and in his 3rd season in charge. But a fantastic FA Cup upset in the club's 2nd season was unbelievably great. When Burton Albion played Championship Middlesbrough in the 3rd round. Burton Albion went a goal down in the second half against a strong looking side. But the underdogs really went for it in the end and scored from an overhead kick with 10 minutes to go to equalise. And just when fans were dreaming of a replay at Middlesbrough, Burton Albion scored the winning goal in the 94th minute. There was absolute pandemonium in the Pirelli Stadium stands, that moment of absolute joy will stay with me forever.

Adam Drew, Burton Albion fan of 10 years

23) I remember the day vividly I was 8 years old! Walking up Wembley way and seeing the crowds.

We were not fancied as we were playing the mighty Man United! Minus Schemichel may it be said who was sent off in the semi! So Les Sealey took over - a former Villa man!

The game did not go to plan for United as Villa stepped up their game! In the two forwards Saunders and Atkinson we had a strike force to be feared! With Dwight Yorke on the bench, Villa went into the game with nothing to lose, and before to long found themselves 2 up through the asformetioned Deano and Dalian. Then the crucial moment... Kanchelskis handled on the line to clear and a penalty to Villa! But Andrei would not leave easily trying to put off Deano from the pen!

The man, the genius stepped up..... No problem at all for the coolest man in football! Villa led the "Famous Man United" 3-0

The usual happened and Mark Hughes reduced the deficit to 3-1! But it was to be our day! And one 8 year old walked off thinking and believing we were the best in the world! (Still Do)

And still to this day we sing.. "Man U, Where's your treble gone!"

Let's hope we see these days again!

UTV

Noel Murphy, Aston Villa

24) Being a Baggies fan is an adventure because there are many ups and downs in our club's history. The memories that mean the most to me are the following four in chronological order.

BEATING PORTSMOUTH 2-0 AT THE HAWTHORNS (15/05/05) - 2004/2005 SEASON

The 2004/2005 season was one to remember, highlighting this game was the one that saved our top flight status. The season had been a rollercoaster and the atmosphere from the crowd was mesmerising, knowing that survival was not in our own hands it was going to be a tense game. But a victory and all the other results regarding relegation sides going our way saw us claim one of the single most important victories in our history, and the history of the Premiership.

BEATING WOLVES 3-2 AND 1-0 OVER TWO LEGS IN THE PLAYOFF SEMI FINALS (13/05/07 & 16/05/07) - 2006/2007 SEASON

Despite losing out in the final by a single goal, I will always remember these two legs as passionate derbies that saw us beat our Black Country rivals on both occasions. In the first game we came from behind and in the second we won by a single goal. Kevin Philips was the star of the show scoring three goals over two legs, to help ensure the Baggies had bragging rights until the next encounter.

BEATING ARSENAL 3-2 AT THE EMIRATES (25/09/10) - 2010/2011 SEASON

Going into this game we were on seven points and most fans will tell you that they don't expect to take anything from the big four teams away from home, but we pray that the players give a good account of themselves. On this Saturday afternoon our prayers would be answered and at one stage West Brom saw themselves 3-0 up at the Emirates. Despite conceding two goals towards the end of the game we held on for a dramatic win and caused a huge upset in the process of claiming all three points.

BEATING ASTON VILLA 2-1 AT THE HAWTHORNS (30/04/11) - 2010/2011 SEASON

Before this game I would have been ashamed to tell you that it had been a colossal 26 years since West Brom last beat Villa. Being without key players Thomas and Dorrans for the game it would be fair to say that expectations from this game were not that high; especially as Premiership survival was all but secure. Despite conceding an early own goal, a strong performance and two very good goals saw Albion finally end Villa's unbeaten run against them in front of their own fans.

Anthony Dosanjh

25) Being a Wolves fan hasn't been easy in recent times but over the last five years things have improved vastly. The memories that mean the most to me are the four below in chronological order.

DRAWING 1-1 WITH BARNSLEY AT OAKWELL (25/04/09) - 2008-2009 SEASON

Not many people would choose a draw as one of their most memorable moments, but this was a special game. The single point was enough in this season to clinch the Coca Cola Championship trophy after a hard fought season against their main title contenders and fellow Midlands side Birmingham City. It was winger and substitute Kyel Reid who came on and got the equaliser that sparked a pitch invasion during game time. Both sides looked unhappy with what they were saying and even manager Mick McCarthy gestured the fans to return to their seats, and when they finally did play resumed and the game finished all square.

BEATING TOTTENHAM 1-0 AT MOLINEUX (10/02/10) - 2009-2010 SEASON

Being our first season back in the Premiership there wasn't too many great victories to choose from but there is one that's my personal favourite. It was the home victory against high flying Tottenham which fell on a winter's day that was bitterly cold and there was even snow on the ground. The weather didn't stop the home fans cheering on their side against an opposition that were at full strength. It was a very tough game but a single strike from David Jones meant we moved out of the relegation zone and completed a memorable double over Spurs.

BEATING MAN UTD 2-1 AT MOLINEUX (05/02/11) – 2010/2011 SEASON

Despite beating both Chelsea and Liverpool in this memorable season, the victory over Man Utd was simply one of those games that you won't forget. Man Utd went on that season to win the Premiership but in this game they were outplayed for the most part. Despite going a goal down early on we dominated possession and made them pay with two first half goals. Despite Utd going all out for a second goal we held on with a dominant defensive display against arguably the best team in England.

BEATING WEST BROM 3-1 AT MOLINEUX (08/05/11) – 2010/2011 SEASON

The Black Country derby is always a tough contest with the game usually a fiery encounter, but this win was the most memorable one of all for Wolves fans. After taking a three goal lead we were pegged back but we held on for one of the most important derby day wins. It came towards the end of the season when we were desperate for the points and this was one of the victories that helped keep us in the Premiership for another season. It was an ambitious and heartfelt performance in front of the home fans who were in full voice behind their team.

Michael Reeman